WINNING
AT PROJECT
MANAGEMENT

WINNING AT PROJECT MANAGEMENT
WHAT WORKS, WHAT FAILS AND WHY

Robert D. Gilbreath

JOHN WILEY & SONS
New York • Chichester • Brisbane • Toronto • Singapore

Library of Congress Cataloging in Publication Data:

Gilbreath, Robert D. (Robert Dean), 1949–
    Winning at project management

    Includes index.
    1. Industrial project management.   I. Title.
HD69.P75G55   1986   658.4′04   85-22642
ISBN 0-471-83910-8

Printed in the United States of America

10   9   8   7   6   5   4   3

For all those in the business community with the insight to ask why the persistence to find the answer, and the courage to change once it is known.

Special thanks are in order for my friends, each a partner with Arthur Andersen & Co., who gave me the opportunity to learn while I was teaching. They are John Smith, Ray Ruona, and Jimmy Jones.

PREFACE

Business projects are exciting and challenging because they take place outside the scope of ongoing, mainline operations. They are temporary and goal-directed, and require a confrontation with the unknown, using the untested, to achieve uncertain expectations. The whole notion of business projects is one fraught with risk and the potential for failure. Those projects able to recognize risks, manage the confrontation, and accommodate the changes it brings are candidates for success. The rest are beset by failure.

The purpose of this book is to expose project failure for what it is: the inability to meet sensible project expectations. Failure is a phenomenon that can be studied—in fact, even demands it. It is shown here as a perceived and a real condition, originating from many sources, using different agencies and often propagating through projects unknown and unchecked. By studying the causes and impacts of failure, however, we derive much more than just an intimate acquaintance with its various aspects, vectors, and symptoms. This alone would prove a scholarly yet senseless pursuit, for knowing failure has no value unless that knowledge, that intimacy, leads to its avoidance.

There are two common ways to gain a better understanding of failure: through personal experience or by vicarious means. Experience in this sense is knowledge gained through practice—a high price extracted by failure for its understanding. In fact, practicing failure seldom leads to its avoidance, but merely to more of the same. We choose here to learn of failure through its examination, assessment, and the recognition of its symptoms—not through practice. Those who insist on practicing failure become quite good at it, a talent most companies do not need and cannot afford.

This book takes a pragmatic approach to failure. It views the condition as an expected, almost certain occurrence that must be addressed continually in order for every project to succeed. It doesn't purport to list specific do's and dont's in a sense of right and wrong techniques, but right and wrong approaches, attitudes, perspectives, and expectations. Given the proper set of each, many errors and misjudgments can be overlooked or judged immaterial to project success. While under their inappropriate counterparts, however, every error (no matter how minor) is amplified and exacerbates project weakness, becoming a failure factor rather than a tolerable imperfection.

How then does this book help us to *know* failure? It does so by first describing common symptoms—indications that any business project is about to fail. Failure *tendencies* attributed to every project are then defined and explored, so that we can distinguish between inherent risks and weaknesses and those particular to each project by virtue of its goals, setting, and management. Ten separate areas of project performance are then examined, each with specific risks, business objectives, and common error, and each encountered in one fashion or another, whenever we decide to embark on a new project.

Special failure factors are identified and described, not just because they are intrinsically interesting or because we enjoy self-criticism or despair, but because *failure understanding* is a condition precedent to *failure avoidance*. This accomplished, the final chapter focuses on approaches and techniques that help our projects steer around the most common and virulent failure agencies—to help us practice failure avoidance rather than failure itself.

Of course the practice of project management always involves compromises, expediencies, and partial failure. The best way to avoid failure entirely is to refrain from project undertakings altogether. To those of us in the world of business this is anathema. Had our ancestors followed this advice, that is, declined project endeavors simply as a means of protecting themselves from possible failure, we would still be living in caves, in both a figurative and a literal sense.

Any reader entering the study of a topic such as business failure deserves a few promises by the author. One of these is a healthy optimism concerning project achievements—an understanding that learning failure is secondary to our ultimate goal of continued project success. So expect no infatuation with failure, but neither will there be unearned or foolish optimism about its avoidance. What is offered in their absence is insight into business problems pertaining to unique project work, with no illustration of failure not accompanied by lessons for its prevention or mitigation.

You will find no vacuous slogans, no universal tools, or magic fixes. These simply do not exist. The book is not intended to sell them. Its only merchandise is ideas. Paramount among these is the concept of failure as a complex and multifaceted phenomenon, one that can and should be understood by all those interested in the management of business projects. Failure can be known, and it can be conquered. It is what makes projects full of risk, management essential, and the effort exciting. It heightens the need to understand project workings and to sharpen project skills. And its very potential doesn't always mean success is impossible, only challenging. For that reason alone, failure, like most other phenomena in life, serves a purpose.

ROBERT D. GILBREATH

Norcross, Georgia
February 1986

CONTENTS

LIST OF FIGURES

WINNING
AT PROJECT
MANAGEMENT

INDICATIONS
OF FAILURE

unmet expectations

The first task for those who wish to avoid project failure is to study its symptoms and to understand what, in fact, failure is. This is not nearly as simple or straightforward as it may appear for failure is an interpreted state, often subjectively defined, and seldom clearly recognizable. People have different views of what constitutes failure; success to one may be failure to another. And what about mitigating circumstances, factors beyond our control, such as the global economy, political environments, and waves of social change, or just bad luck? What was successful under one set of conditions may not have proven so given others.

Add to this the moral and ethical connotations often given the terms "success" and "failure" and it becomes apparent why a determination of one or the other is so profound and yet so subjectively based. Perhaps the error is a rush to judge a given effort as either a success or a failure, a total victory or an abject defeat, with no room for intermediate positions. We all know that any project can succeed in some areas while failing in others, but, when all the facts (or perceptions) are in, we still persist in making a global pronouncement of success or failure; one or the other—no middle ground.

To recognize failure and understand its mechanisms we must stop identifying it through the negative. That is, we must cease defining "failure" as merely the absence, or opposite, of "success." This only exchanges one difficulty for another. Defining failure as the absence of success is like defining darkness as the absence of light. It only leads one to ask "OK, what then is light?"

FAILURE'S MANY FACES

Success and failure are multidimensional measurements, not linear functions beginning at zero (total and abject failure) and ending with 100% (absolute perfection). The variables by which we measure success or failure are neither objectively defined nor independent. When we speak of a project as exceeding its budget we could be pronouncing it a cost control failure. The exceeded budget, however, may have been poorly contrived, erroneously calculated and totally unrepresentative of the work to be performed. Rather than a breach in cost control, this "failure" may be one of poor budgeting. Or given an excellent budget and careful, disciplined cost control efforts the budget may still be exceeded due to schedule delays or technical errors, which almost always have negative cost ramifications. Rather than a cost control failure, we may be merely witnessing a *cost manifestation* of a technical failure. These three primary project performance factors (cost, schedule, and technical) are so highly interrelated and interdependent that any change in one will almost certainly cause (or have been caused by) changes in the others. Failure is contagious.

DEFINING FAILURE

How then do we define failure, if not as merely the absence of success? Let us first recognize failure as a *perception* rather than a physical reality. We have failed only when we, or others, *perceive* that we have failed. No matter how much we feel we have *actually* succeeded, if all those around us perceive failure, then failure has in fact occurred.

People perceive failure when their expectations are not met, when actual accomplishment falls short, for some reason, of expected or planned accomplishment. Whether those expectations or plans are reasonable or not makes no difference for now. Failure exists when what *should* have happened did not happen. This is perhaps the definition of failure most fitting our needs, for it allows us to examine both sides of failure: failure in planning and failure in accomplishment.

> Failure = Unmet expectations

FAILURE'S TWO COMPONENTS

For now it matters not whether those expectations are ours or others, or whether they be reasonable, achievable, low, or high. The fact that they remain unfulfilled means that failure has occurred. In terms of a construction project, it's fair to say that management has failed to meet its expectations (budgets, schedules, specifications) when the finished facility costs more than budgeted, took longer than planned, or operates at less than design capacity. But what if those *planning baselines* (budgets, schedules, specifications) were unrealistic, unachievable or simply out of synchronization with reality (the work necessary)? Failure still exists, but its cause is not necessarily poor performance, just poor planning. What happens in such a case is that *unmeetable expectations* are made, and failure, because it is defined as unmet expectations, is virtually assured from the beginning. This is called *planning failure*, and it haunts virtually every project undertaken. Planning failure is the difference between what was planned to be accomplished and what was, in fact, achievable.

The second component of failure, aside from planning failure, is poor performance, or *actual failure*. This is the difference between what was accomplished and what was achievable. Perceived failure, therefore, is the net sum of *planning failure* and *actual failure*. This relationship is represented by the following equation:

$$\text{perceived failure} = \text{actual failure} + \text{planning failure}$$

Figure 1-1 depicts two situations which show the relationships among perceived failure and its *planning* and *actual* components. In the upper situation (top bar chart) project management has planned a level of accomplishment (C) lower than what is achievable given project circumstances and resources (D). This is a classic underplanning situation. Actual accomplishment (B), however, was even less than that planned. Because perceived failure is the sum of planned and actual failure (the latter being negative in this underplanned case), the following relationship holds:

$$F_{\text{perceived}} = F_{\text{actual}} + F_{\text{planned}}$$

$$\overline{BC} = \overline{BD} + (-\overline{CD})$$
$$\overline{BC} = \overline{BD} - \overline{CD}$$

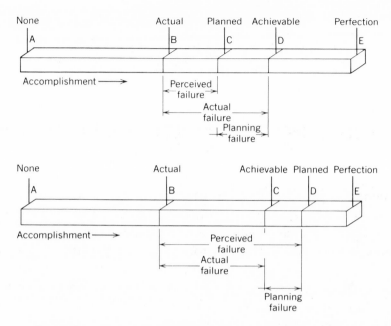

Figure 1-1. Failure having planned and actual components.

A different case is represented by the lower bar chart in Figure 1-1. Here we have planned to accomplish more than what is achievable. Planning failure is assured even if no actual failure occurs. Occur it does, however, and by applying our rule again, we see that perceived failure is the sum of planning and actual failures: $\overline{BD} = \overline{BC} + \overline{CD}$. Note that in both cases (the overplanned and underplanned) *actual failure* ($\overline{BD}$ and $\overline{BC}$ respectively) is the same. Because of its planning component, though, *perceived failure* varies considerably. More discussion concerning planning and its contribution to project failure is found in Chapter 6.

PERFORMANCE FACTORS

Each project has three primary performance factors: cost, schedule, and technical, and a project's success (or failure) is measured by its ability to meet our expectations in each of these three areas. We assess project risks by asking ourselves, during the initial planning phases, "What can go wrong?" in each area. For example:

Cost: It may cost too much money.

Schedule: It may take too much time to complete.

Technical: It may not work as it should.

INTRODUCING THE SUCCESS AND FAILURE TEAM: C, S, AND T

As mentioned earlier, a project may be successful in one area yet fail in another, thus making a general judgment of overall success or failure unjust. While this is true of secondary performance areas it is rarely so for the primary factors of cost, schedule, and technical (C, S, and T). In other words, secondary factors may be successful while C, S, and T fail, and vice versa, but C, S, and T seem always to rise and fall together. They are so closely related and interdependent that either all succeed or all fail.

Figure 1-2 depicts a way of visualizing this close relationship. As seen under condition (a) all three factors are in equilibrium. This represents the initial or planning stages of a project with no planning failure apparent. Should planning failure (positive or negative) exist, some favorable or unfavorable positions would be evident *before* work begins.

Sometime during the course of this model project, performance starts to slip. Whether the instigator of this failure is C, S, or T in nature is not apparent. What is, however, is the interdependence among all three due to the project configuration. They either all fail (condition b) or all succeed (condition c).

What resemblence does this analogy have to real life projects? Let's use the case of a construction project to contrive a few examples where C, S, and T seem to rise and fall together as if linked by an invisible but unbreakable bond.

Condition B: Unfavorable Performance

1.   Major equipment items are late for delivery (S ↓). Contractors begin standby time and inefficient workarounds (C ↓). Temporary methods are used under less than ideal conditions

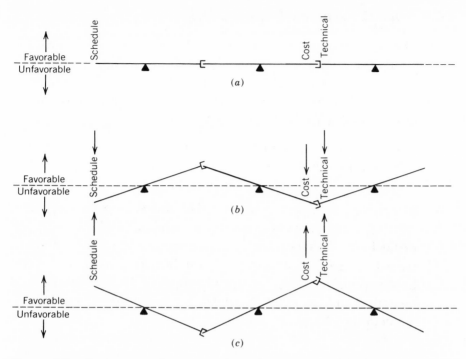

Figure 1-2. Performance factor interdependence. (*a*) Equilibrium; (*b*) Negative variance; and (*c*) Positive variance

(T ↓). Equipment arrives and accelerated shift and overtime work begin to make up lost time (C ↓, T ↓). Because both cost and schedule are unfavorable, the contractor cuts corners on quality of work in order to speed construction time and to save costs (T ↓).

2. Safety inspector discovers improper welds on pressure piping (T ↓). Ripout and rework cause schedule delays (S ↓) and cost overruns (C ↓).

3. Cost reports show cost of engineering and supervision to be approaching budgeted amounts with only one-half of the project completed (C ↓). Owner reduces number of supervisors and shifts to less experienced, lower priced engineering team. Technical problems surface in design and inspection results (T ↓). Redesign and reconstruction of affected areas is ordered (S ↓, C ↓).

Condition C: Favorable Performance

1. Major equipment arrives early (S ↑), allowing for careful installation planning and efficient use of erection facilities to minimize cost (C ↑). Uninterrupted, unhurried installation process allows crews to become more efficient and assures a higher quality of work (C ↑, T ↑).

2. Superior welding process (T ↑) causes much lower rejection rate than planned. This leads to fewer rework welds and less time needed for piping installation (C ↑, S ↑).

3. Standardization and computer assistance help reduce engineering manhours needed for structural design by 30% (C ↑). Project manager requires engineering staff to study alternatives to seismic restraints and snubbers originally specified. Less expensive (C ↑), technically superior (T ↑) restraints are designed and installed. No delay for long lead time snubbers is needed (S ↑).

SECONDARY SUCCESS

Although C, S, and T performance factors do seem to rise and fall in unison, they may show success while other *secondary* factors indicate failure. The reverse is also true. For example, suppose a secondary objective for a major project is to promote long-term stability of the workforce (W). Excellent schedule performance (S ↑) leading to the need for fewer and fewer workers would run counter to the secondary objective (W ↓). What is important to note, however, is that this is one reason why secondary factors are *not* primary factors. Their success or failure is perhaps significant, but not critical to the project. For two important reasons C, S, and T factors are always critical:

1. Failure in any one factor can doom the project in and of itself, and

2. When one fails the other two invariably follow.

Any project manager who strives to achieve secondary success at the expense of C, S, and T is merely cleaning the face of failure. The ugliness remains.

SYMPTOMS OF FAILURE

The reasons for failure are many, as are the methods of failure avoidance. They are subjects of later chapters. For now, however, we must learn how to recognize failure within the context of a project environment—how to sense its presence; how to *know* it. Failure undetected is failure magnified and strengthened. Virtually every aspect of poor performance begins with seemingly minor, innocent origins. These grow in frequency and intensity and reach out to other performance areas very quickly until the symptoms of failure are so evident that detection is no longer a challenge.

The wise manager knows that one cannot wait for self-evident failure because by the time it has become so, it is so extensive as to have caused irreparable damage. The prudent manager practices preventive medicine; hunting for failure, looking for its signs, then seeking out its origins for corrective action. The foolish manager waits until he or she is mortally ill to summon a physician.

Because the origins, mechanics, and manifestations of failure vary so widely, it is meaningless if not impossible to rank its symptoms in any order of importance. Like the common cold, failure is not one disease but a collection of symptoms (perceptions) stemming from literally hundreds of agents acting in a myriad of ways. We recognize the symptoms of a cold though, and should no less recognize symptoms of failure. A cold can be a nuisance; failure can be deadly.

FS 1: By Definition

The most obvious failure symptom (FS) is that which we use to define failure: unmet expectations. Whenever budgets, schedules, or specifications are modified downward to represent less than expected performance ($C\downarrow$, $S\downarrow$, $T\downarrow$) we are witnessing a reaction to failure. This is not always a bad sign though. It may represent the elimination of *planning failure* by bringing baselines back into the realm of reality. Quite often, however, it represents the next symptom of failure.

FS 2: Diminishing Objectives

When you see project goals diminish you are usually witnessing the casualties of failure: lowered expectations. Sometimes this is very obvious, such as the cancellation of a second unit at a two-unit power plant under construction due to extreme cost failure experienced at the first unit. But it may be a bit more subtle, such as the "lowering of design capacity," "stretching out" of schedules, "flattening out" of cash flow, or "smoothing" of staffing levels. Whenever you hear that something is to be stretched, flattened, or smoothed out, be assured that plans cannot be met, so those plans are being changed. Failure is being "redefined" by lowering project expectations and therefore raising the threshold of failure. Unfortunately failure cannot be stretched, smoothed, or flattened out. By the time that happens it has already struck.

Related to diminished objectives is the symptom of failure characterized by a switch from primary success objectives to secondary ones; from C, S, and T to such things as predictable cash flow, elimination of liability, minimized impact on ongoing corporate operations, or providing a good "training ground" for management personnel. When project or corporate management begin to sprinkle their conversations and memos with allusions to these secondary factors one can be fairly certain that C, S, and T are beyond hope.

Projects aren't conceived to minimize liability or to smooth out cash flow. The best way to accomplish these objectives is to do nothing—to never embark on a project effort. Emphasis on secondary objectives is analogous to the references made by announcers during a disastrous football game. When the home team is being defeated 73–0 the conversation turns to such subjects as the weather, lack of congestion in the parking lot, and short lines at the concessions. Failure occurs on the field, where the score (C, S, and T) is always counted the same way.

FS 3: Project Death

This is the terminal effect of failure: the death of the project. No matter when it occurs or for what reason, whenever the project is cancelled it's a sure bet that original expectations are not going to be met. What is challenging, though, is recognizing when death has occurred or is imminent. Some corporations drag the corpse of a project around long after it has lost viability. Often this is done to achieve secondary performance objectives when C, S, and T have expired. These *consolation objectives* may include minimizing the impact of huge layoffs on the local workforce, preserving the reputation of project sponsors in the corporation, looking for a plausible scapegoat, or the fact that everyone left the project so fast that there is no one left to turn out the lights.

Project death certificates are rare. Dead projects seem to drift into oblivion without official proclamation, although recognition is never in doubt. Yet it doesn't take a death certificate to prove that a passing has occurred, it only takes a corpse.

FS 4: Mud Sling

A *mud sling* is a messy dispute among project participants, the type that is bound to happen from time to time on even the best of projects. When mud is continuously and ferociously slung, however, something has failed. When project members are constantly at each others' throats, threatening litigation, pressing claims, refusing work or payments, or even airing private project laundry in public, it is most often a substantial symptom of failure.

The problem with mud slinging is that, rather than focusing on failure detection and its elimination, it is aimed at culpability—finding someone or some group to blame for failure that has already occurred. When mud slinging is epidemic little else about the project gets management attention or project resources, and the result is a continuing slide of C, S, and T for ongoing project work. The effect compounds itself. The more time wrestling with disputes, the less time managing the project, and therefore the higher incidence of failure—which in turn leads to more disputes over culpability.

In advanced cases, the slinging can totally eclipse the project itself. It is as described by a general contractor's representative on such a project: "At this stage we've got two project managers: one to build the hotel and one to build the claim against the owner. And the latter is our best."

FS 5: Process Overtakes Product

Projects are by their very definition temporary and unidirectional. They exist for a definite time and they exist for only one purpose— to produce the resulting product or effect. Once this is accomplished the notion of a project is obsolete, and the project should dissolve. Think of a project as if it were a guided missile, homing in on target. It has been designed, produced, aimed, and fueled for one purpose—to destroy the target. Once the missile strikes its objective, the missile and its reason for existing vanish together.

Major business endeavors of a project nature aren't quite so straightforward or destructive in nature. But it matters not whether the objective is construction of a grassroots oil refinery, a new advertising campaign, commercially viable chemical process, or political campaign. Once the oil is flowing, the commercials are on the tube, the floor wax on every floor, or the candidate in office, the project is no longer.

All projects should be like our guided missile—self destroying. The better they are the quicker they should accomplish their objective and, therefore, the sooner they should dissipate. The duty of each project manager is, then, to make his or her job obsolete. This is difficult to accept for those who are *process*-oriented rather than *product*-oriented. Process-oriented people cling to the security of their function as opposed to the value of their contribution and, as such, make poor project team members. More is to be said concerning this orientation in Chapter 3.

For now let us say that whenever the prevailing attitude of project personnel is one of security, longevity, seniority, roots, or local real estate, danger exists. The conflict between working *well* (and therefore finishing quickly (C↑, S↑)) and working *long* (and therefore enjoying the process (C↓, S↓)) periodically occurs in us all. The astute manager constantly looks for this orientation and tries to counter it by continuous emphasis on the temporary nature of project work and the need to look *beyond* current conditions.

Long project efforts share the propensity for this symptom with those requiring abrupt changes in lifestyle and geographical resettlements. In any case, when people start to refer to the project as if it were an end rather than a temporary means to an end, failure is sure to appear and set up housekeeping for the duration. Unfortunately for them, project parasites eventually kill their host and even they must move on sooner or later. Keep them away from your projects.

FS 6: Corporate Abandonment

Contrary to naval tradition, corporate captains do not go down with the project ship; they jump long before the sailors even suspect rising water. The best way to tell if a project is doomed to failure is not to watch for the rats abandoning the ship but to keep your eye on the fat cats instead. They give a much earlier and more pronounced warning.

We all know that success has many fathers and that failure is an orphan, but it is still stunning to see how this axiom is played out today. A successful project is *everyone's* idea, and because every new project is by definition successful, executives line up to claim association, if not parentage. But let the winds change and these same executives become as scarce as paternal visitors to an orphanage.

Often this abandonment is not only by selected individuals but by the corporation as a whole. This occurs when failure is sensed to be imminent and, *because* it occurs, failure is thereby assured. We see subtle signs of this when the "flagship project" is no longer cited so frequently in the corporate newsletter, when the new building model is taken from the headquarter's lobby, when the senior executives start asking each other "Whatever happened to project X?," and when an assignment to the project is considered an anathema to any aspiring junior executive. It's as if the project had suddenly contracted a fatal disease. In fact it has; the disease is called failure.

At times blatant and unmistakable measures are taken by the corporation to sever all ties between it and the project entity. It is almost comical when, for example, the project is turned into a separate, *autonomous* corporation. The autonomy that project leaders so hungrily sought after at the beginning of the project is finally granted. Except that the granting of autonomy is secondary to the reduction of liability and removal of embarassment. The project is being cut from the mothership and cast adrift, the hope being that it will drift far away before it explodes.

A prime example of this failure symptom was seen during the early 1980s when several electric utilities in the United States created distinct "nuclear corporations" as subsidiaries, then assigned to these new corporations all nuclear power plant projects underway. This was touted as a signal of "corporate recognition of the importance of our nuclear construction effort," however it was plainly liability avoidance. You could almost hear the ropes being cut, and cries of "Bon Voyage" over the waves before the corporate executives hit the deck.

FS 7: Bad Reputation

Every project underway is known to outsiders by its technical expectations and its technical achievements. Because of the uniqueness of each project, these become its trademarks, often its reasons for being. By technical expectations and achievements we mean its size, shape, location, scope, innovative approaches, capacity, physical configuration, and similar characteristics. A successful project is usually one for which its reputation remains technical. This holds for all projects in progress; it is not necessarily true for completed projects.

When we hear of a project's nontechnical performance while work is still underway, the news is usually bad. Either the costs have soared or the schedule has collapsed—or both. Very seldom do we hear of outstanding cost or schedule performance with an ongoing project, and because failure is a perceived condition, a nontechnical reputation often equates to failure.

Of course there are plenty of projects which gain poor technical *and* nontechnical reputations. These are simply disasters, about which everyone seems to know, except perhaps those in charge. These projects have been aptly named "black holes" because of their semblance to the cosmic phenomena that draw everything in their vicinity into their molten centers. Nothing escapes. Black hole projects likewise draw money, material, personnel, and time into their abyssmal cores with a force as certain as gravity.

When looking for failure symptoms one need not search for this extreme. A dependable indication is the nontechnical reputation. The best projects maintain a low cost and schedule profile until their completion.

FS 8: Us Against Them

Successful projects focus on their objectives and the processes underway to those ends. Project management learns from initial errors, adjusts, and continues with minimum disruption. Failing projects do just the opposite. Management attention is shifted away from primary or even secondary performance factors and is focused on error. This focus is often not on failure detection, prevention, or even mitigation. It is on failure *assignment*. People who fail in front of others often try to blame either the circumstances or other people. Projects are no different.

There is no doubt that external influences, the project environment or even project objectives may contribute to failure (these are described in detail in Chapter 2). Failed projects strive to identify these or other external factors as responsible for their poor performance. Its not unusual to see this begin even months before failure actually occurs. Project managers often pick scapegoats and store them in case they will be needed later. A partial listing of these follows.

Government agencies

Economy

Inflation

Declining productivity

Resource scarcity

Bad luck

Lack of corporate support

Technical impossibility

Intervenors

Insufficient time

All these factors have, from time to time, tormented projects; indeed, few projects totally escape their impacts. But successful projects sustain the impact of less than favorable conditions, adjust to them, and proceed in a quest for better performance. Failing projects must cling to them because, with the ability to absorb culpability for failure, scapegoats are, in themselves, precious project resources.

To search for and build a case against a project scapegoat is time and cost consuming. Like mud slinging, it saps management resources and detracts from the attainment of true project objectives. When the search for scapegoats begins in earnest, and dominates project activity, one can be certain that the project is dead. The principal players are merely arguing over its bones.

FS 9: Belt Tightening

A project is in trouble or about to fail when arbitrary restrictions, often in the guise of corporatewide efforts, cut into its operations. These often take the form of personnel limits, hiring "freezes," funding squeezes, and other austerity programs. Their objective is to slow down, stop, or otherwise restrain project activity without being apparent, but their effect is the same. A successful project is immune to corporatewide restrictions and generally allowed to pursue its course within overall, preestablished limits (C, S, and T baselines).

Arbitrary restrictions are useful to those wishing to kill a project without admitting to project-specific failure. Thus, a new power plant can be halted, not because its massive cost overruns make it economically unfeasible, but because "demand for electricity has dropped." And corporate management can avoid a confrontation with a project manager by cutting off his or her organization's growth with "divisional personnel freezes" rather than direct limits on the project staff.

It often pays to look behind such arbitrary restrictions to see if they are indeed across-the-board. They may be project restrictions in corporate clothing. Projects are rarely stopped in their tracks; chopped off with one fell swoop. They are most often slowly strangled.

FS 10: Real Money

Every project begins with a financial examination which leads to some sort of a budget. During the planning stage this budget is an *anticipated* amount, often chock full of contingencies, reserves, extras, padding, and fudge factors of unknown size and indeterminate origin. The fact that these amounts are suspect, haven't yet been committed, may never be expended, and may even represent internal charges rather than external costs lends an aura of skepticism or unreality to them. *Funny money* is not often taken seriously.

When money is spent, however, it is *gone*—both in a real and an accounting sense, and it ceases to be funny. This is when people take notice and often when their interest in project activity peaks—not when budgets are made, not when reserves are shifted, and not when accounting systems are installed—but when money is spent. *Real money*—not funny money.

Project participants are all involved with one express purpose: to make *real* money. The sponsor, often termed "the owner" invests money in order to gain the capacity (new power plant, hotel, etc.), to make more money once the project is over. Other project participants (engineering firm, contractors, consultants, ad agency, etc.) expect direct and immediate payment for their efforts. When any major participant begins to lose *real money,* the project becomes a genuine candidate for failure.

Project management has often been compared to warfare. This is an absurd analogy, for with war one party wins when the other party is killed. With a major business endeavor, however, should one party die all others suffer, if not die themselves. Project relationships are based on *need* as well as *greed*. Each party *needs* the others in order for success to occur. Seldom do we find a project where a major party suffered severe financial losses without the project itself suffering. Those who are drowning in a group of swimmers tend to clutch onto whomever they can. Project members losing *real money* grab like hell.

FS 11: Turnstyle Team

Employee turnover is a fact of corporate life, so why should project efforts be any different? Usually they involve the creation (and, it is hoped, eventual destruction) of a temporary project-specific organization. That fact alone leads to turnover as people come onto and roll off of project organization charts as they and their skills are needed. Additional turnover should be expected due to the mixed and conflicting loyalties, and ensuing dissatisfaction experienced by all project personnel (see Chapter 4). These and other inherent difficulties make the maintenance of a stable work force and long-term group identities virtually impossible in a project setting. This is unfortunate, but successful projects have tolerated the coming and going of key players with minimum strain. They cannot, however, survive a continuous churning of people.

Like most other failure symptoms described here, excessive personnel turnover is both a symptom as well as a cause of failure. And like most, once it begins its impact is continued and compounded—the snowball effect. We see failed projects, or those on the path to failure, when turnover greatly exceeds corporate or industry norms. We also see such pending failure when higher and higher positions are involved. A general rule is that with higher and more frequent turnover, the closer the project is to failure.

Beware of projects with constant references to "the new regime," "reorganization," and "a new team." Often this signifies a ritual dance played out as the project spirals downward. They may be rearranging the chairs on the deck of a new Titanic.

FS 12: Audit the Audit

A number of factors contribute to the growing frequency of project audits and the trend shows no sign of abatement. These include the increase in number of project participants (the more joint owners, for example, the more interests to protect and therefore more audits), today's extreme interest in project controls and management prudence, and the simple truth that despite some pronounced faults, audits have proven effective in surfacing system and operating deficiencies. When well focused and judiciously used, project audits can represent a valuable control effort.

But every good idea can be taken to excess, and management audits are no exception. They are often misused and misdirected, leading to dissatisfaction with their findings and calls for further, unbiased (or better informed) audits. It is not startling, or even unusual today to find redundant, overlapping and even pointless auditing taking place.

Project managements rarely ask to be audited, and those being audited rarely view the effort as an unbiased search directed towards beneficent improvements. Some actual reasons project or corporate managements request (or acquiesce to) an audit include: (1) the need to nail a scapegoat, (2) to expose and punish a business rival, (3) to justify current practices or planned changes, (4) to preempt a more onerous audit or, (5) to satisfy a third party.

It is humorous to see those whose business is auditing attempt to justify their service. Sometimes they change the name of their product to counter customer objections that another audit is not needed. Other names used for management audits are (1) diagnostics, (2) preemptive audits, (3) prudency reviews, (4) organizational studies, (5) operational analyses, and the like.

The point is, where management audits proliferate failure is likely. A project under continual audit is a project in trouble. This makes simple business sense, for no one wants to examine something that works well—only something that doesn't. Projects are like people in this regard, for the more ill a person is the more tests are conducted to determine the extent of the illness.

The sad part about project audits is not their frequency, sometimes questionable objectives, or inefficiencies. Rather, it is the way their findings are ignored or explained away without subsequent improvement. Effort is often spent answering the audit finding instead of correcting the underlying deficiency. A vast number of deficiencies may be due to the fact that the project is simply that—a project, and no project is immune from inherent project difficulties. Like the genes of one's ancestry, there is no escaping their effect. This being the case, it is best to become acquainted with them.

CHAPTER TWO

INHERENT PROJECT DIFFICULTIES

a tendency to fail

Projects are different. This is their most salient feature, and indeed why they *are* projects. And they are different in three distinct ways:

1. They represent unique, one-time-only efforts with singular objectives. Should they be merely repeat performances of what has been done in the past they would represent ongoing operations—not projects.

2. They use a uniquely different set of resources in a unique configuration. Each project is not only distinct from operations, but different from any other project ever undertaken.

3. The environment on which a project effort is unleashed is always different and constantly changing. Conditions vary, jurisdictions change, risks differ, and so do approaches to management and control, regardless of any intentions to the contrary on the part of corporate or project managements.

In other words, each project is different because (1) it *is* a project, (2) it is a *distinct* project, and (3) it exists in a distinct *environment*.

RISK AND CHALLENGE

If there is one word which captures the true nature of every project it is the word *different*. It helps explain why projects are often spoken of in terms of risk. Risk represents the potential impact of unknowns, the negative side of uncertainty. Those wishing to minimize risk, therefore, shy away from unique, one-time endeavors; away from projects.

But the other side of risk is challenge, and these two are inseparable. One does not exist without the other. Every project, no matter how mundane represents challenge, and therein lies the allure of project undertakings and project management. Once an effort has proven successful it is undertaken again and again, and thus is converted from a project exercise to *operations*. Project managers differ from their operational counterparts in their willingness, even desire, to meet and conquer risk.

TO CREATE RATHER THAN TO COMPLY

We often read of highly successful entrepreneurs or project managers, who, having successfully established a new venture, become bored and restless to the point where they leave the ongoing entity they created in search of another new, more challenging concern. These managers are unsuited for operations. They abhor *management by rote*—seeking not merely to husband proven efforts but to begin and test entirely new ones.

PROSPECTORS AND MINERS

Project managers do not enjoy following rules or complying with procedures established by others. They thrive on *creating* rules. When the project migrates towards ongoing operations, as they all do over time, project managers migrate to new challenges.

The distinction between project and operational managers can be visualized by likening the first to *prospectors* employed by a mineral company, and the second to the *miners* who extract and refine the ore discovered by project effort. Prospectors are judged by their results (lodes discovered) while miners are measured by their output, according to established standards. Prospectors are rewarded for *accomplishing an objective*, while miners are rewarded for *implementing and improving a process*. Every successful business enterprise needs both.

Of course, with any new operation much fine tuning, debugging, and optimization still remains beyond the project phase. This is left for operations-oriented managers. Project managers, like projects, are different, and they seek to accomplish not to optimize. They leave optomizers in their wakes.

ACCOMPLISHMENT BEFORE OPTIMIZATION

Perhaps this is one reason why the success of a project is so difficult to measure. We constantly attempt to compare the project experience to operational counterparts, but the comparison is patently erroneous. No equitable comparison can be made because there is no standard, no time honored template against which to judge the project experience. We cannot determine what "could" have been done by comparing it to what has been done before. Again, refinement and optimization are concepts not applicable to a project setting. For this reason we must adjust our methods of rating project experiences from those based on the question "Was the best result obtained?" to something more like "Was the mission accomplished?"

All this means is that we should be discussing projects in such absolute terms as *success* and *failure* rather than quantifiable, graduated indices that rely on comparison to a previous standard, and why even those extremes (success and failure) are not definitive, but perceived and subjectively assessed.

A DIFFERENT STANDARD

Some might contend that this view leaves project efforts and project managers off the hook—unaccountable to any standards. Indeed, the very different nature of project work has been used by some as a sort of universal shield, protecting them and their projects from scrutiny by continually calling "different! different!" at the first inquiry or sign of criticism. On closer examination, however, it must be seen that rather than freeing project managers from accountability, the unique nature of each project actually holds them to higher, more difficult to attain standards. For although they cannot be measured against known levels of compliance and performance, such as quotas, unit rates, unit costs, return on investment levels, or productivity standards, they can and are held accountable for ultimate success or failure, and, more closely, to someone else's notions of prudency, foresight, and reasonableness.

And well they should. Project managers should be results-oriented, achievement-directed, and risk-conscious. They should understand the uncertainty they face and be aware of the many alternatives at their command to avoid, control, transfer, or otherwise mitigate risk. This is why they are needed and indeed, why they exist. It is also why they alone are positioned on the forefront of unique and high-stakes efforts. They must know what risks are possible and be able to distinguish among those they may avoid, diminish, or accommodate.

In order to do so, however, they must first attain a thorough understanding of what projects are, how they differ from ongoing operations, and what difficulties are inherent to all projects simply because they are, in fact, projects. This chapter is intended to help them attain that understanding; not to explain or excuse failure, but to describe an environment where it commonly flourishes.

THIS IS NOT A BICYCLE FACTORY!

As mentioned earlier, comparisons between ongoing business operations and project efforts are patently erroneous and inequitable. However, we can enjoy a tremendous amount of insight into the workings of a project, and more importantly, inherent project difficulties by *contrasting* project experiences with operational ones. This will help us prepare to meet special, project-only risks and to understand which operational controls and approaches are successful in a project environment, and those which should be discarded.

Some differences are self-evident but still critical, for operations are ongoing and are constantly being refined. Projects have only one shot and do not benefit as much from any direct feedback on their performance. Using the example of a bicycle manufacturer embarking on the design and construction of a new plant, we will be able to examine these differences a bit more closely. The ongoing operation of the bicycle company involves the making and selling of bicycles. They constantly tune their processes in order to optimize this function. Cheaper materials are sought, more efficient machines are procured, lower wage workers using less and less labor hours are a goal, along with more efficient plant configurations, shipping, and packaging methods. New versions of these are tried and those that work are adapted. Those failing to bring improvements are tossed aside. Over the years this continuous advancement proceeds to the point where the best, most marketable bicycles (T ↑) are produced in the shortest time (S ↑) at the lowest possible cost (C ↑).

Forepersons, supervisors, and managers in the bicycle company's hierarchy are no different in mission (and treatment) than other ingredients in the manufacturing mix. Those who increase production (in terms of C, S, and T) are kept, others are let go. Survivors, and therefore potential executives, are measured by fixed standards of C, S, and T; what have you done compared to what others have done before?

When the bicycle company decides to locate, design, and construct increased capacity (a new bicycle factory), it is embarking on a project effort whether it knows so or not. Then the project arena is so different that many of the rules, methods, and expectations that work in making bicycles have absolutely no meaning in the "making" of a bicycle factory. Therein lies the crux of corporate versus project battles that rage throughout the business world. We can surely expect, in this example case, that a time will come when the project manager, irate at inappropriate corporate standards and unrealistic expectations will scream "This is not a bicycle factory, it is a project to *make* a bicycle factory!," and he will be right. But because he is right doesn't mean he will prevail. This will occur only when he and his corporate sponsors know the many reasons why he is right and act accordingly.

RULES AND ROLES

For purposes of contrast, let's assume our bicycle company operates a fine factory. That this factory has an existing organization, well defined, and understood throughout the plant. Let's further grant it well established lines of communication up and down the organizational pyramid. Certainly problems will exist in any plant, but let's assume that organization and communication are optimized, like the manufacturing process itself, after years of trial and error. In this plant we can imagine one person at the top of the organization. Call him or her the plant manager and agree that this manager is responsible for the line operations—that the position has all the authority needed to run the bicycle factory and that this is not in dispute.

In such a factory we would expect each worker to understand his or her role, no matter what it is, and to have some long-term objectives of employment that are consistent with those held by plant and corporate management. Ideally each worker aspires to do their best, to move up the organizational ladder, and eventually to retire on a pension made viable by the continued success of the factory. This being the case, each individual's goals are parallel to, and entwined with the factory's goals.

After years of employment, under the direction of similarly motivated supervisors, and working to time-honored and tested procedures, each group in the factory family achieves a good understanding of the roles and relationships they share with other groups and hopefully they "interface" well together. They may not necessarily like each other, but they understand each other. They attempt to meet published standards of efficiency—standards established and attained in the past. They and their managements feel necessary to the continued success of the company, after all, they are *the* bicycle factory of a bicycle-making corporation. They do not then, need to justify their existence. They represent a profit center, the lifeblood of the company, the mainline, the purpose, the *raison d'être*. The factory is the engine of prosperity for the corporation. It's contribution is readily apparent, easily quantifiable, and directly attributable to the people and methods employed—to the *operation*.

NONE OF THE ABOVE

The best way to contrast project endeavors is to say that none of the preceding assumptions fit. Not only do they not fit, they are dramatically opposed to the project context.

First and foremost, the project to build a new bicycle factory must rely on a newly created and temporary organization. Resultantly, it will not be well defined or, at least initially, well understood by those within or without it. It will constantly change as the work scope, size, and nature changes, and as soon as it begins to be recognizable, and understood, it will no doubt change again.

Lines of communication will have to be strung and connected. They will run over, under, and through the organizations involved in project activity rather than simply up and down the operational pyramid. These organizations will include, for our bicycle factory project, the owner, design consultant (architect, engineer), prime construction contractor(s), subcontractors, material vendors, site developer, insurors, sureties, affected governments and regulatory agencies, construction financiers, and many others. Each of these will have its own organizations, methods of operating, procedures, and different—often conflicting—project objectives.

There will be many authorities within the project, with at least one for each cited organization. There will also be overlapping functional authorities, such as the safety engineer, chief mechanical engineer, site officer manager, and labor business agents in addition to the organizational authorities existing in each associated company. As such, virtually every individual involved with project work in any position of responsibility will have different goals; specific goals which often conflict with those of others. All will be temporary, short-term goals so no mutual understanding of roles and relationships among project groups can be assumed. A created, dynamic organization with multiple, conflicting authority embarking on a unique, never-been-done-before project for which communication channels must be established and long-term, mutual goals are impossible. This is a convoluted yet very accurate definition of the typical construction project.

A few other handicaps need to be mentioned (as if we haven't identified enough). Our bicycle factory project will not be treated with the same respect as existing factory operations. They bring in profit today—we bring in *capacity to make profit* years from now. They make money while we spend it. They are profit generators and we are profit dissipators. They are mainline, we are sidetracks. In the short term at least (and this is where most executives live) they *are* the corporation, while we are something different and perhaps, annoying. The corporation understands bicycle making. It is suspicious of bicycle factory making.

The project's contribution to the well being of the corporation is unclear, difficult to see, touch, or measure. If seen at all it may be viewed as a negative; the project as a detractor rather than contributor. Even when a project succeeds, it is difficult to attribute success to project people or processes. Other factors could be involved, such as favorable weather, hungry and competitive contractors, or just good luck.

Some of these distinctions are self-evident and some are a bit more subtle. All contribute to the schism between operations and projects, between operationally minded executives and project managers. If the project is to avoid failure, parties on both sides of this gulf need to understand just how deep and how wide it is; to know which risks, expectations, and methods make sense on each side—and which don't.

THE BUSINESS PROGRESSION:
OPERATIONS→PROJECT→OPERATIONS

It's helpful to view these as two different animals, that is, projects and operations, not as opposing management philosophies or business approaches, but as distinct and viable *phases* in an overall business progression followed by virtually every capitalist entity. Rather than mutually exclusive, projects and operations represent successive efforts with different objectives and different means of attaining them. Figure 2-1 portrays this precedent-successor relationship by arranging projects and operations (or enterprises) in an end-to-end pattern. Beginning with some sort of *resource base*, initial capital investment, ideas, and talents of risk-taking individuals are combined to explore potential enterprises. This is a *project* effort, with a set of expectations (return on investment), some limited resources (C, S, and T), along with some degree of freedom and autonomy needed to achieve results. This mix may achieve new capability to return profit through increased production capacity (new factory), broader market share (advertising campaign), new product sales (research and development), or even acquisition of existing capability from others (merging, buying, etc.)

Once the project's objective is achieved, it is termed a success.

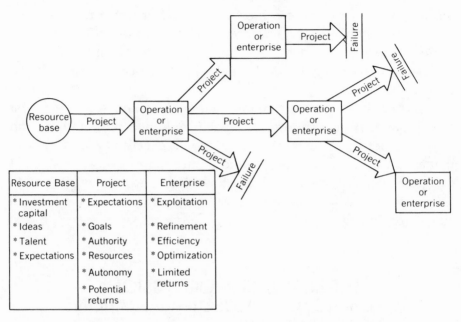

Figure 2.1 The project-operations progression of business.

Operations then takes over. They refine the process, consummate the acquisition, and otherwise optimize the possible results by thorough exploitation of the project result. After refinement is well underway (repeated operations produce less and less improvement), the company seeks once again to expand its profit. A new effort (project) is mounted, with hopes that it will result in a net increase in the operational base of the firm. Again, this increase may be due to expanded capacity, markets, products, services, or efficiencies. Each represents the end result of successful *project* efforts. In this fashion, projects represent the searching and, when successful, seizing of new profit *opportunities*, which are in turn *exploited* through successive operations.

It matters little whether the project in question is a bicycle factory, a research and development effort seeking a cure for a disease, or a marketing campaign aimed at introducing a dramatically new product to the public. All suffer enough on their own merits, in addition to the problems of inherent project difficulties. But in order for them to succeed at all, their sponsors, from projects and operations alike, must know the difference.

THREE REASONS FOR FAILURE

Failure is difficult to define, isolate, and eventually avoid. We analyze failure in order to do all these and we cannot analyze it without making further divisions of failure; looking at failure's components, indications, and tendencies. Add to this the differing reasons for failure to occur. For every project, there seem to be three major reasons:

1. General failure potential by virtue of it's being a project (inherent risks).

2. Specific failure potential attributed to it's particular mission (accepted risks).

3. Specific failure generated by the project organization and activity (created risks).

Because it is impossible to discuss specific projects and specific, accepted risks (item 2) in the context of one book, we will focus our attention on failure bases 1 and 3; inherent and created risks. We begin by examining inherent risks, those pertaining to all projects simply because they are projects. These will be called "failure tendencies" (FTs). The second category, created risks, will be termed "failure factors" (FFs) and are described in Chapters 3 through 12. But first, let's address the tendencies.

FT 1: The Project Is Nonoperational

Projects have a tendency to fail because they are not operations and they do not respond well to operational measures and controls. One of the greatest errors a project manager or corporate executive can make is to transpose operational concepts to project settings. They simply do not work in most cases, and those that can work must be tempered and tailored to each specific application by someone knowledgeable in the differences. This is easy to understand but so difficult for most of us to obey. We have a built-in mental set that tells us to optimize and to measure against existing standards in order to determine what has happened, what is happening, and what to expect in the future.

Some of the cornerstones of operational management simply fall apart when used for projects. A good example is the principle of economy of scale. We all have been taught that a bigger machine using more resources at a faster rate is more efficient than a smaller counterpart; that we can achieve more economy with a process producing 5000 nuts and bolts an hour than one producing say, ten. This law applies well in a factory making nuts and bolts, but when we turn to the process of making the factory, we cannot use it. We have only one factory to be made.

Trial and error doesn't help us much either. Should the first 100 nuts and bolts turn out incorrectly we can fine tune the equipment and check the next 100, and so on until optimal results are obtained. With our project example, though, we benefit little from past mistakes. We have no margin for error, no second, third, or one hundredth attempt at perfection. We are given only one. Sure, we can use economies of scale and trial and error within certain parts of our project, certain elements, but even these are so infrequently occurring and limited in number that both concepts help little. And they can be misleading.

Let's suppose that our nut and bolt factory requires a foundation of reinforced concrete containing approximately 20,000 cubic yards of this material. The nature of the construction process is such that, once the first few cubic yards of concrete are poured we learn very little about how well the excavation, reinforcing steel, embedments, penetrations, formwork, and hydration process are performing. We may learn how to improve the placement and distribution of concrete in this particular formwork, but this aspect of the foundation construction represents only a small percentage of the work. We seldom are able to efficiently rearrange the hole, reset the rebar, redesign the formwork, or change the water content of the concrete simply because these work items must be done so far in advance of pouring that process adjustments are uneconomical. We do our best to prepare for concrete pouring, but once it's started, no further economies are achievable.

Add to this the fact that concrete placed in a massive foundation is not the same as concrete placed on the 14th floor, for example, and the use of pouring rates to predict and measure economies for future work becomes erroneous if not meaningless. That is, pouring rates in terms of cubic yards per hour experienced in the foundation area must be drastically reduced for the elevated deck on the 14th floor.

What about other operational assumptions? Let's examine the roles and relationships existing in an operational setting. Because they are usually well established and universally understood, little reliance is placed on explicit procedures, organization charts, job descriptions and the like. The opposite is true for project efforts. Because there are virtually no "understood" roles and relationships, these communication tools (charts, procedures, descriptions) not only cannot be taken for granted, they are essential.

Operational work results in fairly self-identifying, self-correcting variances. Projects do not. A variance is any difference, favorable or unfavorable, from expected results. Repeated operations allow these "abnormalities" to be seen and their sources corrected for the benefit of future and similar work. With one-of-a-kind efforts, any variance is merely a variance from plans, not from past results—simply because past results are not accurate predictors. So identification of a variance (C, S, or T) usually occurs after the one-of-a-kind effort is completed, leaving no allowance for application of lessons learned to similar, following work. It simply isn't there.

We can use the example of *usage variance* to point out another, sometimes subtle difference. With line manufacturing (operationally oriented work) a good manager attempts to reduce the waste and rejections under his or her control. If 200 pounds of steel were required to produce 150 pounds of nuts and bolts when the same weight of product is usually produced using only 180 pounds of resources, we call the extra 20 pounds a "usage variance." In this case it is unfavorable for more steel was used than the optimum. Manufacturing systems provide usage variance data to managers in order to identify the offending process, technique or manager. Without sometimes sophisticated information systems to detect these variances, these data are lost. It is easy to "lose" 20 pounds of steel in a manufacturing process. With our construction project example, however, a usage variance of 10% cannot be lost. Excess concrete cannot be hidden, it has a way of making its presence known.

Again the concept of usage variance has little meaning in a project sense because operations which waste or economize on input material are not often repeated. No sophisticated reporting techniques are needed to identify these variances (a huge pile of wasted concrete will suffice), and once identified, there are no other foundations to be poured—no need to correct pouring methods.

We cannot leave this nonoperational notion without pointing out one additional contrast. Most operations are conducted internally, with company-controlled personnel and methods, while most project activity is performed (at least in the short term), by outsiders. This is because project activity is performed outside the mainstream of the company's operations, using skills the company does not normally possess, and so infrequently as to make staffing of those skills uneconomical. Once we go outside for help we loose (1) understanding of roles and relationships, (2) long-term leverages over performance, (3) total visibility as to cost, schedule, and technical performance of outsiders, and (4) direct control over performance. We rely more on indirect controls, short-term motivation, created authorities, and simple trust. By necessity we turn over critical project responsibility to "others," and hope that they meet our expectations, both express (contractual) and implied (hope).

FT 2: Untested Expectations

Because project work is unique as to size, scope, and setting, our expectations must also be unique. We cannot simply expect what happened last time to happen again and measure project experience against it. These rules do not apply. Surely certain portions of the project work have been completed elsewhere, and we have some idea as to their cost, schedule, and technical parameters, but for the project as a whole we cannot use the past as a guide to the future. Very little intermediate feedback is gotten as to how well we are doing as the project progresses, and what little is learned from this feedback is often inapplicable to the remainder of the work. It is nice to know, but worthless.

Can we compare this project to others? The answer is a very qualified "yes," but these comparisons must focus on similar work done under similar conditions the same way. They also can only help us when there is a large amount of work and for those cases when performance can be determined on early elements in time to apply the knowledge thus gained to later elements. This rarely happens.

All of this should not be construed to imply that simply because our expectations remain untested we need not have expectations. We can and must, or we wouldn't be able to determine if a project can be accomplished within our required C, S, and T baselines. Untested expectations should not be read as "no expectations." They are valuable, but not immutable.

FT 3: The Funding Hurdle

No project is undertaken unless it is expected to meet certain corporate criteria. These are most often based on some sort of funding threshold. Those projects expected to exceed that criteria are approved and the others are rejected. This *feasibility* determination can be the result of an exhaustive study or a simple management judgment backed by a few figures. Corporations cannot do everything, and they decide, in most cases, to do certain things over others based on the payback expected. This is called the *funding hurdle*.

Let's suppose we are in the business of making and selling home cleaning products. We would like to enter new markets and expand our gross margin. There are a number of ways to do this, some better than others, and there are an equal number of *product champions*, that is, people within the company who sincerely believe in certain new products. We have decided to undertake only those new products which can be expected to return 14% of our investment after their first year of introduction. This is our company's new product funding hurdle.

Product champions constantly request authorization for investment of company funds in new product development and marketing. We grant each request only when it can be reasonably expected to return 14%. A common tendency is to underestimate startup costs (what it takes to develop a new product and penetrate the market) in order to increase the chance of clearing the funding hurdle. The other common tendency is to overestimate the profits returned.

The product champion, knowing that his or her pet project will not clear the funding hurdle, purposely or unconsciously minimizes the C, S, and T required while maximizing the return. Expected costs are trimmed, schedules are fast tracked, and technology requirements are downplayed until, at some point, the project is approved and begins. When this is done to excess, planning failure (at least) is almost assured.

To visualize this process better, compare the project under review to an athlete preparing to clear a hurdle on the track. He can better his chances by (1) losing weight and strengthening his jumping muscles, or (2) cutting off the hurdle's legs and thereby reducing the height he must clear. Product champions often do both. They lose weight by paring down the required resources needed to achieve project objectives (C, S, and T baselines). They strengthen their muscles by placing an inordinate amount of confidence in themselves, their proposed staffs and their methods, and they lower the funding hurdle by overestimating the return expected of the finished product or facility.

The funding hurdle phenomenon is a fixture of project life, and many projects that clear the hurdle should have been left standing in the starting blocks. Even those that sail far above it are not guaranteed success. Conditions will change, markets shift, competitors act or react, and consumer preferences wander. The longer the project takes from inception to final delivery, the less effective the initial funding hurdle test can be. Sometimes this initial hurdle isn't enough. Perhaps long-term projects need to confront continuous funding hurdles; to rejustify their existence periodically, based on current conditions, performance, and expectations. Maybe this should even be done as a matter of course, not just for those extreme cases where a black hole begins to develop.

FT 4: The King of Change

Anyone who has ever built their own house knows that the biggest maker of change is themselves. Customers seeing their purchase evolve tend to see ways to improve it, strengthen it, make it more safe, more efficient, more attractive. This continues with each incremental change, on its own merits, appearing justified in terms of increased C, S, and T. The cumulative effect however, is often overwhelming.

Project work seems particularly prone to the meddlings of the sponsor—the corporate owner. When we purchase a new automobile, for example, we don't visit the assembly plant, witness the fabrication process and make on the spot changes to color, fabric, structural integrity, or design capacity. We don't see the product until it is finished, and at that time either accept the result (buy) or reject (keep looking).

How different it is with projects, where the sponsor is the first player in the game, the originator of the project itself. As the project progresses, this authority is often used to initiate change. More is to be said concerning the role of change in project success or failure later on (Chapter 10). For now, just acknowledge that change can wreak havoc on a project, and the project sponsor often earns the title "king of change."

FT 5: Fast Tracking

To *fast track* a project is to overlap certain activities that are traditionally performed consecutively. For a construction project we often see the major phases of design and construction overlapped in regard to time. Design of the foundations is completed so that foundation construction may begin early, before the design of the building's mechanical and electrical systems is complete. As foundation construction proceeds, design of the superstructure can begin, and construction of the superstructure can commence before the interior finishes (carpet, wall coverings, etc.) are selected. Fast tracking simply implies that what is ideally performed consecutively (design, then construction) is performed concurrently.

The benefit of fast tracking, when it works, is strictly a savings of time for project work. Overlapping of stages allows overall schedule *compression;* less time required for overall performance, even though some elements of the work may take longer. Most proponents of fast tracking point to schedule compression and associated cost savings attributed to a shorter funding period and a new capacity (the object of the project) being available sooner as benefits that counter-

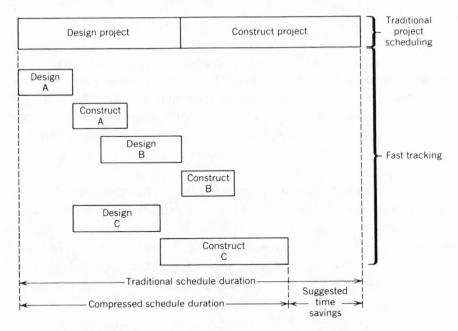

Figure 2.2. The concept of fast tracking: Fool's gold?

act any lesser inefficiences required. An illustration of fast tracking is shown as Figure 2-2. In the construction example, foundations designed early in order to facilitate immediate construction may be overdesigned to accommodate any potential equipment loadings that are unknown at the time. Fast trackers say this is a small price to pay for schedule compression. If it were the *only* price they would be right, however, it isn't.

What often happens in a fast tracked project is that the early work must be redone in order to accommodate unforeseen changes and unexpected results. Equipment may have to be rearranged and extra, heavier equipment ordered. This may cause the foundations to be inadequate, and thus necessitate complete redesign, ripout, and rework that would have been avoided had fast tracking not occurred. Projects are difficult enough to manage in a fairly static environment. Adding the fluidity of fast tracking tempts failure to occur. Only the most skillful, fully staffed, best informed and resource-rich project sponsors can accommodate the added demands of fast tracking. Its benefits don't accrue to amateurs or to risk avoiders.

Many project sponsors know the perils of fast tracking and deliberately eschew its use. What they may not realize, however, is that try as they may, fast tracking is almost inherent to projects. That is, we must fast track regardless of our intentions to the contrary. Why is this so? Much of the impetus to fast track comes from the funding and feasibility exercise mentioned earlier. Projects are defined and initiated up to the funding authorization point, and then held in waiting for approvals to be granted. As this continues, original C, S, and T targets begin to grow stale and are seriously jeopardized. By the time enough corporate sponsors are in favor of the project, these targets are often difficult to meet without fast tracking. Like life in the army, project initiation is often a game of wait, wait, wait . . . hurry up!

There are other examples of fast tracking besides our construction project. When a new product is to be introduced, we often start titillating the sales staff or the eventual customers about its merits and availability. The marketing effort often begins before the product has been developed and tested. The best example of project fast tracking might be President Kennedy's promise to put a man on the moon "by the end of the decade" (1960s). Note that in this one phrase he effectively set the project goals of S and T without ever mentioning the needed C. We all know the result. That project teaches us that, yes, given the right amount of C (unlimited funding) any reasonable S and T can be met—even with fast tracking. Unfortunately the rest of us must operate with finite resources.

FT 6: Moving Targets

Technology is moving, social mores are changing, information is exploding, management techniques are multiplying, and visibility into project inner workings is increasing. Each factor aggravates project effort and makes success more elusive. We are expecting more and more from projects and willing to give less and less in terms of resources and C, S, and T limits. Why is this so?

There are a number of explanations, and perhaps truth in all. The first might be the expanding population of alternatives each company faces in its business. There are just many more activities within access of each company, many more markets, many more services and products they can supply and exploit than in the past. There are also many different ways to supply and exploit each. More accessible alternatives means there is more pressure on those that are chosen to succeed. If the only way we can grow is by building a new factory, the factory-building project has little competition in the funding hurdle, and little need for constant rejustification as it progresses. There are few detractors and reasonable expectations. But given the fact that growth can be accomplished through other alternatives such as acquisition, merging, diversification, or prudent investment, the choice of a new factory is not automatic nor is the project without detractors once chosen.

Technology not only allows us to do things better, it brings more alternatives to doing them. Unfortunately technology doesn't halt its progress once our project and its goals and C, S, and T baselines are fixed. Long-term projects are more prone to becoming obsolete or suboptimum before they are completed than are short-duration efforts. And projects which require massive commitment during their early stages are also more susceptible to the impact of moving technology.

Because of the pressure of competition for the funding dollar, many companies are looking at operational improvements rather than new projects. Today more than ever before, a greater portion of the construction dollar is spent on plant modifications, as opposed to grassroots projects. People are looking for ways to apply the "slaughterhouse theory" to existing operations as an alternative to undertaking new efforts (projects). The slaughterhouse theory attempts to take the raw material in a production process and extract more and more product with less and less effort. As the meatpackers used to say, "we try to get everything out of the pig but the squeal." All this means is that projects have competition during the approval process and built-in critics during their implementation phases. These critics are the champions of nonselected alternatives, and most of these alternatives deal with increases to ongoing operations—contributing to that classic battle between operations and projects.

FT 7: Big Brother

Projects make good targets for regulators. These might be governments, their agencies or their representatives. Without going through the entire alphabet soup of possible government intervenors (OSHA, EPA, DNR, NLRB, PUC, FCC, FTC, etc.), let it suffice to point out that, despite promises by politicians to the contrary, their presence and impact show no sign of abatement.

There are many "little brothers" which may intrude upon project life. These aren't government agencies necessarily, but often represent corporate, or nonproject interests. At times they are helpful, but we must remember that the role of corporate staff is to assure consistency and uniformity in corporate endeavors and this goal often conflicts with project operations in a dramatic way. Little brothers which can impact a project from the corporate home include *internal auditing, legal staff, personnel, risk management, data processing, public information, training, treasury, accounting, engineering,* and *marketing* to name a few.

The impact of little brothers increases as the project gains visibility and as the project manager tolerates their intrusion. The wise manager "manages" these internal outsiders as carefully as he or she manages the project. They keep them happy, informed, and feeling useful, and they cannot ignore or antagonize them unnecessarily. Each has the ability to wound, if not kill the project.

FT 8: Is Everybody Happy?

Projects are often ill defined concerning what benefits they will bring. For this reason and many others, projects are often overvalued and end up promising everything for everyone. We all know that a major corporation is comprised of a multitude of special interest groups, and that no idea, effort, or project will satisfy all of them. In their zeal to gain corporate acceptance of the project concept, project champions must restrain themselves in this regard. They must promise only that absolutely necessary to clear the approval hurdle, and no more. Unnecessary promises create more expectations. Failure to meet expectations is failure itself. Why ask for it?

An entirely new group of parties become involved once the approval hurdle is cleared and the project effort begins. These are the principal project participants. Often these represent divergent or even conflicting interests. Here are some principal participants on a construction project, along with their specific objectives:

Player	Goal
Owner	Available as soon as possible (S)
	Low cost (C)
	Operates well (T)
Architect	Operates well
	High fee
	Referred work
Contractor	High profit
	Quick cash
	No hassles
Subcontractor	High profit
	Quick cash
	More work

Keeping in mind that there are often many contractors, subcontractors, as well as nonlisted players, such as consulting engineers, insurors, sureties, material vendors and others, glaring discrepancies can be seen already. The most obvious one is the owner's desire for low cost contrasted with the architect's goal of high fees and the contractor's and subcontractors' desire to maximize profit. We might also have, and frequently do, a conflict between the contractor's desire for high profit and the subcontractor's wish for high profit as well as quick cash. These are just a few very obvious conflicts. Construction projects are replete with them. They represent another inherent project difficulty; one not confined to the construction industry.

FT 9: Fishbowl

Major projects have a high and unmistakable profile. What might be private undertakings among business associates in an operational sense become very visible, spotlighted efforts once we define a project. Project work is work in a fishbowl, open for all to see. We have pointed out some common project detractors while describing other failure tendencies (little brothers, big brother, champions of unchosen projects, operational enhancers, etc.). This high profile only serves to illuminate the project for those wishing to fire on it.

Sometimes project managers and their staffs simply ask for trouble by calling attention to their work. Often this is done during the promotional effort required to clear the authorization hurdle or to recruit new project members. Regardless of the motivation, however, a high profile only serves to heighten expectations and provide a more visible target. Many corporate executives view virtually every new project with suspicion, as either a budget hogger or a management pet. A wise project is a secretive one, hidden from view, coming up for air only when absolutely necessary. In this sense a project is not unlike a hippopotamus resting under the surface of a pond. The larger the hippopotamus the longer it must stay under water and the better target it makes once it breaks the surface. Once there and exposed, it takes deep and rapid breaths, for it knows that along the rim of the pond, hunters are waiting and taking aim.

FT 10: The Invisible Project Manager

Each project has two project managers. One is very visible while the other remains inactive and hidden. The former is responsible for bringing the project's concept into reality; the latter is the author of the concept. Typically the concept's author is operationally motivated, often representing the eventual owner of the completed project.

Some examples may be in order. For an electric utility, the hidden champion of the new power plant project may be the power generation department—the eventual users of the completed facility. A chemical salesperson may detect a potential market for a certain adhesive among existing customers and prompt a research and development project aimed at providing it. This salesperson will not become the project manager during the development phase, but stands to inherit the finished product and to benefit by it. Just as in a political campaign, we know who the hidden project manager is—the candidate. He or she inherits the project's benefits but does not personally run the campaign. This is left to the campaign manager (project manager).

Why should the existence of a hidden, often operationally minded project sponsor detract from the success of any project? In theory, this adds more support to project undertakings, but in practice it can cripple the project. For while cheering the project from the sidelines and having perhaps the greatest stake in its outcome, the second project manager tends to load more and more expectations on the project, and these often increase C, S, and T as well as chances for failure. The generation department may wish for more sophisticated instruments and controls in the new power plant—adding C, S, and T. They surely will want to accelerate the completion schedule—the sooner to get their hands on their facility. In any case involving tradeoffs between capital costs and operating requirements, they are sure to campaign for better equipment, more sophisticated processes and maintenance-free devices (all increasing construction C, S, and T) in order to trim annual operating expenses and effort (lower operational C, S, and T).

Operational sponsors tend to load more and more "weight" onto the project, weight that, had it been added during the feasibility phase, would have kept the project from clearing the funding hurdle. Operational sponsors are sometimes the point people on the owner's team—representing the "king of change" to the best of their ability. Once they see their project taking shape they can think of hundreds of enhancements that, in their mind at least, "must" be made. Identifying each change and tracking its impact on C, S, and T is a major challenge to the actual project manager. This is the only way the project can be protected from uncontrolled growth, which like a cancer, spreads until it eventually kills.

FT 11: What Worked Last Time

Given all that has been said regarding the uniqueness of each project, little value should be placed on existing concepts, processes, procedures, organizations, contracts, systems, and *expectations* if these were borrowed from previous projects. They simply will not apply without extensive modification. If they work as is, without any changes or adaptations, then we are not applying them to a project but merely to another *operation*.

This advice is easily given but seldom applied. The problem is that human beings cannot erase their memories and mental sets as quickly or thoroughly as magnetic storage media. We remember, we assume, we understand, we forget, or make light of differences between last time and this time. Often this presents no problem, but it just takes a minority of these transpositions to create damage. The subtle distinctions which give us so much trouble are often overlooked. No project is "Just like last time." If one motto can be applied to all projects it might be this: "There Was No Last Time."

FT 12: Trust Me

Because project expectations are subjectively made and untested, because most existing policies and procedures are not transferable to new project efforts, and because quantification of project success is often impossible until late in the effort, a great deal of confidence must be placed in the people in charge. We must *trust* project management.

People operating in a trusting relationship, whether it be in business or their personal lives, are reluctant to divulge detailed data to their counterparts. Project managers are no different. Requests for even the most innocuous information are sometimes rejected as representing a challenge to that trust. Even the slightest insinuation that all project activity is not totally under control or perfectly managed is met with an immediate stonewall effort on the part of project members. This is why it pays not to go into business with your relatives. It also points out the danger of basing any project relationship on trust. Both parties (project and corporate) benefit from objective performance criteria carefully and intelligently applied to the project. Any success in reducing the natural reliance on *trust* will benefit the project.

FT 13: Short and Sweet

One simple axiom will explain the undoing of many a project: *The longer a project continues the more susceptible it becomes to inherent risk.* Although there is no quantifiable limit (one year, five years, or ten years) there is a point in time beyond which the project will fail of its own weight and momentum. There are some projects which are feasible, make economic sense, are practical, and will clear any other hurdle placed in front of them except the hurdle of time. At some point, and it varies with the nature of the project undertaking, the cumulative effect of imbedded and created failure tendencies and factors will finally overtake the project and crush it.

We can think of this effect as similar to the aging process in humans. A normal, healthy individual will invariably succumb to old age. No matter how flexible, malleable and adaptive it may be, a project will soon bend one too many times, become fatigued, and break. In this regard a project is like a piece of cheap, soft metal. When stressed by bending it shows no sign of failure—it bends with the stress. This may occur repeatedly, with constant bending back and forth until, sooner or later, the point comes where it bends no longer, but snaps apart. Material scientists refer to this phenomenon as *fatigue stress* or *creep loading*. We could use these terms to describe the effects of project old age. Perhaps it is best to avoid long-term projects altogether or to insist that they be divided into a series of self-contained, short-duration efforts: little projects, less susceptible to fatigue stress or creep loading.

FT 14: Ripple and Collateral

Two terms need to be defined before continuing. *The ripple effect* refers to the impact of one group's work on other groups, or of one activity on other activity. *Collateral* means simultaneous or concurrent work. In a project context, considering the many interdependencies involved, there is no shortage of situations where someone's effort (or omission) has a deleterious ripple effect on collateral work being performed by others.

Project work is by its very nature collateral and prone to rippling. Not only does it ripple internally but it ripples due to waves emanating from external sources, such as governments, third parties, or more often, its sponsoring organization. This effect is most pronounced in a fast tracked effort. The propensity toward collateral work and the vulnerability to ripple effects also increase as the number of players (principal project participants) increases.

FT 15: Baby It's Cold Outside

A final inherent failure tendency concerns the position of most projects *outside* the normal chain of events within the sponsoring organization. As an outsider, the project is often out in the cold, so to speak, when it comes to the protection afforded by the company. Such ongoing services as transportation, personnel, accounting, graphics arts, word processing and the like make up the company fabric of services that often go unnoticed until they are gone. Many projects live outside their reach, and cannot effectively use corporate services. These end up with their own mini-corporate services residing within the project organization. Here again is another potential for conflict—project versus project services. Another reason (as if one were needed), to keep projects small, short, and secretive.

SUMMARY

Like an organism inheriting defective genes, every project brings with it certain inherent risks, or failure tendencies about which we can do little. Many of these tendencies stem from the distinctions, and conflicts between projects and their operational counterparts. Others can be attributed to unclear, untested expectations and methods that are characteristic of all projects.

We have defined and discussed these tendencies not to excuse project failure nor to cast disparagement on those striving for project success. On the contrary, one must understand inherent failure tendencies in order to differentiate them from those which may be avoided. Inherent tendencies are there, we cannot manage them away. We can only recognize their existence and learn how to side-step each as we travel down the project path, for they cannot be eradicated. Sometimes it is best to dodge one's enemies than to insist on confrontation.

Inherent failure tendencies can be best thought of as the background props on the project stage. They constitute the failure setting, giving all projects the propensity to fail. There are other risks of a more active sort. We call these *created risks,* or failure factors. Sometimes failure factors act independently and sometimes they amplify or extend the impact of failure tendencies. Either way, they are many and they are potent. They are also the subject of the next ten chapters.

PEOPLE

most demanding, most giving resource

For any business endeavor to succeed it must be blessed with the right amount of resources at an acceptable level of quality. Among these are material, equipment, money, information, authority, time, and *people*. People are the focus of this chapter. The topic of people is too broad, volatile, and sensitive to handle without certain understandings. A listing of these follow.

1. All companies and projects have a mix of outstanding, average, and poor performers.

2. People cannot be totally replaced with machines, computers, or processes. We must have them.

3. The majority of persons are well-intentioned and interested in project success.

4. People have all sorts of talents, problems, needs, goals, and indifferences. We care only about those which impact project success or failure.

5. The grouping and positioning of individuals in a project or corporate organization are subjects of the next chapter. Here we direct our attention on the individual, what influences his or her performance of project tasks, and what built-in failure factors are attributable to individual perceptions and performances.

As the most valuable and necessary ingredient of any project, we need first recognize that this resource begs to be managed, and that its management is the largest challenge to project success. It's important to understand, however, that people represent a very special resource, one very different from the rest. Unlike material or equipment, people cannot be stockpiled until needed. They are a very *perishable* resource. Each individual is so unlike the rest that people cannot be treated as a commodity. Their quality, skills, motivations, and effectiveness are not uniform nor should they be taken for granted. Like other perishable items, people do not remain the same over time. They either improve or deteriorate rapidly.

All these characteristics apply to people whether they are located in a corporate, functional setting or arranged together for some project-specific purpose. The wise project manager understands these special characteristics and devotes a disproportionate amount of management attention to this resource. This manager also understands the special relationships between people and project success, and more to the point, the failure factors brought to any project by the people assigned to it. No examination of project success and failure would be complete without addressing people. Unfortunately, this topic is most often overlooked by those who practice and analyze project management; a practice which may represent the largest failure factor of them all.

FF 16: Unskilled Leaders

Given the importance of people as a project resource, the temporary nature of the work involved, the lack of long term associations and loyalties, and the conflicting interests represented by principal project players, it's shocking to note the lack of "people skills" among today's project managers. A great number of those responsible for project success either (1) underestimate the criticality of people, or (2) are totally unequipped to manage people.

There are a number of reasons for this consistent inadequacy. First and foremost among these could be the startling discrepancy between the skills necessary to *become* a project manager and the skills required to successfully *manage* a project (people skills being the most important of these). Realizing that all industries and all projects are not the same, some generalizations are still in order in this regard. One of these is the fact that outstanding individual contributors in an organization are those most likely to be chosen to husband a new project. They may be trained as engineers (construction project), scientists (research and development), or computer systems analysts (new software offering). We pick the good engineer, scientist, or systems analyst because they know the process or product we are attempting to create and we throw them into an entirely new environment, one for which they have little training or inclination. In fact the talents and characteristics that made them successful at their previous positions are often the antithesis of what it takes to succeed in a project environment.

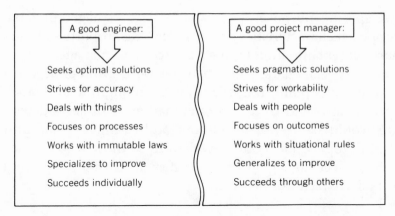

Figure 3-1. Why individual contributors make poor project managers.

Without apologizing for the exceptions, and there are always these when the topic is people, Figure 3-1 attempts to point out a few of these opposing characteristics and perspectives. Although it contrasts the qualities of a good engineer with those of a good project manager, the figure could just as correctly substitute the words "scientist," "systems analyst," or even "accountant" among several others and the comparison would remain valid. It seems that project managers are chosen, often at least, from a pool of good people, but often people skilled at the wrong things. These tend to be technically oriented and product (thing)-concerned.

Those choosing project leaders should rethink this practice and perhaps consider the selection of candidates from another pool. These might include teachers, communicators, sales managers, or even attorneys with courtroom experience. Those who make good individual contributors are those who make poor project managers. This is one area where operational leaders may prove to be better suited to project management.

Regardless of the source, project managers tend to need but not have people skills. Why is this so? One answer may involve the acquisition of people skills. We all know they aren't taught in colleges or universities. They are learned at the teacher's knee—by listening to and emulating successful leaders with whom one is lucky enough to come in contact. Leadership (and related skills) is an acquired ability. In the field of project management, few of us have the opportunity to see it in action, much less to copy it.

There are a number of reasons for this. One is inherent to the transient nature of project life. Good leaders are so rare that they cannot be assigned to one project for any length of time—they are constantly shifted to others so that their value can be leveraged. Their skills are seldom reduced to writing or even communicated orally; they work intuitively, and when they leave they carry their talents with them.

Some scholars of this trait called leadership insist that leaders are born, not created. They add that good followers make poor leaders. But our corporate societies seem to promote to the position of leader (or project manager) those who have proven their ability to follow for years, and under any circumstances, over the ones who blaze their own trail. It's an old saying, but true. Those who follow the rules well are sooner or later put in charge of rule-making, and this is when they fail.

FF 17: No Generational Tradition

Many successful business leaders, from all industries, learned their trades at the knee of their fathers, mothers, or surrogates thereof. Even when the child enters a trade totally different from his or her parents, there is often a set of transferable skills and perspectives that were somehow passed down from one generation to the other. This is rarely the case with project work.

The reasons are fairly obvious. For one, projects are so different as to eliminate knowledge transference. Another reason lies with the growth of new specializations within the project framework—specializations that did not exist 20, ten, or even five years previously. A partial listing of these might include project managers themselves, planning and scheduling engineers, contract managers, quality assurance specialists, media manipulators, information systems designers, and risk managers. When these folks visit their parents for Christmas the conversations regarding their work are surely limited. It used to be common for small children to not know exactly what their parents did for a living. Now parents do not understand what their children do.

Because most of us working at the project level are in such ecclectic and new roles, we have few (if any) role models to follow. We have to continually define and redefine our roles, and these change from project to project, industry to industry, and company to company. Very few assumptions are valid. We are not *what we are*, but *what we do*. And what we do changes almost daily. This need to understand one's role on the project team and to feel confident that it is appropriate and accepted is a theme we will come back to again and again.

FF 18: The Cupboard Is Bare

Because companies embark on major projects infrequently, it's understandable that they might not have a staff of potential project managers in waiting, ready to take over the effort from the beginning. But where can they go to find these leaders? One might think that companies offering project management services would be well stocked. They aren't. Their cupboards are often bare, and this demands an explanation.

Project management firms, architect/engineering firms, ad agencies, and others on whom we may call for project-specific expertise are notoriously cheap when it comes to investing in their own people—their most valuable resource. They typically hire talent away from others rather than nurture and groom it internally. They live on fees generated by full assignment of their experts to the accounts of others, and spend very little time or money on internal skills development—preferring instead to let their clients "teach" their people on the job.

These companies traditionally operate with a fluctuating work load and a similarly fluctuating skills base. Their staffs suffer drastic peaks and valleys, with frenzied recruitment (piracy from other competitors) as soon as a big project is landed, and almost immediate layoffs as soon as the assignment is completed.

As a consequence, project-based people in these types of companies are continually shifting from one employer to another. This has nothing to do with the value of each individual, but is a simple fact of life attributable to the nature of the project business. In this regard, these firms are little more than "job shops" or talent agencies. They add little value to their inventory, especially in the area of project training. They broker talent, but do little to create it. This attitude extends beyond people, to such areas as standards, procedures and quality control. But those are explored in other chapters. Suffice it to say that they don't create leaders, they merely rent them out.

FF 19: Transits and Ledgers

If one divided all project skills into two categories, with few spanning both, these might be labeled "technical" and "commercial." Good people well versed in each category are needed and are usually found. What is missing are good people with skills lying in both categories. For some reason our educational system and the demands of the occupational marketplace seem to divide the flow of people into one or the other camp, and seldom do we see someone with a foot in both.

It's this synthesis of technical and commercial skills and awareness that is so necessary to project success. Each project is a blending of needs and activities that cross and recross these imaginary barriers between the technical and the commercial. We need transits *and* ledgers to make any project work.

It's helpful to have some common understandings among project leaders existing in both camps—a common project "language"; one transcending this functional wall. This is seldom found. What's seen in its absence are technical people who don't understand, care, or relate well to commercially oriented people, and vice versa.

It wasn't too many years ago when the president and CEO of any major industrial concern was more than likely an engineer, particularly if there was a technical base to the business. Later the pendulum seems to have swung back to the point where operational elements of industries were eclipsed by financial considerations, and more and more accountants, controllers, and general financial managers took over the reins of corporate leadership. Today, with increased emphasis on operational effectiveness, the pendulum seems to be returning to the engineer's camp. Perhaps it will keep swinging between these two extremes until we become wise enough to find a third choice—the leader able to synthesize technical and commercial acuity. Someone not intimidated by the technical challenges and yet aware of commercial risks and controls, and most of all, blessed with the people skills required to assure project success. When that occurs failure will have met its match. Some companies try to bridge the gap by appointing two project managers, one in each camp. This is total folly, for a project can afford only one project manager, and while project responsibility may be delegated, it surely cannot be shared.

Many a failed project became so because those responsible for *driving* performance factors (C, S, and T) were not those responsible for *controlling* performance. A good example is cost performance. The project manager and his or her subordinates who are actively directing project work are the ones who *drive* project costs up or down. They spend or save money. A project controller or "cost engineer" merely quantifies, reports, and forecasts eventual cost outcomes, but does not cause them. As long as this distinction is understood it doesn't cause a problem. Whenever a project manager, when asked "who controls cost?" points to the cost engineer, or for that matter anyone besides him- or herself, he or she is heading for trouble.

FF 20: Fruits of My Labor

A true craftsperson enjoys the sight of his or her product; the fruits of labor. Project personnel are no different. They seek the sense of pride and accomplishment this brings, and rightly so, for they seldom get this opportunity. When they see the end result of the project effort, it is often difficult to isolate and identify *their* individual contribution. This is an unfortunate, but albeit a very real fact of life.

On long-term projects it is rare to find many people at the conclusion who were there at project initiation. People come and go. People who are needed at the beginning are not necessary towards the end (planners, designers, copy editors, researchers, and so on). People needed at the end are not needed during commencement of project work (startup engineers, sales representatives, operations). Few of us get the opportunity to see any successful project be born, live and die.

Our work is so interrelated and sometimes so nebulous as to prevent the matching of effort to results. How can the person who agonized over the budget and tracked the costs of a high rise office building "see" his or her work in the finished project? What about the person responsible for finding the insurance coverage and construction bonding? Or the drafter of the construction contracts? All of these are vital and demanding project functions, but when viewing the finished facility it's tough to see their result. In this regard, most of us envy the mason, or the electrician. They can point to the building and tell their grandchildren "I did that." Most of us can't.

Pity even more those whose job it is to prevent problems from occurring. How can someone point to a problem that didn't surface and say "I prevented that?" In this category place the building's construction security guards, safety engineers, and the clerk who assured that all subcontractors were covered by adequate construction insurance.

At the top of our pity list place those poor souls who labored long and hard over alternatives to project activity or approaches that were not chosen. Or those who worked for months or even years only to have the project cancelled in mid-life. None of these achieve the thrill of seeing their labor come to fruition.

And finally, consider those people who performed exceptionally well for projects that miscarried, or failed dramatically and publically. The survivors of a black hole are often tainted with its reputation; victims of guilt by association. It's safe to bet that there are hundreds of engineers who were associated in some way with the design and construction of the Three Mile Island nuclear plant, but who don't mention that project on their resumes.

FF 21: Banished to the Boondocks

Sometimes an assignment to a project effort means a refreshing, challenging mission. At other times it may mean banishment to the corporate boondocks. A sensitive project manager, and a selfish corporate boondocks. A sensitive project manager, and a selfish one, makes sure project personnel view the assignment in the former fashion. Regardless of the reason, however, many people feel that working on project tasks places them outside the corporate mainstream, away from their functional "nests" and, as the expression goes "out of sight, out of mind."

By virtue of its temporary nature, project work can't usually generate long-term loyalties or supplant those existing between the individual and the company. Often the individual sees the project as being a "taker" of his or her time, effort, loyalty, and commitment while the company functional base (accounting department, engineering division, manufacturing operations, legal staff, and so on) is seen as a "giver" of such benefits as training, salary, prestige, and advancement. Any reversal of this perception by the project manager will accrue to the project's benefit.

One final note in this regard. While some may unfairly see project assignment as condemnation to the boondocks (literally or figuratively so), it often is just that. Many functional managers see project assignments as a convenient way to offload or dump undesirables— to transfer their problems to the project manager. This is a constant temptation often followed, and the only defense from the project's point of view is insistence on quality and rejection when appropriate. Herein lies yet another skirmish in the corporate-project battle. There are many others.

FF 22: Different Tools

Every project needs a judicious combination of people and tools. A problem with project work is that different people are usually involved, and they are forced by necessity to use different tools differently on each project. By tools we mean those processes, procedures, instruments, and other devices (paper being the most common) used to accomplish project activity. People are very adaptable, but constant changing of procedures, methods, and objectives can be very disturbing to most. This is why successful project members are those oriented towards outcomes and not towards processes—those more concerned with results than methods of achieving them. Project managers need to seek out and reward this orientation—it is one that is generally punished in the rest of the operationally minded company.

Put simply, those who live by rote don't fit into project life. People with flexible, adaptive skills or *skill bases* do quite well. Project work is transient, temporary, dynamic, ecclectic, and often inefficient. Sometimes immediate or even final (fruits of my labor?) feedback on performance is elusive if not meaningless. These characteristics usually create a constant atmosphere of anxiety among project members. Those unable to exist in this condition will not find happiness at the project level.

FF 23: Carrots and Sticks

In view of the inability to identify one's personal contribution to project accomplishments (or disappointments) we are typically unable to offer direct rewards and punishment. This causes a good number of project members to suffer from an identity crisis. They seldom know exactly what their roles are, what they have produced, or how well they have done so. Project management can counteract this feeling (and its resulting negative impacts) through constant emphasis on the individual's contribution, no matter how tenuously defined, and by rewarding *level of activity* and *commitment* in lieu of identifiable *results*.

When this isn't done to the satisfaction of the individual, a strange but common phenomenon begins. People seek, unconsciously sometimes, to establish their identity via the project. This usually involves *change*. They try to make their individual mark on the project by championing such causes as a new purchasing procedure, new computer system, revised accounting approach, new scheduling methodology or revised quality assurance program. Whatever the subject of change, the fact that it will be "my idea" is often enough to justify it, at least to its sponsor. (Incidently, this is how many a worthless *project* is generated). Whenever we find a champion of change, it might serve the project's interests to determine if the reason a new thing is being touted is based on its merits alone, or merely to reinforce the identity of the champion.

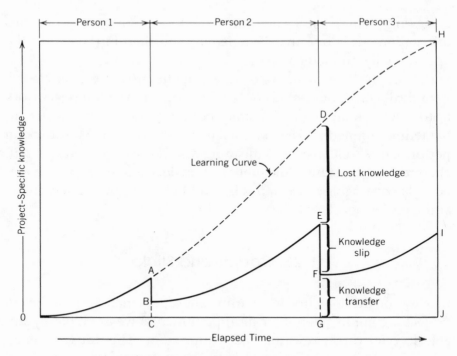

Figure 3-2.   The broken learning curve.

FF 24: The Broken Learning Curve

Project-specific knowledge is valuable and it is acquired through project-specific experience. Whenever a key project player is replaced with another, the learning is interrupted, with the second individual having to take up, not where the first left off, but somewhere below that point. This is best depicted graphically, as shown by Figure 3-2. The growth of knowledge over time is called experience, and Person 1 begins the project with none. He or she gradually builds experience and, if never replaced, does so at a faster pace, finally tapering off towards the end of the assignment. This ideal is shown as the rising curve OADH.

When the first person is replaced, the replacement receives only part of the accumulated experience gained by the first, and begins at a point such as B on the chart. He or she in turn begins to adapt to the project and become more experienced in its operations until, as before, a replacement is sent. When Person 3 shows up, the *knowledge slip* between person 3 and his or her predessor is represented by the difference between point E and point F on the chart. The knowledge represented by the difference bewteen point D and point E is *lost knowledge*—knowledge that would be there had Person 1 never been replaced. This depiction could be viewed as generous by some, for the *transferred knowledge* is always fairly substantial (line BC or FG). This represents that knowledge which was successfully transferred from Person 1 to 2, or from 2 to 3—sometimes called *hand-off knowledge*.

This effect is seen at virtually every position and skill level within the project organization. It can be minimized by (1) reduction in replacement frequency and (2) reducing personal knowledge to written or procedural form whenever possible; increasing the knowledge transfer by shifting emphasis from people to tools.

An anology, or vivid application, of this broken learning curve notion was experienced by the U.S. armed forces during the war in Vietnam. Since soldiers and officers were sent to Vietnam on fixed time assignments (one year) rather than for the duration of hostilities (as in past wars) the transfer of skills from short timer to newcomer was critical, but never complete. In many cases it took a good six months for a man to become proficient in survival skills and mission methods. At that point he often began to focus his attention on surviving as opposed to accomplishing something, whatever that was defined to be. When a replacement arrived, there was no one-to-one match—people came and went, there was no individual replacement. Hence, minimum hand-off knowledge.

FF 25: Jacks of all Trades

Projects can't be run by committees, (what can?). But the skills required are often so eclectic and multidisciplinary as to preclude their possession by a single individual. Compromises are often made, but the truth is that new, changing, and difficult-to-define positions are always found in project work. A good example of this might be the emerging discipline called *contract administration*.

Common among the construction industry and major contract manufacturing projects, the function of contract administration is inconsistently defined and often unrecognizable. It is generally meant to represent the commercial handling of contracts for performance, such as those to construct a power plant, hospital or highway, or to build a new military jet or weapons system. Persons working in this neophyte profession are deemed to be proficient when they possess knowledge in a majority of the following fields:

Law

Accounting

Engineering

Insurance

Suretyship

Construction (or manufacturing)

Information systems

Estimating

Planning and scheduling

Finance

Procurement

Auditing

Project management

Quality control

Records management

Quite a full plate! It would probably be a safe bet that nowhere in the world is there one man or woman possessing all of these skills. The point is that today's project positions require eclectic skill bases and generalized awareness in addition to specific abilities. These roles are often ill-defined and poorly understood throughout the project—much less between the project and the rest of the company.

As the positions are ill-defined, so are the qualifications for each. This all leads to a very project-specific understanding, made on a case-by-case basis, as to just exactly what everyone should be doing. In addition to this, we must note that responsibilities of each individual are *situational* in nature—not carved in stone. Again, those needing stability and consistency should pass project work by.

FF 26: The Marine Hymn

The Marine Corps may need only a few good men, but major projects need more—not only more men (and women) but the proper tools to support and leverage their abilities. Every successful project contains just the right combination of good tools and good people. Those who scoff at reliance on tools by stating that "all I need is a good project manager; he or she will make it work" are fooling themselves, or are speaking of a small, one-person project.

Given the assumption that every company is composed of outstanding, average, and poor performers, how can tools impact project success at the least cost? The answer lies in the ability of good tools to make a difference between favorable and unfavorable performance on the majority of people—the average ones. Figure 3-3 illustrates this concept.

Let's suppose the project represents the population of the company (and indeed, of the business world), with something on the order of 15% outstanding performers, 70% in the average category, and the remaining 15% termed "poor" or nonperformers. The message is that outstanding performers will be successful whether given good tools or not. They succeed with very little assistance from the outside, very few tools need to be given. This type of person will create their own tools if not given any—and work well. On the other extreme the nonperformers probably will remain so regardless of the tools they are given. Give them good tools and they won't know how to use them nor be inclined to do so. The impact, that is, the difference between success or failure, is with the large group of average performers. Given poor tools their work is poor. Given good tools, they are effective contributors.

All this is not intended to diminish the importance of people or the role they play in project accomplishments. They play the key

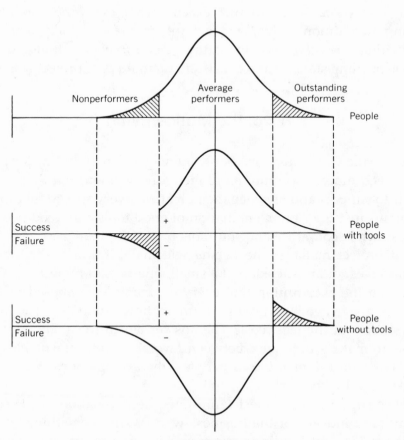

Figure 3-3.   The balance of people and tools.

role, the most critical one. But the wise project manager realizes that this role can be improved and amplified (leveraged) through the judicious use of the right tools at the right time.

SUMMARY

People are, without a doubt, every project's most valuable and most perishable resource. They demand to be managed, and their management is the biggest challenge to project success. They cannot be stockpiled, treated as commodities, or otherwise neglected. In order to be used, people must be informed and respected.

Unfortunately many otherwise good project managers understand how to manage every resource but this one. If we are to find fault with people we must begin at the top. Many good technicians make poor project leaders. Whether through lack of training or interest, they often focus their attention on the tangible or the technical at the expense of other project elements. Good individual contributors are not necessarily good project managers.

Those with superior project skills probably didn't pick them up through generational lineage, nor are they stored among the staffs of companies providing project services. These typically broker rather than create the required skills. The demands of most business projects require both technical and commercial expertise; a synthesis of skills that is rare and valuable.

Most people perform best when they can see the results of their work, when they can ascertain their individual contribution—the fruits of their labor. Steps taken to fill this need are recommended, as are those to identify and reward excellence or to bridge the learning curve that is often broken when project personnel move into and out of the effort. This is often difficult to do, especially considering the eclectic nature of many of today's project positions.

No study of people in a project setting is complete without considering the role of good tools and the combination of tools and people so essential to success. For the vast majority of our companies, the best way to leverage human performance is to equip people with the proper tools, the information needed to use them, and the authority to do so.

Projects are little more than organized people working with tools to meet certain expectations. We have discussed expectations, and now, people. It's time we tackle the second most sensitive and volatile topic in the project mix—organizations.

ORGANIZATIONS

only contrivances, temporary and weak

The topic of organizations is one ripe with conflict, friction, misunderstanding, and management dissonance. We shall attempt to penetrate the veil of myth and personal bias covering organizational theory in order to understand the burdens placed on project work by the need *to organize* in order *to accomplish*.

Project organizations are nothing more than temporary contrivances aimed at structuring and leveraging the work of people. They are necessary evils, none without structural flaws and implementation difficulty. The search for a perfect project organization is a never-ending but pointless one. As in all other aspects of project life, perfection is not a valid goal—accomplishment is. This is the way we will treat the topic of organizations. Not by seeking the best or the most intrinsically interesting, but the workable.

Nor will we be concerned with the best, or most workable way to organize company forces for the continuation of ongoing, operational work. That's the goal of the optimizers. Neither will we dwell on the functional arrays in which ongoing services are performed for the benefit of the entire company. Our interest is projects, and our interest in organizations is a very selfish one. We are looking for organizations that help us achieve. We need to understand the characteristics, strengths, and flaws of all available alternatives in order to choose among them and to make our choices work.

WHO CARES?

Organizations make very attractive scapegoats for project failure and very popular reasons for project success, and everyone seems to have a personal, often exclusive, favorite. There may be some readers who don't share this interest in organizations, so perhaps a good way to start our analysis is to identify those who may have little or no interest in the topic.

Those not needing a better understanding of the role of organizations may include people representing a company or division thereof for which:

There are no jurisdictional disputes.

Individual responsibilities are well defined and understood by all.

There are no gaps or overlaps in authority.

Each person's skills are used effectively with minimum organizational friction.

Each person has a defined and acceptable identity, role, authority, and career path.

There are no conflicts of loyalty or multiple allegiances.

Staffing levels are never inadequate.

No one ever discusses "the last reorganization" or "the next reorganization."

Anyone answering "yes" to all of this list can be excused if they turn to the next topic. The rest of us have experienced some or all of these problems, and realize they are endemic to project life. Where did they begin?

THE EVOLUTION OF PROJECT ORGANIZATIONS

Major projects require more than one individual to operate, hence the need to organize the efforts of several and the use of a "project organization." Four such typical organizations are depicted by Figure 4-1. Here we see some of the earliest attempts in industry and commerce to structure project forces, beginning with a *functional* array, or a *project island*, leading to some more recent, fairly innovative approaches, including the *matrix* and the *network*. A general rule is that each of these structures has been tremendously successful given certain project applications and each has failed miserably given others. The trick is to understand the strengths and weaknesses associated with each in order to pick an approach best fitting the project conditions at hand. Let's begin by analyzing the features of each.

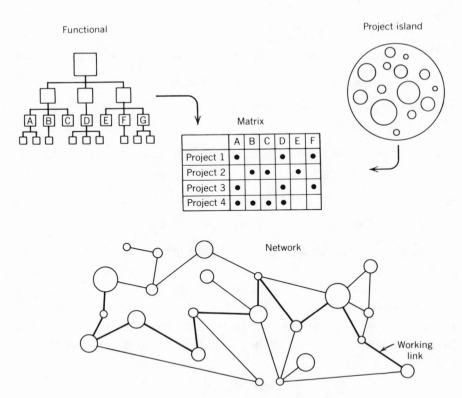

Figure 4-1. Organizational structures.

THE FUNCTIONAL BASE

We see this organizational approach represented by the all too familiar branching organizational tree found in most companies. It is often used to define ongoing, static, operational *functions* performed throughout the entire company. These might be finance, treasury, manufacturing, sales, personnel, administrative services, general counsel, engineering, accounting, shipping, and so on. It's safe to assume that everyone working on a project began project work from one of these functional "nests," and will return thereto upon completion of his or her project-specific tasks. Regardless of the scope or volume of company efforts, the functional organization remains structurally the same as time passes. The size and number of boxes, and their relative arrangement may vary to accommodate change (the ever popular "reorganization"), but the distinctive top-down hierarchy remains.

The functional organization is founded on the concept of division of labor, and works well for repeated operations requiring sustained support of various skills (accountants, purchasing agents, shop foreperson, and so on). It is a process-oriented approach to organizing and distributing talent. In other terms, it's focus is on *tasks* rather than *goals*. It is the most unsuited to project work for this simple, yet fatal characteristic.

When confronted with a major project effort, many companies insist on treating it from the functional basis, without any need to reorganize or redirect people just because a project happens to come along. This approach is blind to the distinctions we have and will continue to make between operations and projects. The functional tree is based on the segregation of specialists into distinct nests, with very few crossing over organizational boundaries (seldom does an engineer spend a few years in accounting).

In addition to its process orientation, the functional organization is characterized by tunnel vision among its supporters. They seek to define each box, or person, within the organization by rigid rules and responsibilities. This attitude often leads to organizational disputes, boundary squabbles, and territorial suspicions. A successful project cannot withstand this drain of time and talent. It must direct all its effort toward results, with little concern as to who accomplished them and how much "credit" is given them. However, these concerns seem to be critical to many functionally based managers.

For all its faults, the functional basis does have value. It provides consistently directed and trained personnel for project applications. It assures at least a minimum level of consistency and control, in each functional area, from project-to-project. It also allows for the somewhat painless interchangeability of people. All of these benefits are attractive and even essential when accruing to processes or continuous operations. They have little currency in the world of projects. Again, we leave consistency, interchangeability and minimum levels of control to the optimizers. They are not project goals.

So if the benefits of the functional approach are not important to projects, and its best application is to ongoing, operational work, why use it for projects? Alert and resourceful managements do not. They opt for one of the remaining choices, any one of which is superior in a project setting.

Before describing the better choices, however, a few words need be said concerning the reasons we still see the functional base applied to projects. One may be the fact that it avoids creation of a new organization, or auxiliary force within the company. It avoids the selection of leaders, and therefore, the assignment of ultimate responsibility to any one person, or group of persons. It presents minimum change and refuses to grant the project organizational status. It doesn't threaten the personal empires of others. These are obviously not valid reasons. They are selfish, inane, and stupid. But they are very real and common. They torment projects.

THE PROJECT ISLAND

A response to the flaws of the functional approach is to gather all project personnel, detach them organizationally (and often literally) from the remainder of the company, and place them in what is called a *project island* organization. This project island consists of project-specific personnel working solely for the benefit of the project, either full or part time. A separate project-only organization is formed, with some reporting to the company hierarchy, typically at the project manager level. It is a temporary, goal-oriented fabrication very popular with project managements.

The project island response carries certain benefits as well as disadvantages. It's main attractions include freedom to direct skills towards the project and *only* the project, fairly straightforward and one-dimensional loyalties (to the project and the project manager, at least temporarily), and a focus on outcome rather than methods or consistency. All of these make it an attractive candidate for project success.

But the project island is not ideal, for a number of reasons. The allegiences to the project and the project manager are there, but they are often diluted, part time and temporary. Each individual must constantly remember that the project doesn't go on forever, and sooner or later they must return to their functional nest. The project island is also characterized by short-term planning and short-term relationships; perishable ones. The formation of ongoing *networks* that help to transcend artificial organizational barriers requires time and patience. Neither are bountiful in a project setting. And finally, though consistency of controls is not a project objective, it is often an overriding company concern. The project island approach flies in the face of consistency.

So we find two very popular, very different responses to the need for a project organization, the *functional base* and the *project island*. Each has strong disadvantages. How do companies, when faced with a new project choose between them? Often they try to gain the advantages of both by adopting a hybrid of the two: the *matrix* organization.

THE INFAMOUS MATRIX

Figure 4-1 illustrates the marriage of the project island notion with the functional base to create the matrix. As shown, it is a simple matching of functional skill *suppliers* with project skill *users*. Projects 1 through 4, in this case, use various types of skills from functional nests A through F. Each dot on the matrix represents a part time or full time person or group of persons, who are temporarily assigned to project-specific work. On completion of their special contribution, each person returns to the existing, continuous functional base (in a figurative if not literal sense) to await assignment to other project uses.

The theory behind the matrix is sensational. We gain the best of both worlds. From the functional world we gain specialization of skills, division of labor, immediate application and reduction of personnel, levels of consistency through each project (and across all projects), and transfer of knowledge, via the persons in the matrix, from one project to another—a sort of cross-pollenization of ideas. We also receive the benefit of checks and balances between the operational and project sides of the house, and a bit of long-term consideration that transcends the temporary project lifespan for the benefit of the people in the matrix.

Unfortunately, when we get the best of both worlds we also inherit the worst, and the matrix is loaded with problems. Chief among these is the divided loyalty it requires of every individual; loyalty up the top of the matrix (to the functional head) and across the left side (to the project superior). This tugging and pulling can be very upsetting at times, and extremely hazardous to the individual concerned. Because the assignment is temporary and skill-based, there tend to be many "experts," each working in their own little area of expertise. In other words, too many chiefs and too few Indians. The fatal flaw is that of divided loyalties, and this extends not only to the people caught in the matrix, but to the tools they use. These include those procedures, processes, methods, documents, reports, and records that allow work to be performed. Often they are not the same from project to project. We end up with different people, working for different bosses, using different tools differently at different times. And it's not uncommon for the matrix to have more than two sides, as shown in our figure. There may be occasions where someone is serving the needs of more than one project, and even in more than one capacity; in effect working in an n-dimensional matrix. The matrix can be a mindbender.

The appeal of the matrix could be its attempts at organizational *synthesis*, as incomplete and inefficient as it might be. There's little doubt that, although the execution of the concept is often faulty, its intentions are exemplary. For the matrix attempts to break down artificial organizational barriers, use skills directly where needed, focus on product over process, and put simply, to get things done *despite* the organization. In this regard it represents the precursor to the next, most recent, and most difficult to define organizational approach: the *network*.

THE NETWORK PHENOMENON

The network phenomenon looks at organizations from an entirely new perspective. It is unlike the other approaches in that it doesn't attempt to structure people into an organization, but to exploit the natural structures that exist among people. This is why we call it a *phenomenon* rather than a *structure*. Networks aren't purposefully created, they are used. Our Figure 4-1 shows a typical network as a grouping of separate *links* between people throughout an existing company or project. This is another characteristic of the network: it is not a separate approach but an overlay of relationships lying on top of existing organizational structures.

The network can best be thought of as the collection of friend-ships, acquaintances, favors, debts, grapevines, cliques, mutual in-terests, social ties, and all the other dashed, dotted, and invisible lines *not* drawn on the approved organization chart, but there none-theless.

There is in fact more than one network overlaying the approved chart; there are dozens of them, and they tie together at different points (individuals) who are in turn plugged into different net-works. The end result is an entire *fabric* of human relationships. In most companies this fabric has been woven over many years, from strong material, and in a tight pattern. Each network is a very egal-itarian society made up of individuals with mutual interests.

Can we *make* a network to achieve our selfish project interests? The answer is no, we can't. So why worry about networks, then? They don't replace an organizational approach and they can't be created. Why concern ourself with them? We can *use* networks that exist to further project objectives. We can nourish beneficial net-works, encourage their growth and well being. Networks represent our alternatives to existing organizational channels. They are the safety valves of an overheated, stalled project. No successful man-ager alive has not recognized the value of networks in accomplish-ing something quicker, cheaper, and with less hassle than the alternative: going through the proper channels. This is not to im-pune the use of networks but to congratulate it. Process-oriented managers may lose sleep when "procedures" aren't followed. Product-oriented managers lose their jobs when goals aren't achieved. Hurray for networks. May they flourish.

We've already mentioned the goal-orientation of networks, now let's address their other characteristics. They are first and foremost dynamic and ever changing as new individuals, new interests and new relationships develop. The links among network members run most often bottom-up through organizations, or sideways, rather than top-down. Networks emphasize the individual's value and contribution based on *what he or she does* as opposed to *who he or she is*. They are self-sustaining, with little or no management overburden, and in this regard have no use for "empires" to be built, destroyed, or feared. And as seen from Figure 4-1, there are no jurisdictional boundaries, just links between members. One uses a network by finding and tapping into the *working link* that connects source to user. It matters not whether there were alternate or even shorter links, connection is what counts. Again, product over process; accomplishment over optimization.

With all this going for them, you might wonder where these networks are, and if they are rare. They are all around us. We see examples in the "old boy network," the "survivors of network" (whose members are former associates, co-workers, project members, etc.), and in social networks centered around schools, churches, clubs, teams, neighborhoods, mutual interests, hobbies, political parties, citizen committees, and the like.

For all their many uses, networks have dangers. It pays to be aware of these. Networks are based on the concept of free and open access to information—the mutual and unencumbered sharing of ideas and data. Those projects that find this distasteful cannot use networks to their fullest. Also, as previously mentioned, there is an emphasis on "what you do" in a network rather than "who you are." Those comfortable with being identified by where they work or who they are *with* or whom they supervise will not like networks. In fact, the egalitarian nature of networking makes it difficult to tell who's who—there are no badges, stripes, uniforms, or other signs of organizational status.

The fatal flaw of a misdirected network may be the inability to assign total responsibility to any one person or group. Network participants consult, advise, touch base and connect, but seldom lead, or take the consequences of leadership. In this regard, networks resemble spineless, shapeless webs. They cannot exist without actual, contrived organizational structures (functional, project island, matrix) to lend support. Networks are not logical, nor are they symmetric, structurally aesthetic or managerially attractive. But they get a hell of a lot of work done quickly. They are a free resource, and only a fool ignores their potential.

FF 27: Functional Malfunction

Unless the project is so small as to preclude any organization at all, the functional base is better avoided. Those who insist on managing projects from such an ongoing organizational structure are making the very simple and very erroneous assumption that projects can be treated as if they were operations. Enough has already been said to point out the fallacy in this assumption.

In addition to a fallacious premise, the functional base malfunctions because of its own structure. It lacks an identity, a "center" around which project-specific efforts, expectations, processes, and achievements can be wrapped. No civilization can exist without some sort of culture, and this organizational approach leaves a project with no cultural attributes.

Functional bases are adept at shifting responsibility. In its truest sense, a functional organization assigns no overall project responsibility. It presumes that the whole (project) is nothing more than the sum of its parts (functional contributions). This invites failure.

Finally, this approach provides few mechanisms for transcending organizational boundaries. Any project manager knows that, no matter how cleverly the organization is arranged, or how well staffed it may be, no project succeeds without some way to climb over, or knock down, organizational barriers.

Sometimes functional cultists name a project manager to assume all project-related responsibility. This works well, but only when that manager is fully equipped with a flexible, dedicated staff and the autonomy to pursue the project goal—despite the existing organization. When this manager is part time, or represents the interests of one parochial "box" on the organization chart, the designation "project manager" is a misnomer.

Companies with continuing project work sometimes go so far as to establish a "project management" *function* within their existing organization. This helps, as long as it is not treated as merely another operational function in practice. As soon as it becomes self-perpetuating, empire-building, or process-dependent it ceases to deserve the project designation.

FF 28: The Isolated Island

When the project team is totally divorced from the sponsoring company it may encounter a whole new set of dangers. One may be the swift and certain severance of network ties between individuals on the project team and the rest of the company. A second handicap is the confrontational stance this extraction often produces: us (the project) against them (the rest). It may also isolate the project team to the point where potential contributors are lost because they cannot make the total commitment necessary for project assignment. They may agree to visit the "corporate boondocks" occasionally, without wishing to set up permanent residence there.

FF 29: Matrix Gridlock

We have described some handicaps attributed to the matrix organization, but a few more need to be mentioned. One of these is the result of divided loyalties (among personnel) and conflicting objectives and methods (among the different axes of the matrix). When the divergence is wide, a factious atmosphere prevails. Often this leads to intractable positions taken by both sides to a dispute. The result weakens or even stops project effort. This is known as *organizational gridlock*, and like the traffic conflict for which it is named, people get angry, no one gives an inch, and consequently, no one gets anywhere. The only way out of gridlock is through decree from a higher source (one side "wins") or through compromise by each party locking horns. Pragmatic project leaders are experts at compromise.

This constant, and very common friction between functional and project-specific sides of the matrix organization can be mitigated. One such method is to shift people from functional assignments to project-specific ones frequently, with the anticipation that understanding of one will benefit performance of the other. People on lower levels of the organization chart are shifted in this manner very often. It is their superiors who are most intransigent, and most in need of an assignment on the other side of the fence.

FF 30: A Transient Contrivance

The temporary nature of any project organization is a major and potential contributor to failure. All organizations are contrived (only networks are inherent and self-sustaining). Project organizations are not only contrived but self-destroying (like our guided missile example). This leads to temporary lines of communication, temporary authorities, temporary procedures, and short-term relationships. Network development and exploitation take time. Project life affords little of this resource.

A curious phenomenon takes place on very temporary projects. Behavioral scientists have shown that a small group of people, when placed in an isolated environment, react differently depending on their perception of how long the isolation will last. Take a group of ten individuals, none knowing another, placed in a closed room. Given the knowledge that they will be in that room together for four weeks duration, they will soon take organizational steps, and individual leadership initiatives will surface. In other words, someone will be granted or take charge. But if the same group were told they would be together for only thirty minutes, none of this occurs. No one proposes the need for leadership, much less a person or method to provide it. Why bother?

Project organizations are the "rooms" in which these people will temporarily dwell. The shorter the project (or the shorter it is perceived to be) the smaller role leadership and mutual interests will play. This explains the tenuous and tentative nature of project work often seen during the planning stages, and why planning usually gets off to a slow, shaky start.

FF 31: Double Agents

Some people play one side of the matrix organization against the other for personal gain. These may be likened to double agents in the world of project-corporate espionage. They are rare, but worth mentioning and considering. They carry the notion of divided loyalties, inherent to a matrix concept, to an extreme. This is not to suggest that each individual should be "patriotic" to one side or the other, but merely to recognize that there are those who profit in the conflict. Keep them away from your projects.

FF 32: Second Shift

Not only are project responsibilities passed from one person to another (this is commonplace), but quite often from one organization to another (this is extremely hazardous). A classic example is the transfer of project duties and momentum from the engineering organization to the construction counterpart for a project to design and build a new facility. And as in any other handoff, there are slippages and things are dropped. These include information, controls, procedures, perceptions, and knowledge to mention a few.

Whenever one "shift" takes over from another a gap in responsibilities develops. The old defense of "it didn't happen on my watch" is heard again and again. The solution to this problem is to avoid shift work entirely. Place one person in charge of *all* aspects of the project—from beginning to end. Even when this is done properly, more positive steps can be taken to avoid failure in this regard. They are all ways to transcend the responsibility gap. Such transcending factors or forces may include a comprehensive *plan* for the project, one which includes all phases and demonstrates their interrelationships. A transcending project *language* and *culture* are helpful. But most effective is the practice of including representatives of the second shift on the first shift's team. That is, include construction engineers on the design project. Include operational managers on the construction team. Let people transcend the gap. Avoid end-to-end responsibility assignments.

FF 33: Spatial Separation

Some project members or groups operate by remote control; physically separated from the results of their labor. We all respect the need to see the fruits of our labor, and two factors which interfere with this are time and physical or *spatial* separation. We can coun-

teract the first by shortening project efforts and creating more frequent, often smaller achievements. A ten-year project should be
broken down into much smaller, shorter duration "pieces," each
with identifiable achievements. Few of us can exist for ten years
without seeing accomplishment. Wise project managers recognize
and provide for this need.

They similarly understand the negative effects of spatial separation. If the design engineers are in an office in Los Angeles and the
construction site is in Texas, the workers tend to become isolated
from their product. Surely, they see design drawings and specifications—the intermediate products of their efforts, but never the final
result, either in its intermediate or completed stages. Anything that
can be done to eliminate this separation will contribute to project
success. Some enterprising managers have gone so far as to physically relocate the entire design team to the project site. This achieves
a multitude of benefits, not the least of which are a compression of
the communications float and a more clear understanding of the
problems encountered by both design and construction forces. The
hidden and most valuable benefit is the direct matching of effort to
product. Very few other changes produce such a positive and sustained impact on morale, solidarity, and efficiency.

Bridging or eliminating the time and spatial gaps separating
people from their physical accomplishments is critical to the success
of most projects. It gives visibility to goals, it showcases performance (and failure—which is also beneficial), it strengthens project
allegiances, it short-circuits communications (reducing information
lag and error), promotes learning by tying cause to effect, and it
enhances network building. The alternative is remote control,
which, because results remain unseen or indeterminate, tends to
focus more and more on process rather than product. Encourage
physical proximity and project intimacy. The returns can be dramatic.

FF 34: Stirring the Pile

Will businesses ever permanently destroy the mystique of "reorganization?" It seems that no company exists wherein the topic of conversation doesn't invariably shift to the last reorganization or the

next reorganization. Executives seem fascinated with the need for and the process of reorganizing. Perhaps this is due to their optimistic nature; most view reorganization as a chance to move up. It is commonplace for a reorganization to be announced in which, we are told, everyone moves up—no one loses! This seems too good to be true—it is.

The mystique of reorganization needs to be understood so that it will not infect projects or impede their progress. We need to know why the mystique exists, how to counter it, and how to minimize the impact of reorganization once it occurs. Let's begin with an understanding of its allure.

The textbook answer to the mystique question goes this way. Suppose the organization extant is viewed as a pile of people occupying various company positions. If we could somehow intelligently wield a large, figurative spoon and commence stirring these people and positions, the resulting pile would be better able to achieve company goals. How often, however, do we see hidden motives, not quite so altruistic, at play?

Some actual reasons many companies or projects reorganize are that reorganization (1) excuses past actions by providing a "clean slate," (2) allows upgrading of positions and salaries for certain selected individuals, (3) stalls difficult but substantive decision making, (4) removes undesirables by placing them where they will do little harm, (5) counteracts or confuses an externally originated audit or reorganization, (6) allows corporate muscles to be flexed. Of these, the effect reorganization has on decision making is probably the most damaging. Pending, potential, ongoing, or recently consummated reorganizations effectively *freeze* companies, preventing any other decisions, organizational or otherwise, from being made or even studied. This is why many executives order them—they make good blocking devices.

Reorganizations hurt projects, even when the result is a better project organization. They destroy or maim valuable personal networks. They paralyze prior and subsequent work—work that is carried on in suspense by people waiting for the other shoe to drop. They slow project momentum. And they dissipate real project responsibility. Project organizations (temporary contrivances that they are), need to develop and blossom rapidly to be effective. They are always "fast tracked." Continuous reorganization is disruptive at best, and often fatal. There are many times when it is better to continue to operate with a faulty organization than to suffer the shock of reorganization.

FF 35: A House Built on the Sand

One need not possess an engineering degree to recognize that house builders avoid sand when choosing ideal foundations. An insightful project manager uses this understanding to the project's advantage. How so? By keeping the project dynamic and fluid, by placing little strength in organizational structure or positions, and by so doing to discourage empire builders. They seek permanence and stability. We should show them neither.

Empire builders are those individuals who measure their corporate worth by the number and status of persons working under their supervision, or by the decisions that cannot be activated without their approval. It is easily seen why project work is not attractive to empire builders. Projects should be like shifting sands, dry, and nonnutritive—the better to discourage these characters from putting down roots.

To use a nautical analogy, a wise project manager keeps the ship moving at a high enough speed as to prevent barnacles from attaching themselves to the hull. When this proves unsuccessful, he or she periodically lifts the ship from the water and scrapes them off. This is called "reorganization," but it is really housecleaning.

FF 36: Warm Bodies

People aren't commodities and neither are they interchangeable parts in some giant machine called an "organization." They perform at vastly different levels depending on their motivation, skills, direction, and the ways their talents are leveraged by project leadership. With this in mind, it is safe to say that project problems don't go away by throwing warm bodies at them. Though most frequently cited as a significant project problem, understaffing is generally not the persistent evil it is held up to be.

There is no question that there are understaffed projects, and ones where the number of people assigned is totally inadequate to meet the need. For every one of these, however, there are probably ten others where the difficulty is not lack of people, but misdirection, misapplication, and misunderstanding of the people assigned. Or poorly leveraged people, people organized incorrectly, or given the wrong tools with which to perform. No increase in absolute quantity will solve these problems, but, to the contrary, it will serve to exacerbate them.

Throwing bodies at a project is akin to throwing money at a social injustice. It never works. It represents the blunt object wielded at a problem, when precise instruments manipulated with a high degree of articulation are needed.

Those needing more "bodies" often circumvent corporate or project restrictions by relying more and more on temporary help, consultants, or job shops to perform project work. This is understandable, but dangerous. There is no project loyalty, and many hidden agendas in the makeup of these people's motivation. Better to examine responsibilities and skills within the existing project and eliminate redundancy, inefficiency, misunderstanding and unnecessary tasks. In other words, be concerned with the match among skills, responsibilities, and level of effort that "warm bodies" represent—not the number thereof.

FF 37: Finger Pointing

This failure factor pertains to unassigned, misdirected, unfocused, uncommunicated, or just generally poor responsibility assignment. We have discussed the need for people and tools to make projects work, but people with unfocused responsibilities cannot use good tools. This is an immediate and sustained need of all projects, and project management must satisfy it quickly and continuously.

How can responsibility assignment go wrong? Simply put, it can go wrong hundreds of ways, but go right only one. It goes wrong when two or more people share responsibility, when there are gaps and overlaps in processes and controls, when *authority to perform* is not granted concurrently with *responsibility for performance*, or when responsibility assignments are ignored or in dispute. All these are common but well understood in terms of impact by both operational and project-oriented managers. One deserving particular attention concerns the concept of "joint responsibility."

Anyone working in a manufacturing plant has seen signs on the wall giving some sort of industrial slogan such as "Safety is Everybody's Responsibility," or "Every Worker is Responsible for Quality," or perhaps "Sales are Everybody's Business." What these really mean are "safety is *nobody's* responsibility," "*no one* is responsible for quality," and "sales are *nobody's* responsibility." Taken literally, these signs attempt to spread responsibility over everyone. This cannot be done. Responsibility for specific work is effectively *unassigned* when it is assigned to more than one group or person. It is dissipated, diluted, and dissolves.

This is not such a radical concept. We've made several distinctions already between process and outcome, between activity and results. The same kind of distinctions can be drawn between *functions* and *responsibilities*, or between *activity* and *duty*. Projects work very well when people are given responsibilities and duties rather than merely functions and activities to perform. An analogy will help clarify this point.

Suppose you are staying in a hotel on a business trip and telephone the night operator at the front desk to request a 7:00 A.M. wake-up call. The night clerk logs the name, room number, and requested time. This information is given to the day clerk who arrives for work at 6:00 A.M., and this clerk begins to call the rooms requesting the service at the appointed time. The day clerk calls your room. The telephone rings, but there is no answer. He or she calls once more, still no answer.

The clerk fulfilled his or her duty; he or she performed his or her assigned activity; even reperformed it. But you do not receive the call. Several things may have happened. For one, your room telephone may be defective, so that it gives the sound of a ring to the clerk on the other end but makes no noise in your room. Or maybe the clerk's telephone works incorrectly, dialing the wrong room exchange even when the proper number was entered. Perhaps the night clerk taking the request entered erroneous data on the wake-up log (wrong room, wrong time) or even failed to enter your request at all. Suppose you were ill, occupied, or for some reason incapacitated, and unable to hear the telephone. Given time we could come up with dozens of other reasons why, even though the day clerk performed his or her activities properly, and fulfilled his or her function as required, the wake-up call still did not achieve its objective—did not wake you.

Here is the difference between function and responsibility. The responsibility of the day clerk should be to achieve results—to waken the guest at the appropriate time—*regardless of the method*. Should no answer be forthcoming when he or she calls, he or she should check the status of the telephones—his or hers and yours. The clerk could walk to the room and pound on the door, recheck the log, or verify the name and room number against the registration records to assure their accuracy. There are many other steps that a *responsible* individual would have taken beyond the mere minimum required by his or her *function*.

What does this distinction mean in the context of projects? It points out the reliance we must place on responsibility assignment as opposed to functional assignments or procedures to get things done. We could have written each of the alternatives the day clerk *could* have taken into his or her job procedure. This would prove tedious, time consuming, and dangerous, for even after careful consideration we would probably miss one. In addition we would have to assure that all day clerks read, understand, remember and comply with all procedures, and constantly revise and perfect these procedures as times and conditions change. Taken to extremes this would be ludicrous and fruitless. We would spend more time writing and teaching procedures than managing the hotel.

Unfortunately, this little story is repeated on a grand scale throughout the business community, on project after project. It is much easier and more effective to assign responsibility than to dictate detailed activity that may or may not achieve desired objectives—to prescribe *results* rather than methods: *product* over *process*.

SUMMARY

The subject of organizations is full of controversy; rather than one best alternative, project and company management should search for and seize any one of a number of "workable" organizations. All have advantages and all have faults. The challenge is to understand these and to make a wise selection. Success lies not only in making the choice, however, but in *implementing* it once it has been made. And therein lies the potential for organizational failure.

We have cast many a disparagement on the functional organization base. It should be the least chosen alternative; working only for small projects for which no project-specific organization can be afforded. We have also pointed out failure factors inherent in the project island and matrix approaches, and described the value given any project by the multitude of networks between individuals. Any action taken to expand, nurture and *exploit* networking should benefit the project.

Organizations can be analyzed *in vitro*, but they must operate *in situ*. This means with a complement of people to fill the boxes, circles or lines on the charts. People accomplish objectives—not organizations. The latter exist only to leverage the skills and motivations of our human resource. We can tap these skills by best recognizing individual contributions, matching those to achievement, assigning focused *responsibility*, and blocking the negative aspects of human nature. These include empire building, the infatuation with reorganization, double agents, and the like. We can encourage mutuality of interests and physical intimacy between our people and the project for which they toil. This last accomplishment may represent the highest objective of any organizational contrivance.

PERSPECTIVES

viewing the cube

There appear to be two types of concepts which present the most trouble when trying to apply sound management principles to a business endeavor. The first set are those that are so obvious as to be overlooked and thus ignored. These might be called *unused concepts*, and we need to constantly remind ourselves of them so they can be used whenever possible. The second set of troublesome concepts are those difficult to define, to shape, or to package. These can best be thought of as *unformed concepts*, those that are so nebulous or shapeless as to lack a definable, and therefore memorable identity.

An example of a simple but often unused concept has been given in previous chapters: "projects are different than operations." Another might be the concept of people as different from commodities. Everyone recognizes these as soon as they are spoken or read, but often they are not applied to daily business activity. An example of the second category might be this: "Achieving and maintaining the proper perspective when dealing with projects is a major element of success." What does this mean? It is not unlike the famous quote from Woody Allen, who stated that one "has an 80% chance of success just by showing up." This might help us remember the concept, but does little to promote its understanding. Again it is an *unformed* and difficult to remember principle.

The challenge of this chapter is to give the notion of *perspective* shape and meaning; to crystallize the concept, illustrate its use, and in so doing to assure its memorable identity. As with other analyses, there is a touch of pragmatism in our motivation. We care little about this concept, or any others, if its understanding doesn't help avoid project failure.

The concept of *perspectives* qualifies for our attention in this regard. To give structure, form, and application to any type of project effort, we will use several devices. These are designed to help coalesce the thoughts behind the notion of perspectives into something solid and useful. Among these devices are analogies, figures, and graphically depicted relationships.

VIEWING THE PROJECT *CUBE*

Major projects are baffling. They are often so large, so time consuming, so expensive, and so full of interrelationships and different facets as to render them incomprehensible to the casual observer or even the seasoned manager. Often the first challenge to those attempting to control projects is to understand them. This is a greater chore than it seems, for projects represent huge, constantly changing collections of objectives, roles, responsibilities, expectations, methods, perspectives, needs, resources, activities, and measurements.

We are often tempted to see a project as one giant amorphous blob, devoid of shape, tumbling or floating through space and time with no apparent destination. While this might be true for some projects (black holes) this depiction doesn't give us much help when it comes to control. In order to control project activity and outcomes we need to create a better mental picture of a project; the better to get our minds around it.

One way to visualize a project is to define what it represents and see if any working generalizations are apparent. Projects are collections, and they may be viewed as collections of any one of the following:

Activities

Responsibilities

Resources

People

Processes

Objectives

Tasks

Assignments

Relationships

Physical results

Limits

Plans

Experiences

Work scopes

Data

Accounts

Unfortunately this list could go on for pages without solving our dilemma: How best to reduce a complex process to a shaped form and thereby identify our underlying concept of *perspectives*. Perhaps this is the answer: to view each project as a collection of different perspectives. Everyone has a different way of looking at a project— of getting his or her mind around it. It also makes sense that the perspective of each viewer should correspond to the viewer's role in project effort. We shall take this approach.

Figure 5-1 depicts our way of illustrating the major project perspectives we will examine in this chapter. Beginning with the project "cube" at the top, we see the three major roles project participants will play: (1) *performing* project activity, (2) *understanding* project activity, and (3) *controlling* that activity. Sometimes these perspectives are all held by one person (as with small projects having only one participant), sometimes by groups representing many thousands of people. Sometimes they are correct perspectives, that is, in line with the roles of those who hold them, and sometimes they are incorrect. And sometimes these perspectives change, whether they should or not. It is not difficult to see the source of many project failures in this concept of perspectives. We shall explore several. But first, we need to become better acquainted with the project cube.

Figure 5-1 shows the three major axes along which a project may be viewed. These are *performing*, which we may think of as resource management, *understanding*, which we call information management, and *controlling*, another term for project management. The large cube illustrates some of the elements of each different perspective, giving examples of activities, tools, and objectives that would concern someone taking each particular view. A few qualifications are in order when describing this cube:

1. Three views doesn't necessarily imply three different people, organizations, or companies.

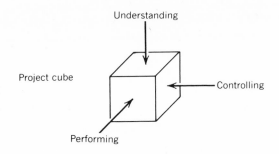

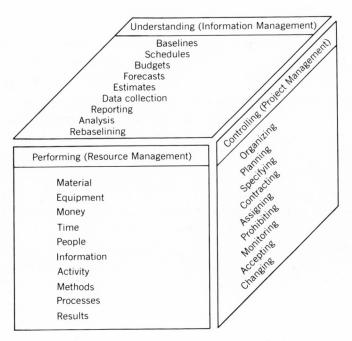

Figure 5-1.   Principal project perspectives.

2. The views are not mutually exclusive, that is, someone look-
    ing from the top down (understanding) would be interested
    in the resource of time. However, this interest is not in the
    use of time (this is the performing view) but in the *planning*
    and *measurement* of time usage (such as when we schedule
    and report activity durations, late or early completions and
    the like).

3. The project cube shown here is merely a *contrivance for under-*

standing—a device helping us to shape and remember the concept of perspectives.

Keeping these in mind, the cube is very helpful to us. We can use it to understand why people's actions may be based on different perspectives rather than unsound motivation or lack of skill. We can use this concept to focus and direct information in the right quantity and quality to those who could best use it (Chapter 7). It will help us see why different organizations plan differently (Chapter 6), and how changing roles are often not accompanied by changed perceptions—a key failure factor (Chapter 10).

Every project requires performance, understanding, and control to succeed, and virtually every failed project has lacked some element of one or more of these. For this reason, performing, understanding, and controlling can be seen as not only three different perspectives, but three *roles*—three sets of responsibilities. Their interrelationships are very close, intimate, and complex. We have illustrated them in terms of components, now it is time to understand their relationship to time. Figure 5-2 helps us do this. If we plot the amount of effort required in each area throughout the project's life, we may see performing, understanding, and controlling in an end-to-end fashion, as shown in the top of the figure. Or we may see them as parallel activities, each unchanging throughout time. These two views are incorrect, for although each activity continues throughout a project's life, they are not always constant in amount of effort required.

A better depiction is found at the bottom of Figure 5-2. Here we show the activities (and perspectives) of controlling and performing as continuing at varying levels depending on the project lifespan, with the need for understanding remaining constant. During the initial stages of the project, the need for controlling is great. This is manifested in the *planning* that goes on during this period. Very little *performance* has begun, however, as the project progresses, more and more direct work is performed and the need to control anticipated work reduces. Contracts have been let, information systems have been installed, procedures are in place, and responsibility assignments have been made. Less and less control is needed the more the project progresses, simply because the remaining work

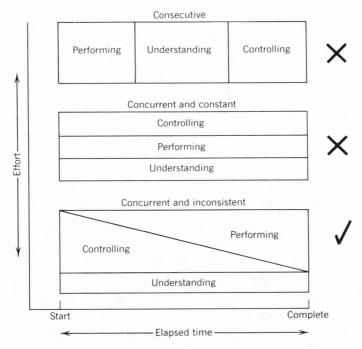

Figure 5-2. The distribution of effort over a project's life.

dwindles, the uncertainty as to completion diminishes, and the risk of exceeded baselines decreases. This is not to suggest that C,S, and T may not be in horrible shape, but as the work remaining decreases in volume and complexity, the direct effects of it being done late, at too great a cost, or of poor quality diminish. The time for maximum project control is during the initial stages, when failure *avoidance* can be practiced. The purpose of control towards the end of a project is one not of avoiding failure, but *mitigating* its negative impacts. It is surprising to see so many projects for which this concept is misapplied.

CONTROLLING THE CONTINUUM

A *continuum* can be defined as: something which is continuous, of which no separate parts are discernible. An example of a physical continuum may be a globule of water floating freely in zero gravity, or perhaps a barrel containing thousands of earthworms. What a fitting name for some projects! So many of them do seem to defy discernment, to resist shape, and to elude our mental grasp. These are true "continuums," and many times it is difficult to guess in which direction they are oozing.

Although "continuum" is perhaps a good way to visualize a project, it doesn't help us understand, perform or control project work. We cannot manage a continuum; we can't predict its path. Another representation is needed.

Regardless of the perspective they hold, successful project participants have shown that projects are best managed in pieces, with the continuum being reduced to or represented by a collection of elements, each having defined shape, predictable characteristics, and responding to management intervention. They break the project into pieces, manage each piece, and thereby manage the project as a whole. Put another way, they manage a forest by controlling the growth and health of each tree.

There are times when the art of management can benefit from a few methods used in the pure and applied sciences. This is one of them. Structural analysts, when trying to predict the behavior of a physical object, often model the object as a collection of connected "finite elements," each having specified physical properties (strength, elasticity, mass, etc.). They then subject this mathematic model to some sort of stimulii (perhaps the recorded accelerations produced by a historic earthquake) and determine how each element will act and react. By modeling the action and reaction of each element to the input acceleration and to the subsequent and compounding reactions of adjoining elements, a grossly accurate representation of the behavior of the entire object (skyscraper, pump, pipeline) is obtained.

Figure 5-3 shows how this concept may be applied to project management. In the top left we see our amorphous blob: the continuum that is the project. Our challenge is to represent it by a collection of discrete, finite "elements." Model #1 uses triangles which, when connected as shown, achieve a fairly close resemblance to the size and shape of the project. Thirty three elements (triangles) are used. Model #2 uses triangles as well, but only eight of them. We see this model as easier to form and identify (and therefore to plan

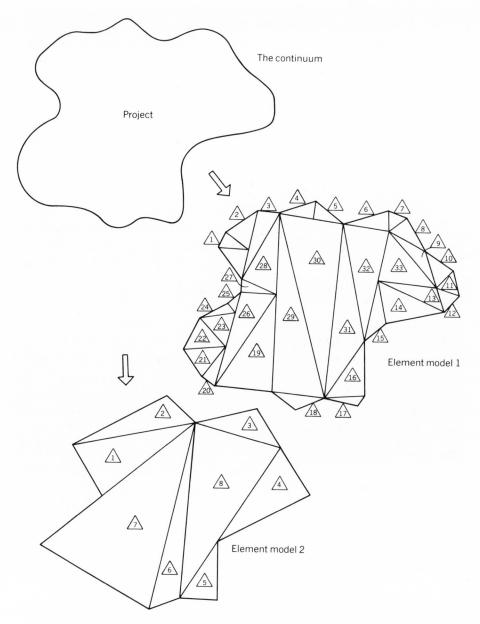

Figure 5-3. Breaking the project down into comprehensible elements.

and track its reaction to project stimulii) because it is simpler and easier to construct. However, it is also less accurate than Model #1. Therein lies the tradeoff in many project models we use in the real world: accuracy versus expense. The more accurate our models of the project, the more costly, time consuming and detailed they must be; the more difficult they are to manage, the more complex and detailed the resulting information will be, and the more precision required when a change is made.

What does this finite element analogy have to do with project management and project perceptions? It shows, in a physical way, how a difficult-to-define project can be reduced to a collection of simple components. It hints that we can plan and control each component fairly easily, and by so doing plan and control the project. And it demonstrates that we can go to many levels of detail when "modeling" the project; thereby gaining a more accurate but more costly representation.

The analogy is not as farfetched as it may first appear. We all form mental representations of projects in order to better understand, perform or control work. We model projects when we prepare cost estimates or budgets—these are cost "models," and we constantly wrestle with the need for accuracy in our budgets as compared with expediency and time required to produce and use them. We model the time element of project work with simple or extremely complex schedules. The more accurate they are the more costly they are to produce, time consuming and difficult to understand and use. And we model the project as a series of responsibilities given to participating organizations (contracts, purchase orders, job orders, etc.). Again, the tradeoff between accuracy and effort is always involved.

VISUAL PROXIMITY: FOCUS

It may help to think of the degree of detail in our modelling attempts as analogous to optical "focus." The more discrete we model the project (more elements) the closer our focus becomes. When we see it as a collection of five elements, our focus is from a distance. Moving closer we may see each element composed, in turn, of ten "subelements," making 50 components in total. Upon closer examination (and modelling) greater and greater numbers of components are possible. The same is true when we reverse the process: the farther and farther our vantage point lies from reality, the fewer and fewer components we are able to discern—the more inaccurate our perception becomes. We can zoom in from forest to tree, to branch and to leaf, and as with experiments in optics, the clarity of our object increases as the visual field under study decreases. The converse is also true: the farther away from the project the more we can see, but with less resolution. This principle will become very important when we study other areas of project failure (see Chapters 6, 7, 8, and 10).

Perspectives vary. So far we have analyzed only two dimensions of any given perspective: direction and focus. That is, whether we view the project cube from the front (performance), top (understanding), or right side (control), and when so doing whether we see it composed of a few, many or a multitude of components. These aspects pertain to our view of a project: from which direction and at what distance. Both are characteristics of *direct* view. Sometimes it helps to follow an *indirect* approach.

PERIPHERAL VISION

Night vision is different than day vision. Because of the architecture of the human eye, that which we can see best by looking directly at during daylight is not best seen directly at night. In fact looking directly at something during periods of darkness is the worst way to see it. That portion of our eyes directly behind the pupil doesn't contain the mechanism nor the chemicals necessary for night vision, so we "see" things at night out of the "sides" of our eyes—with peripheral vision. Soldiers training for night missions are taught to focus their vision around the intended object rather than directly on it. Could we benefit from the same training? Could our perspectives sharpen and prove more informative when they become indirect, or "peripheral?"

Yes they can, and the best way to demonstrate this is through another figure. This particular one, Figure 5-4 makes use of what might be called "the analogy box," a simple figurative device we will use from time to time to portray elusive points or notions that have project application.

THE ANALOGY BOX

This device is best thought of as a flat wooden structure consisting of a plywood base bordered by wooden planks on the outside edges, with two L-shaped walls inside the box. Figure 5-4 shows two such boxes, identical in size and shape. Each contains a number of ping pong balls, and each is divided into three zones, labeled with the triangles and numbered 1, 2, and 3. Each box has been oriented so that its top corner is pointing due north, and the entire box has been lifted from the surface of the paper at that apex, so that the angle the box makes from the paper's surface is about 30 degrees. These are the physical "facts." The remainder is management analogy, conjecture, opinion, and demonstration.

THE STRUGGLE TO SUCCEED

Look at Figure 5-4 and focus your attention on the top box, labeled "A." Let the balls represent people, each trying to succeed. The rules of this project define success as attainment of the northernmost position possible, while still remaining inside the box. All the people are placed in Zone 1 and told to achieve success. An alert individual looks around and sees that the apex of the first interior wall is the most northern position and scrambles for it. Others, seeing this leader move, follow—hoping to participate in and share success. The result is a group of people huddled against the first interior wall, each experiencing the satisfaction of being in the most northern possible attainable. They have found what is called "the local solution," the highest positions in Zone 1.

Using a compass, or by constantly walking uphill (the direction

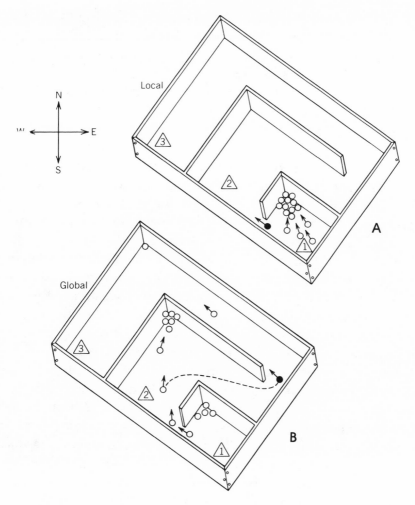

Figure 5-4. "The analogy box": local versus global solutions.

of success), each has attained a modicum of success—the most success available in Zone 1. Any movement away from this apex is in the downward direction, thus confirming the fact that they have obtained the optimum position, according to the rules.

There is one exception: this person shaded a darker tint. He or she has broken the project rule, by following peripheral vision. He has seen around the first interior wall into Zone 2 and has ascertained that the local solution may not be the best solution. Given time, this outsider may pursue his vision by climbing to the Zone 2 apex, or more probably, some other enterprising individual, borrowing the concept, may leave the pack long enough to spot Zone 3 and a higher, more northern position. These possibilities are shown in box "B" in the figure, representing what we might call attainment of "the global solution."

A number of project-related lessons can be derived from this example. First, it pays to take an outside view from time to time—to let our vision wander off the accepted objective. Quite often this is the value a consultant or other project outsider will bring to our effort—the ability to take a different view, to remove the project blinders and discover a whole new approach, method, or result.

If we follow the example of the dark balls, the enterprising individuals, we might also conclude that, at times, one must fail in order to succeed. Each discovery of a higher zone was preceeded by stepping backwards (south) or to the side (east or west) and thus away from the direction of apparent progress (north). Small failures are sometimes prerequisites to larger successes. No ultimate success can be gained without a few temporary setbacks. Apart from being cute slogans, these are facts of project life.

Note each group of balls following the leader (darker ball). Is this a sign of management, or perhaps something else? It might be argued that there are two different phenomena occurring here. The first is when the unshaded balls follow the movement of the shaded one from the bottom of a zone to the top of the same zone. Think of this as motivation—the manager has motivated the group to achieve higher levels. The second phenomenon concerns the shaded manager's discovery and pointing out of a higher zone of achievement for the group to pursue. This could be analogous to management "direction" or "guidance" or what we like to call "vision." A good manager (project or otherwise) should provide both: *motivation* to achieve the highest position attainable in a given situation, and *vision* to point out new situations offering even higher attainments. A good project manager also realizes that there are always local solutions and global solutions, and knows when to pursue each.

The box also shows us that some efforts are best approached head-on, while others can be attacked circumfrentially—using peripheral vision. But most of all it points out the value of the outside view—the unencumbered perspective.

THE MANAGER AS MOVING CAMERA

A good manager understands the importance perspective plays in project success and failure. He or she realizes that perspectives are often unannounced, inconsistent, and fluctuating among principal project members. They also realize that any fixed perspective, no matter how well founded and clear it may be, is a poor perspective, for our views must be constantly moving in order to keep up with changing project risks, responsibilities, and environments. In this regard, the best project manager is not unlike a moving camera, shifting position, angle of view, focal length, and exposure frequency as it moves over, under and around the project, which in turn, is always in motion itself.

It's also important to note that, as a manager gets farther and farther away from the object of his or her attention (the project in this case) the more that manager must rely on secondary or tertiary input regarding the project. That is, the farther away the less available and reliable primary data (such as that attained through sight) become.

Managers can be removed from projects in two principal fashions: spatially and by time. The first refers to simple physical separation. A project in India being managed from New York is an extreme example of spatial separation. When that happens the manager must rely on reports to determine what is occurring. When these reports become one, two, or three months in arrears, the manager is removed from the project *in terms of time* as well. Again, as proximity to the project increases, direct and reliable information and control links are feasible, whereas indirect, unreliable, and summary level links characterize a lack of management proximity. Anything that encourages physical proximity in terms of space and time is therefore beneficial. The only exception involves the tendency for management to get so close as to preclude peripheral vision—the outsider's perception. This should never be traded for the benefits of intimacy. Both can be had.

We have described perceptions as they may vary according to direction (performing, understanding, controlling), mental modeling (size, complexity, and number of elements), and focus (visual proximity to the object). Perspectives may also, and frequently do, vary with time. That is, each project member's perception must be dynamic, shifting with the circumstances and needs that are both current and *forecasted* for the project. The project manager is not the only one who should resemble a moving camera.

FAILED PERSPECTIVES

Now that we have described the characteristics of and importance given to perspective in a project context, it's time to explore ways in which perspectives can go awry.

FF 38: Wrong Perspective

The most obvious and most frequent failure factor is that of having the wrong perspective, and acting accordingly. We see this when a project owner hires a general construction contractor and then proceeds to dictate *how* work will be performed. This owner is looking down the wrong axis of the project cube; thinking *performance* when it should be thinking *control of performance*.

Often the wrong perspective is confused with the wrong motivation, or wrong objective. All are harmful to project health, no matter who their holder, but the first is most insidious. Wrong motivations or objectives are fairly self-evident, while incorrect perspectives are not so easily detected. The best people, well intentioned, skilled and provided with the proper tools often plunge ahead in the wrong direction because they carry the wrong perspective around in their minds. This is a critical management deficiency. Every project manager should communicate the right perspective to all team members at the very beginning of each project effort. And that expression needs repeating from time to time, because (1) people move in and out of the project organization, (2) perspectives can change to match changing conditions and objectives, and (3) people tend to forget. The proper project perception should never be assumed.

Another example of the wrong perception might concern a construction management firm hired by the owner to "manage" the contractors performing construction work. If the management firm is staffed with former construction superintendents whose careers have been spent directing construction performance, they might carry that perspective into the new, very different position of construction management. Sometimes this distinction is little more than a nuance, but more often it shapes and directs every aspect of the participant's effort. The duty of the construction management firm in our example is to plan, organize, schedule, budget, and report on progress of work performed by the contractors, not to supervise or direct their work. They have been engaged to *understand* and help *control* rather than to *perform*.

It is important that everyone on their staff recognize the distinction, lest they step over the fine line separating *performance monitoring* from *supervision*. Should they do so, the firm (and the owner it represents) may inadvertently forego the benefits of an independent contractor relationship and assume many risks and responsibilities normally carried by the contractor.

Not only do positions and responsibilities change with changing perspectives, but so do the tools required to fulfill the roles involved. A good example concerns information systems. All contractors maintain some sort of manual or automated systems that allow them to plan, status and forecast their work at a level of detail commensurate with their *performing* perspective. These systems typically give them data concerning labor hours expended, quantities installed, installation rates, equipment usage, crew compositions, set-up times, and production rates compared to (1) past work on other projects, and (2) forecasted work for the project at hand. These systems are intended to satisfy the information needs of the performer. These needs are not the same as the controller or the one wishing to understand the project (the other two perspectives).

Supposing the contractor in question is operating on a lump sum, firm-fixed price contract, unit rates, labor hours, equipment usage and related data have no meaning to the owner (controller). All the owner needs to know is: (1) is the work proceeding according to schedule, (2) is the work being performed correctly, and (3) how much is payable to the contractor at any given time (C, S, and T on a very summary level). In this sense, we can think of the contractor's information "model" to be much more closely focused (more elements) than the owner's model of the same project. This is not only acceptable but desirable, for each has different perspectives and different information needs; hence different tools to satisfy them.

FF 39: Out of Focus

When management, regardless of their principal perspective, is too close or too far away from the project its vision is blurred. Its focus is incorrect. This occurs when we scrutinize the leaves or the branches of a project but should be watching the trees and forest. Or when the opposite takes place: looking at the "big picture" when its components are begging for attention. In these cases the manager's "finite element model" is either too fine (too many small elements) or too coarse (too few). This causes local solutions to be seen when global ones are not, and vice versa. A manager with vision is capable of seeing both.

Proper information and reporting systems allow a manager to change focus almost at will, and to zoom in or out of the project data forest without losing focus. These employ structured, tiered approaches that allow summarization of data without loss of information traceability, down through successively lower levels of detail, to the source of project difficulty. This is a topic best treated in Chapter 7. It should be noted here, however, that the best project management tools are those allowing for this adjustment of focus—for this selectivity based on perceived risk, management objectives, or overriding concerns.

FF 40: Specifying Process, Not Product

There is no better way to stifle innovation or penalize ingenuity than to specify the process you wish someone to follow rather than the product you expect to be its result. When a cosmetics concern hires an ad agency for project-specific work, it errs by selecting the media, preparing the advertising copy, choosing the spokesperson, and designing the point of sale displays. It is for the agency to select, prepare, choose, and design—other words for *perform*. Often we see owners, in their zeal to assure performance, specify methods of performance in lieu of expectations, or both. This is wrong, and the error is based on improper perceptions. Here is another example.

A construction project owner wishes to have a tremendous amount of soil removed from the job site and specifies in the construction contract that it must be dumped at a preselected site located 12 miles away. All prospective contractors include this added haul cost in their bids, and the low bidder is chosen. Once work is started, the contractor notifies the owner that an equally acceptable, authorized dump site is located only one mile from the site, and that had it been allowed, several million dollars could have been saved by the owner simply by not specifying the prescribed site—by relying on the bidders' ingenuity.

Should overriding concerns (different perspective) predominate, a different verdict might be had. For example, the soil removed from the site might be contaminated, with government permission for disposal granted for the prescribed site only. Or the excess soil may be needed there to serve as structural fill for a different owner project. In these cases, the owner's need is to have the spoiled soil dumped at the specified site. Absent them, however, the owner's need is merely to have the soil *removed* from the project site. Regardless of our perspective or project role, it is almost always better to specify results than processes. This pertains to dealings with other companies (contractors, advertising agencies, etc.) as well as to internal transactions (managing our own people).

FF 41: Risk-Free

Every project entails some degree of risk for each participant, regardless of their perspective or role. The very nature of project work is one laden with risk, and the primary mission of each project manager should be to to reduce, transfer, avoid, or otherwise lessen the impact of risk in a manner consistent with the achievement of project expectations. This is natural, and there have evolved many tools and techniques designed to do so.

Contract pricing strategies represent examples of risk transfer techniques. They allow the owner and contractor (buyer and seller) to shift risk from one to the other, and hopefully this is done in a fashion consistent with the capability of each to control risk. In any case, they decide to shift almost all cost risk to the contractor when agreeing to a hard money, lump-sum price. The owner assumes virtually all cost risk when they agree on a cost-plus-percent-of-cost pricing methodology. These are the two extremes, and we know there are hundreds of variations in between—each designed to distribute cost risk differently.

Any project manager who thinks it possible to dump all project risk on another party is a fool. This simply cannot be done—we cannot participate without sharing some element of risk. Of course, the best way to avoid risk completely is to forego projects altogether. Those choosing this option need not turn another page. The rest of us realize that, try as we may, the transfer of risk to others is never complete. We realize as well that, along with the transfer of risk, we must transfer authority to deal with it and freedom to do so. This rule applies to outsiders and to insiders, to those other companies we join for project work and to the individuals we choose to perform, understand, or control it.

FF 42: Fixed View

Sometimes perspectives are so firmly ingrained in people's minds that they cannot be easily modified. These people need to be identified and "re-educated," or placed in positions aligned with their permanent perspective. A similar problem exists with those of us not willing to change perspectives (or roles) as a project progresses—even when to do so is essential for success. This problem is most often seen on long-term projects (*perspective stagnation*), first-of-a-kind efforts (*unformed perspectives*) and when dramatic changes in position occur among the principal project players (*perspective shock*).

FF 43: Mixed Views

Because project work occurs sporadically, many participating companies cannot carry established organizations fully staffed and ready for project deployment. These must be created as the need arises, and often they are staffed with agents, contract workers, consultants, or borrowed staff from another company. It is essential in these cases to recognize the potential of blurred, mixed, or inconsistent perspectives (not to mention motivations and allegiances). We see this frequently with so called composite organizations, when the project sponsor relies on others to supply talent or labor underneath its management umbrella.

It's conceivable that one or more of these helpers may be, intentionally or not, organizational "moles" (to borrow a term from the world of espionage). Without being too skeptical, managers in charge of composite organizations should not take monolithic perspectives for granted. Members of the composite staff may have hidden agendas; motivations not consistent with those of the team.

FF 44: Project Arrogance

One perspective that should never be tolerated is one of arrogance; a feeling that the project is better than the rest of the company, untouchable, supreme, or somehow immortal—that it will live indefinitely. Often seen on large projects with noble goals, this can be likened to organizational or mission *hubris*. It is almost always a fatal flaw, for to be successful each project must recognize that it is temporary, based on need, and thereby unnecessary if (1) the need changes or vanishes, (2) the prospect of fulfilling the need diminishes, or (3) the price of fulfillment is deemed too high (C, S, and T).

Sometimes this perspective is manifested openly, but often it is imbedded in the minds of principal participants. Regardless of its visibility, it seems prevalent with those projects for which the end is used to justify any means. These are the ones that appear to be destined for completion, to hell with C,S, and T. While this attitude may persist for a time, it almost always results in poor management, sloppy processes, and failed expectations. No project effort, short of total war, is exempt from the requirement to justify itself in terms of performance factors. The greater the effort, the more prevalent the arrogance, the more prone to failure it becomes. Failure seems attracted to large, proud targets. The landscape of business is strewn with their carcasses. Despite their size, strength, and apparent invincibility, even dinosaurs vanished when they no longer remained feasible.

FF 45: Eye to Eye: Toe to Toe

There is a large difference between maintaining a healthy skepticism and insisting on confrontation. Some project participants presume, even demand adversarial relationships from the very beginning. Because people and companies involved with projects have different perspectives does not mean they must have opposing motives. Because we do not see eye-to-eye (along the same axis of the cube) does not mean we must exist toe-to-toe.

We must constantly remind ourselves that projects are temporary relationships, based on *need* as well as *greed*. We need each other, and must have a common perception that transcends all others, a joint perception surmounting parochial ones: the desire for a successful project. Almost never does one party survive a disastrous project experience while others fail. Like a ship overturned, a failed project assures each passenger of an equal chance of drowning. In this regard we should approach each project as a win-win proposition, one in which individual success is rarely achievable without mutual success.

Owners sometimes forget this principle when they insist on pressing lawsuits against a contractor still at work, or threaten to remove a principal player from the project. No matter how well founded and deserved this action might be, it will almost certainly result in temporary or permanent setbacks to the project. If these can be tolerated, and if the long-term result is beneficial, then they should be pursued. Otherwise they represent folly. The owner in these cases should ask itself: do I prefer a finished project or an enforceable claim in court? Most wise owners swallow their pride and opt for the latter. Abject failure is like a grenade, once it explodes everyone in the room is injured.

A certain amount of give and take, flexibility, and compromise is always needed, especially when high risk, performance-critical efforts are undertaken. In these cases a pragmatic perspective is better than a righteous one. As Ben Franklin once said, "Everything one has a right to do is not best to be done."

FF 46: Project Drives Company

If there is a single fear bordering on paranoia among functionally anchored managements it is this: that the project, once created by the company, will grow in size and strength until one day it will devour its maker: the "Frankenstein syndrome." We see this fear manifested by operationally oriented executives who refuse to allow or even to consider project-specific controls, methods, or systems to infiltrate company life. They are often overheard making statements such as "That may be acceptable for the project, but not for the rest of the company," or "If we let that persist on the project, pretty soon we'll have to do it everywhere!" What does this perception mean to us? Simply put, we can never forget, nor become insensitive to the *differing* needs, objectives, and perceptions applying to non-project life.

There are many times when company-wide objectives are vastly different than project-specific ones. A partial listing of these follows:

Company Concerns	Project Concerns
Funding sources	Funding uses
Predictability	Unnecessary
Uniformity	Uniqueness
Standard controls	Risk-based controls
Constant staff levels	Fluctuating staff levels
Asset accounts	Cost control elements
Reporting to outsiders	Reporting to insiders

Any time project management can weave project-specific objectives into company objectives, making them one and the same, chances of success are enhanced. The ideal condition exists for those projects where company perspectives are parallel with, if not identical to, those of the project. This rarely occurs, particularly if the project holds itself up to be immortal, superior, or dominant (arrogance). Or for those projects that attempt to confront corporate sponsors out of spite. The next factor involves one such type.

FF 47: The Project from Outer Space

From time to time a project holds itself up to be so vastly different, so unique and unprecedented that no existing standards of management or business acumen apply to its conduct. Scorn is heaped upon any attempts by the sponsoring company to control or even to understand project performance. It's as if no rules apply, or so the project would have the company believe.

This perspective almost always leads to misunderstanding, mistrust, and eventual failure, for not only does the project need outsiders, it must have inside support—not just to clear the funding hurdle, but throughout its existence. And proven business controls *do* apply to project environments. Perceptions may change, objectives may be specific and unique, but the time-honored principles of planning, organizing, and managing are always applicable. Like physical laws of nature, they are inviolate. The law of gravity always holds, even for the project from outer space.

SUMMARY

The concept of project perspectives is difficult to establish and to apply because it often lacks shape, form, and a memorable identity. Like many other *unformed* concepts, it is typically addressed only when its absence or misunderstanding causes failure. Three principal project-specific perspectives are those based on a need to *perform*, *understand*, or *control* project work. These are illustrated by the three dimensions, or axes, of our figurative project cube. Other factors influencing perspectives include the use of mental models to represent the project (finite elements), focal length (management proximity) and the use of indirect, *peripheral* vision to achieve a new, sometimes refreshing perspective.

Project and company management is often ignorant of or uncomfortable with the entire notion of perspectives. This may be due to its unformed condition, or perhaps to the difficulty with which perceptions are understood, established, or changed. Unlike organizations, which are the easiest to see and manipulate of all management elements, perceptions are hidden, indeterminate and often unresponsive to direct management intervention. This explains why the most rare and valuable project manager is one sensitive to the role of perspectives, and tireless in his or her quest to shape and direct them. This is the manager who sees the global solution while all others are scrambling for the local version. This is the manager with vision.

PLANNING

outguessing and outsmarting failure

Most treatments of this topic typically begin with repetitions of trite, overused statements such as "Proper planning prevents poor performance" or "You can't get to your destination without a map." These are hollow and useless admonitions. They don't help us plan more or plan better. In fact, the banality they represent often turns project and corporate management away—away from the very valuable exercise that good planning represents. They tell us to plan, but never how to plan, why to plan, or who should plan. They focus on the type of planning that is usually done well: performance planning. Note their use of such terms as "performance" and "are going." These are anchored in only one axis on our three-dimensional project cube: performance.

Planning in general, or for that matter performance planning, doesn't eliminate failure, the *right kind of planning* does. Here is the seed of many a failed project: misdirected planning, planning those activities that need little of it, and ignoring the others.

WHAT'S THE SCHEME?

The British have a wonderful term for performance plans. They call them *schemes*. We plan our schemes well. Typically we focus on *how* something will be accomplished to the detriment of plans concerning project understanding and project control. We scheme, but don't plan, and the distinction is critical to project success.

WHEN WILL WE EVER LEARN?

"Why is it that we always have time to do it over, but never enough time to do it right from the beginning?" This is a quote that echoes around corporate boardrooms the world over—the response to failed planning. The value of planning as an integral part of any business enterprise has been known for centuries, and is proven again and again by project failure each year. Yet for some reason we tend to begin each project bouyed by optimism, only to find ourselves hopelessly pessimistic as the project spirals downward over time. The value of planning is measured by its ability to reverse this process—to begin with a certain pessimism and, through confrontation with potential failure and positioning adequate controls to counter it, end the project experience on a note of optimism concerning the future. Planning is the process of *outguessing* and *outsmarting* failure.

EARNED OPTIMISM

The knowledge that one will face many failure factors during the course of a project is reason enough to begin the planning phase with some pessimism (just imagine all the things that may go wrong!). When followed by intelligent, carefully selected measures taken to sidestep failure (what we call *controls*), this essential pessimism is transformed into an earned optimism. Planning, then, is the process of converting justifiable pessimism into earned optimism. Not a bad way to begin a project.

Surprisingly enough, this view is not universally held. Two alternatives (neither of which is recommended), thwart the need for planning. The first is a fatalistic view, best, and often expressed by the statement "It's going to take as long as it takes and cost as much as it costs." This view presumes that failure is preordained—that there is little we can do to prevent it or reduce its effect. Fortunately those holding this view have slowly removed themselves from the ranks of project management, for not only does this position denegrate the value of project management it tends very strongly to be a self-fulling prophecy. That is, the more one holds that it will take what it will take (in terms of C,S&T), the more in fact, it will.

THE POLLYANNA PERCEPTION

Another popular view might be termed the *Pollyanna Perception*. It's characterized by unearned, if not unbridled optimism during a project's early phases. Pollyanna managers can't be faulted for their optimism, per se, but for not taking steps to enjoy an *earned* optimism. These are the steps of planning; steps taken to circumvent failure. Often the spectre of failure is crowded out of their field of vision by other, more pleasant thoughts or is suppressed by their faith that somehow things will work out best in this case. Lack of experience contributes to this outlook. So does ignorance of the potentials and mechanics of failure. And among these failure factors are ones emanating directly from the planning experience itself.

FORGET PERFECT PLANNING

Some executives are keen on planning and insist that it be done perfectly. Two situations result. First, so called perfect plans will be created: plans incapable of implementation by imperfect organizations and personnel. Secondly, so much time and effort is spent on creating perfect plans that there is no C,S, and T left for actual project execution. These are extremes pointing out the fallacy of insisting on perfect planning. There are other, more common reasons for perfect planning never to occur.

To begin with, each project effort starts tentatively, with a certain degree of hesitation. This may be due to the uncertainty of its feasibility, the search for funding sources, an unfamiliarity with the project scope on the part of company management (operationally aligned management), or the concurrent consideration of other projects (competitors for the funding hurdle). In any case projects never march off decisively. They drift around the company, stumble, stutter, and then start. Once they start their sponsors want to see something tangible immediately (yesterday was too late). They want to see intermediate results, not the beginning of planning. They confuse feasibility studies with planning, although these are two entirely different animals. Feasibility studies answer the question "can it be done?" while planning answers "how are we going to perform, understand, and control what can be done?"

Because of the tentative nature of every project's beginning, most companies don't commit project-specific personnel or other resources until the very last moment. This hampers advanced planning by depriving the effort of knowledgeable managers, money and company resources necessary to ensure valuable plans. The individuals or group assigned to project planning are often unassigned, available, and expedient rather than our best. They are not commonly those who will carry out the plans they make. Another factor involved with less than perfect planning is this optimism mentioned earlier. Everyone *knows* this project is a great idea, so why place a great deal of emphasis on guessing what can go wrong and building controls to protect it? Again, this attitude confuses *feasibility* with *controlability*. It may be a great concept, but it will get nowhere unless we have the skills and resources to manage it to fruition. This focus on feasibility rather than execution, coupled with an unearned trust in existing tools and procedures works against planning.

These are some of the reasons why planning is never done as it should be done, in a timely manner, with plenty of funds, personnel, and other resources, and under the direction and close participation of actual project management rather than surrogates. Most successful projects manage to survive these handicaps and develop good plans despite them. Unfortunately many failed projects began to fail right from the beginning, during the planning phase. Sometimes the very fact that perfect planning is unobtainable causes management to abandon the concept of planning entirely. They misunderstand the objective of the exercise. Planning doesn't allow us to draw blueprints of project perfection—to design a successful project. It simply allows us to rationally focus our controls and information tools where they will give us the most value—on *risk*. Plans not centered on risk are not plans at all, not even schemes. They are dreams, with the same chance of coming true.

RISK ASSESSMENT: OUTGUESSING FAILURE

Plans represent potential controls. They don't necessarily support standard controls, fixed controls, or general controls. They help us create and point *specific controls* at specific risks. Hopefully we end up with highly developed controls easily deployed should the occasion for their use arise. It's best to think of planning as the creation of contingency controls, ones that can be used when needed and changed to meet ever current project conditions.

Information systems (understanding) and controls cost money and take time to develop and use. Those not giving us value should be abandoned. There is no sense in spending project money and time on misdirected systems or controls. The challenge of planning, then, is to determine just what systems and controls will give value, will work, and can be implemented in time for their project-specific use. Successful projects accomplish this objective through the practice of *risk assessment*.

Risk assessment involves mutual estimations, on the part of the planning group, as to what can go wrong with project performance, understanding, and control activity. It is an attempt to list risk factors that may impact elements of the project, rank them in order of importance, and assign particular systems and controls to counter them. Often these controls are grouped into categories, such as (1) organizational controls, (2) procedural controls, and (3) contractual controls. This grouping is not important, however, it merely points out that there may be, and often are, more than one way to prevent or reduce risk. Sometimes these overlap, and sometimes one or more controls are never needed.

The result of a careful assessment of risk followed by a plan to implement controls, on a selective basis, as they match risk is a sound basis for project initiation. This concept of risk-based controls is shown graphically by Figure 6-1.

SPECIFIC CONTROLS: A PROJECT FOUNDATION

One way to visualize the entire risk-based planning process is shown by Figure 6-2. Each of the three views shown (*a*, *b*, and *c*) are a cross sectional look at a building foundation site. Shaded areas represent soil, with bedrock shown spotted. During the initial phase of the project (*a*) we see the subsurface conditions undisturbed, with a need to determine the extent of soil and rock below. Soil will make an unsuitable foundation material, while rock is pre-

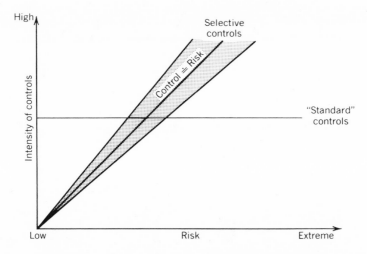

Figure 6-1.   Planning selective controls to match risk.

ferred. The task of project planning in this analogy is to determine the risk below the surface (extent of or depth of soil) and to build solid controls to eliminate that risk (blocks placed where soil is removed). As depicted by scene (*b*), risk assessment may include a general area excavation down to a certain level (analogous to removal of general risks found with every project) followed by spotty drillings through the soil to determine how many blocks will be needed and where (controls). This is the "what if" modeling done by considering just what can go wrong for each aspect of potential project work. Once this is completed, a solid foundation of controls can be installed (Scene (*c*)). The risk assessment process is performed not simply to reveal potential risks, but to point out the types, locations, and strengths of controls needed. We identify and attempt to quantify risk in order to better build systems and controls to counter it.

THE PROBLEM WITH STANDARD CONTROLS

The problem with standard controls is they don't block specific risks in an efficient way. They either over control or under control, either too much or too little. Many companies spend millions of dollars on

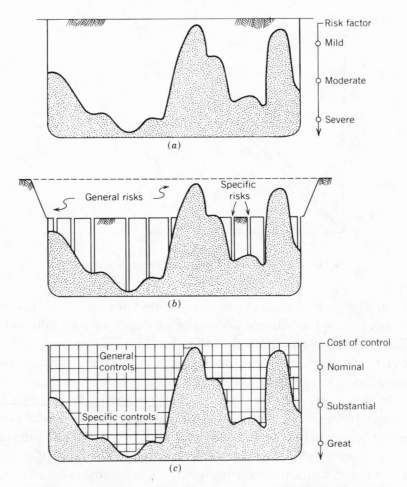

Figure 6-2. Risk assessment: Outguessing failure. (*a*) Project initiation (unknown risks, no control); (*b*) Risk assesment (probing for potential problems) and (*c*) Planning (building controls to meet risk).

extensive, complex and exhaustive information systems, procedures, contracts, organizations and the like, expecting to apply these to every project, regardless of risk. This is their "universal tool." We all know that universal tools never work. Neither do standard controls. If we think of risks as threatening animals, a severe one may be a charging elephant and a nuisance a buzzing housefly. An elephant gun (extensive control) works well for the elephant but is a bit overkill and inefficient when controlling the fly. And while a flyswatter (minor control) may stop the fly it will do little to keep a charging elephant at bay.

Supporters of standard controls would dispense with both the elephant gun and the flyswatter, preferring instead a middle-weight weapon, such as a baseball bat. Needless to say, this wouldn't stop the elephant or the fly. Risks (the elephant, the fly) are almost always specific, and projects almost always fail for specific reasons. If standard controls are to be used at all, they should only serve as *minimum* controls, providing a base on which specific, risk-targeted measures can begin.

ATTACK OF THE SPECIFIC RISKS

The field of immunology provides a fitting example of the adaptation of specific controls to specific risks. Our bodies develop very precise antibodies designed to attract or attack certain foreign objects in our bloodstreams, objects such as viruses, bacteria, and the like. While their structures and chemical compositions are complex, we can visualize both general and specific antibodies in a simplified way with Figure 6-3 and 6-4 respectively. Looking at Figure 6-3 we see four different types of foreign bodies invading, only to be met by an equal number of general antibodies, each designed to attach itself, and thereby kill, a certain type of intruder. Unfortunately these general controls only stopped one, whereas with Figure 6-4, specific antibodies were far more successful. The unsuccessful, general antibodies shown in Figure 6-3 are not harmful in themselves, but they represent a waste of resources. The same is true for so called general controls, but worse. For general controls often supplant the use of more effective (often cheaper) specific versions.

INCREMENTAL PLANNING: THE FOLDED MAP

As mentioned earlier, some executives cite the fact that planning cannot be perfect as reason to devalue its use. In the same way,

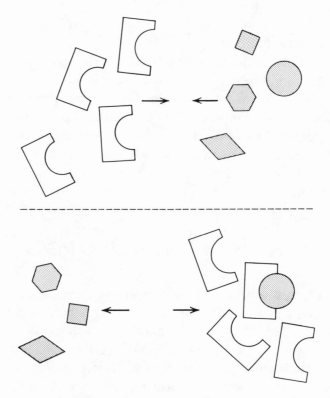

Figure 6-3. "Standard" controls attack risks.

others complain that because long-term risks can't be seen with the same degree of acuity as short-term problems, the planning process as a whole is faulty. These views ignore the incremental nature of planning, and assume that just because all project activity can't be planned to the same detail there is little need to plan at all.

A more progressive and realistic view considers the fact that long-term risks occur in the long term, and by virtue of being far away, need not be known to the same extent as near-term risks. The same is true for controls designed to confront risks. The closer the risk the more required the control. There is little need to tailor specific controls to fit long-term risks when those risks may change, diminish, or evaporate. Better to cross one bridge at a time, and allow the detail with which we design future bridges to decrease as the distance to them increases.

A depiction of this philosophy is provided by Figure 6-5. It rep-

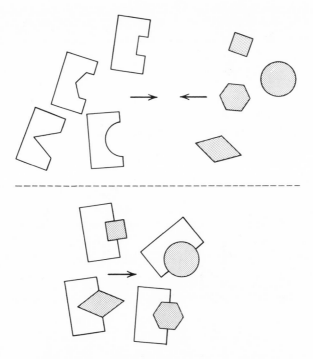

Figure 6-4. "Specific" controls attack risks.

resents the project under study as a large sheet of paper, on which we have drawn a map (our plans). During the initiation of the project (*a*), we are able to foresee the risks involved with near-term efforts (say for the next six months) with quite a bit of detail. After that, however, our vision and the value of our predictions concerning risk diminish. Our intermediate-term map is not as detailed, and our far-term version is even less so.

As we proceed down the project path, to a point six months in the future (*b*) we refocus our examination of risks expected in phase two, and refine our assessment based on new and more detailed information available at that time. We also refine our assessment of the remaining work as well, but with a little less information and therefore less detail. Finally as shown in (*c*), we move into the time span originally deemed far term, but now near term. Once again we refocus our risk assessment and redefine and deploy our controls accordingly.

The concept depicted by Figure 6-5 is analogous to a traveler

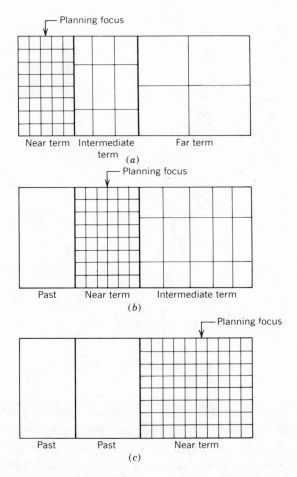

Figure 6-5. Incremental planning: The folded map. (*a*) Project initiation; (*b*) six months later; and (*c*) eighteen months later.

using a map of the country in which he or she is located. Not wanting to constantly scan unnecessary portions of the large map, he or she folds it into a small square containing only the area the traveler expects to traverse for a few hours or days at a time. Once the traveler reaches an edge of the square he or she refolds the map to another, adjoining square to keep the viewing area consistent with his or her physical location. While the traveler may scan the other areas of the map with some degree of concern (he or she needs to know where he or she will be later), the traveler concentrates attention on the minute details of the folded portion—the near term.

We can think of the map shown in Figure 6-5 as our project plan, folded and refolded as our project team travels through time and we carry our high degree of resolution from near term to near term as we go. This folded map example is not unlike our concept of focused perceptions, or finite element modeling, described in Chapter 5. We model our effort in terms of risk, and near-term risks are certainly more pressing than long-term potentials. Our degree of resolution (number of finite elements) should therefore vary in proportion to risk. This is another reason for discarding standard controls (fixed focus lens) and for periodic updates of risk assessment and controls selection. Failure cannot be spotted once and forgotten. It moves, waits, changes its angle of attack, and strikes unexpectedly elsewhere.

FF 48: Unbounded Optimism

Projects are expected to succeed or they would not be undertaken. This simple fact gives rise to a not-so-innocent result: a contagious disease that spreads downward from project and company sponsors and affects virtually every project-assigned individual. The disease is *unbounded optimism,* and it can be deadly.

The very process of clearing the funding or feasibility hurdles sometimes gives a project the reputation of being immune to failure. It has proven feasible, therefore it will be successful. Unfortunately, this simple but erroneous leap in logic is more common than we would assume among project and company management. There is a great deal of difference between a feasible project and a successful one. Nonfeasible projects are not undertaken, so they can't fail. The only projects that fail are those once judged feasible. Feasibility then, far from protecting a project from failure, only makes it a candidate thereof.

But it is the feasibility process, the "judgment by fire" that gives many a project this aura of invincibility. This is often intensified by publication of project intentions to the outside or internally, among the company family. Public announcements of anticipated joy do not promote risk-based planning, especially when that planning will take time, cost money, and surface potential problems. Risk assessment is sometimes viewed as a wet blanket thrown over the feasibility party.

Another reason for this initial project optimism is the new project organization: the new team. These players, the project manager in particular, need to build confidence in their project and themselves, and pointing out a set of risks is not generally the best way of doing either. They exude optimism, and in so doing limit their ability to achieve it. This is because their optimism often precludes the understanding of risks they face and the formation of expensive, tailored controls to meet the challenge ahead. Once the new team has predicted success, it is difficult to return to the sponsors and ask for more time, money, or personnel to assure that success. A final factor contributing to this unearned optimism, as mentioned before, is an ignorance or underestimation of failure itself; how it starts, how it acts, and what it can do. Whether gained vicariously or through actual experience, nothing contributes to thorough planning more than an intimate knowledge of failure.

FF 49: Intrigued by the Scheme

When project members become so infatuated by the physical accomplishment ahead, by the *performance* perspective, that they fail to give due consideration to *understanding* and *control* plans, they have become "intrigued by the scheme." This is common and very easy to understand. After all, the scheme is the most interesting part of any project plan—how something is going to be done. It is action-oriented, tangible, gives visual results, and reflects the fruits of labor in a very real way. Methods taken to understand project activity, or to control it, are not so tangible. They go unseen, many of them contingency plans never implemented. They can't be shown to visitors, nor can they be photographed and printed in the company newsletter. No models can be made for the president's office. Plans for understanding and control take a back seat to performance plans. The scheme is the star. Unfortunately the scheme is often the best understood, simplest, and easiest to accomplish of the three project objectives. It needs the least management attention, but gets the most.

This infatuation with the scheme to the detriment of the other critical plans is similar, in a way, to the process which occurs when we buy a bright, shiny new automobile. It comes with an owner's manual (understanding) and a warranty booklet (control). But who, on bringing a new car home to the family, ignores the vehicle and concentrates on the accompanying paperwork? Most likely these items are shoved into the glove compartment and looked at several hundred miles down the road, and then only when the car has failed. This is when attention to understanding and control become critical to the owner, but like the analogous projects, little can be done in terms of prevention. Managements tend to care a lot about project information and control once the project is failing, not before. Because projects begin with optimism, and management tends to focus on "what is to be done" (performance) rather than "what can go wrong" (risk assessment) it is easy to see why planning for understanding and control is overlooked. Few of us want to be the one to tell the emperor he has no clothes.

FF 50: Paralyzed by Risk

Carried to an extreme, risk assessment can be a self-defeating process. There are projects for which so much risk was uncovered that the advisability of the effort itself becomes an issue. This is after it has been proven "feasible" considering expectations, rewards, and performance strategy. The fear of risk causes us to either ignore it or treat it as insurmountable, unpredictable, and therefore unassessable. We become paralyzed by fear.

Under these conditions we may succumb to an *unearned pessimism*, playing the "what if" game to the point where every project is a potential catastrophe. There is little need to proceed with a project so full of risks that it is best left unpursued, but on the other hand, there is little benefit to the practice of project phobia. Some middle ground is needed. A healthy respect for risk leads to constructive actions designed to minimize failure factors. Risk phobia leads to the abandonment of lucrative potential—unpursued project opportunity.

FF 51: Insisting on Perfection

No plans can be perfect, and no assessment of risk is totally accurate. For this reason, those who insist on identifying every conceivable risk and controlling every possible failure factor often end up studying projects to death and pursuing none. Another common result of this insistence on perfection during the planning process is the degradation of plans themselves. When we finally realize, as we must, that plans can't be perfect we sometimes abandon planning altogether.

There are other reasons for plans to be abandoned during the course of a project, reasons which we shall explore with other failure factors, but to abandon planning during the initial phases of project work simply because it is imperfect is a critical error. The structuring of controls around risk assumes that risk is a perceived, subjectively assessed characteristic—not a quantifiable certainty. Risk assessment is educated guessing (what *might* go wrong), not objective determinations of what will go wrong. Again, some controls based on risk will never be needed, some will be redundant, some too much, and some too little. Perfection is an operational objective, with no meaning in the project environment. Those who insist on optimum plans are often struck by the next failure factor.

FF 52: Planning Infatuation

Planning takes time, costs money, and delays tangible, physical, identifiable project *performance.* This is why most planning is cursory and incomplete—something experienced project managers have learned to live with. At times, however, the planning team becomes infatuated with the exercise of planning itself, not realizing that plans are a means to an end (project success) rather than an end in themselves (good plans). Planning can be interesting, exciting, and sometimes just plain fun to those responsible. It is not unlike the ever popular war games—pretend exercises in which all of the thrill of the actual battle is realized, with none of the harmful consequences—no one gets hurt. An undue infatuation with planning is sometimes a cover for a greater problem—a reluctance to begin project work; to face real risks and real challenges.

Planning is fairly failure-proof. There is little risk of failure, or at least apparent failure, during the planning process. And planning often delays or tables actual, difficult-to-make decisions. Choices can be postponed, or studied indefinitely. It is often used as an excuse for inaction, with the alternative of "let's study this some more," or "let's form a committee to check into this aspect" used to duck issues and delay decisions.

Finally, the extension of planning often extends the rein of the planning organization itself. If we use a separate manager, or group, to create the plan and will turn the project over to others once it is complete, the planners may attempt to stay in control as long as possible. This leads to drawn out plans, more studies, further analysis, and consideration of every conceivable alternative except one—turning the project over to the "doers" rather than the planners. This is another reason to include the doers on the planning team. Hopefully they will force planning to its logical conclusion—the beginning of performance, understanding and control: the project.

FF 53: Deification of Plans

Planning enthusiasts, sometimes called "cultists," may promote an aura of sanctity regarding their plans. They may present them to the project or company organizations as untouchable, unchanging and therefore not to be tampered with. They do this by (1) seeking and achieving high management endorsement of plans, (2) strict or prohibitive revision procedures, or (3) creating detailed, *rote plans* which do not allow room for individual or management judgment and situational application.

A goal of any planning organization should be flexible, risk-oriented plans, plans capable of being implemented. The more stable, strict, and unchangable they become the less value they have for the project. Plans are tools, means to an end, not objectives of the project. They should always be subservient to project expectations. To that end, they need not contain extraneous restrictions, prescribe byzantine processes, or promote petty jurisdictional disputes; often the result of people using plans to solidify power.

Plans exist to accomplish project goals, and anything else they promote only serves to weaken their influence or contribute to their abandonment. Plans containing embedded "power elements" should be stripped down to their cores, exposing only what is needed to perform, understand or control. The rest is excess, and often fatal. The offspring of plans, what we call *procedures,* are even more susceptible to this tampering. More shall be discussed about them in Chapter 8.

FF 54: Dust Collectors

Every company and every major project has them; usually residing in large, three-ring binders positioned on bookshelves or credenzas throughout the office. They are called plans, but they are actually dust collectors—unused plans. The reasons for this are many, but the result is the same: wasted time, money, and management talents. There are very few physical examples of planning failure. Frozen plans are some of them.

Here are some reasons for this condition: (1) plans are so obscure, inappropriate, and unenforced as to be meaningless, (2) plans have been superceded by a much different reality, (3) plans are changing so quickly that no one can keep up with them, (4) attempts at revision have proven unsuccessful (the "Act of Congress" revision procedure), or (5) plans have been ignored for so long that any attempts to follow them at this late stage would prove embarrassing.

There are only a few acceptable reasons for allowing plans to gather dust. Among these is the fact that, for certain purposes, the very act of planning, or the process that preceeded the physical plans, was more important than the result. That is, by virtue of going through the production of plans the plans that result are no longer needed.

An example concerns the issue of responsibility. Often it is difficult to ascertain who is responsible for what with a new project and a created organization. Some companies use what is called a "responsibility matrix" to depict assignments of duties, functions, or responsibilities among internal groups or individuals. This is typically a graphical depiction of a matrix matching a list of activities (duties, functions, etc.) on one axis of a sheet of paper against a listing of groups, personnel, or organizations on the other. In this fashion what is done is matched with who shall do it. The preparation of a responsibility matrix is highly recommended, for it achieves two important objectives. First, it points out responsibility gaps, those activities or functions for which no one has been assigned responsibility. Secondly, it surfaces redundant, overlapping, or miscommunicated responsibility assignment.

The purpose of creating the matrix is not merely the object (the paper map) but the *activity* of assigning responsibility correctly in the first place. The goal is to surface responsibility errors and to communicate their correction. The fact that a physical object results (the matrix) is secondary. It is the outcome of an understanding, not as important as the understanding itself.

There are cases when it is entirely appropriate to throw the matrix in the waste can after it has been completed, for its value is in its making. The same can be said for some plans. By forcing a physical product, we are often best able to assure that the activity necessary for its production is performed. In other words, when we tell someone or some group that we want them *to plan*, we often have less chance of that occuring than if we had told them *to produce* a plan.

This is true for many other areas besides planning. When we want someone *to study* alternatives, we get better results if we tell them *to produce a study* of alternatives for our review. The end forces the means. The need to create a physical result often drives the more important processes needed to produce it. The need to produce a project plan causes the team to assess risk, select controls, form organizations, assign responsibility, design information systems, and produce procedures for implementation. The alternative, stressing the activity without the product (telling the team *to plan*) is often about as fruitful as telling them *to think*, or *to try hard*, or *to do well*.

FF 55: Planning Millstones

It is surprising to see how many long-term projects carry obsolete, outdated plans around on their backs, or more fittingly, around their necks. Obsolete plans work against a project in a number of ways. First of all, they make it difficult to tell where the project is going in terms of C,S, and T, or to determine where the project has been. They embarrass the project team when dealing with outsiders (obsolete C,S, and T baselines are almost always exceeded ones). They also prevent the implementation of current, achievable plans: obsolete plans block effective planning.

Some reasons for obsolete plans, or *planning millstones* are the difficulty with which planning revisions are made, the erroneous assumption that replanning is a symptom of failure (not planning when needed is a factor in failure), and the fact that millstones block knowledge, and publication, of what might prove to be unacceptable information (information shock).

FF 56: The Myth of Standard Controls

Standard controls help avoid standard risks. Unfortunately, most project risks and reasons for failure are anything but standard. They are project and circumstance-specific, and because projects vary so widely from one another, project-specific risk means very different risk.

The myth of standard controls fails to recognize this. It presumes that virtually every risk can be countered by some sort of a magic bullet—some broad network of controls capable of addressing whatever may or may not occur. Were project controls to meet this criterion they would be needlessly complex and expensive in almost all incidences. In order to be effective in 1% of the cases, they would have to be totally overeffective in the remaining 99%. Few projects can afford the attendant time, costs, and skills required for effective standard controls. Instead, what is generally found where they are espoused are controls that are woefully inadequate in most cases and overadequate in others. Like a standard business suit, they are too small for most customers and too large for the rest. Just as the standard person doesn't exist, neither does the standard project. If standard projects did exist, we would gather them together under the same organization, perform their tasks over and over again, and optimize the outcome. This done, we could quit calling them projects and start calling them operations, for then that title would be more fitting.

So standard controls will not meet our needs entirely; each project is different. But there is a limited place for standards, for there are some problems most projects face, regardless of their differences. And companies who frequently embark on projects should try to isolate these standard problems and institute a set of *minimum* controls or minimum procedures that serve as a general basis for the development and deployment of project-specific counterparts. More about standards is contained in Chapter 11.

FF 57: Second Stringers

Because planning takes place early in the project lifespan, because actual project management teams are often occupied with actual project difficulties, elsewhere, or because project planning is done by nonproject personnel, we often find second string management in charge. This is a terrible mistake, repeated often and in many places. No one follows the intent of plans as carefully as their authors, and no one resents plans as much as those who inherit them from inferiors, or less experienced personnel. Planning is a critical, line activity—not some filler work for those on the bench between assignments or those not fitted to perform actual work. Planning is actual work, of the highest priority.

If he or she has been identified, the project manager should take charge of assigning and leading the planning team. So often this is impossible, for the selection of the project manager is not made until late in the planning process. The plan is often developed concurrently with the "courtship" of the project manager. The sooner the selection is made the better. Assigning the eventual project manager to direct the planning achieves a number of important benefits. First, it assures the consideration of actual risks—risks identified through the experience of one who has been in the project arena. It promotes use of the ensuing plans by fitting them to the manager's style and sense of priority and making use of the inherent pride of authorship in us all. We are simply more likely to follow our plans than those we inherit from second stringers. Most sky divers would prefer to jump with a chute packed by themselves than one given to them by someone who has never been off the ground.

FF 58: Planning in Different Languages

This is what happens when plans are inconsistent with the way the project will be managed, or when plans are inconsistent with other plans. The first instance is a result of a lack of understanding regarding the role of plans. Plans help us control. If we make assumptions in our plans regarding organizations, authority, conduct or business transactions that bear no resemblance to the activities we will perform or the environment in which we will work, these plans are meaningless. By the same token, if each organizational entity involved in project work plans differently, based on different assumptions concerning performance, understanding and control, we will end up with unsynchronized plans and project discord from the beginning.

In order to be effective, planning needs to take place in the open, in full view of those who will bear the resultant impact. Often, however, we find small cells making plans in hiding, waiting until they are fully developed or approved by higher management before springing them on the rest of the company or the remainder of the project team. Birthdays aside, few of us like surprises. There is no reason for secretive planning, except in those cases where the nature of the work is in itself confidential (such as military projects, speculative land development, or perhaps some types of industrial research). But even in these cases, the performance of project work is what is confidential, not necessarily the plans to understand and control it. Secrecy usually doesn't apply to the project members, only to outsiders.

Why then do we find secret plans? They are commonly used to disguise and legitimize power grabs. These include procedural restrictions favoring one internal player or party (department, division, group, etc.), the dispensation of authority, the formalizing of heretofore informal control, or other assorted power grabs and empire building attempts. This explains why so few people want to *create* plans, but so many insist on the right to *review* them. They just want to assure themselves that no power is snatched away from them under the guise of a plan.

That project-specific plans, so valuable to the effort at hand, can be manipulated and delayed in order to satisfy parochial organizational purposes is unfortunate, but it is as common in our corporations as the executive suite, the coffee break and the annual Christmas party. It occurs often and projects fail because it occurs. It is analogous to two or more dogs fighting over a bone, who spend so much effort and blood fighting that the bone is lost before the fight is over.

Planning in the dark to meet selfish organizational objectives has two detrimental effects. First, it leads to late, meaningless, and uncoordinated plans, for often more than one set of plans is being grown in the dark. Secondly, should plans be made in the light of day, so many power grabs and esoteric organizational interests surface that, in order to satisfy everyone concerned, only spineless, general, and otherwise useless plans are produced. They offend no one. But in order to avoid making a stand on key project issues, these plans have no substantive content, no detail, and no enforceability. They contain broad generalities, such as "the project manager shall check with all affected parties," "this shall be done in a manner consistent with established company procedures," or "higher approval will be obtained before proceeding." To be useful plans must be uniform, coordinated, detailed, specific, and decisive. A project sponsor not able to meet these criteria when preparing plans has no business undertaking a project which will in turn require uniformity, coordination, detailed work, specificity, and decisiveness.

FF 59: Blue Sky

Blue sky plans are not specific, detailed or decisive. They are too general to be meaningful. Sometimes this occurs because management mistakes *policy* for plans. They are very different, in that policy is a management expression of what will be achieved, while plans are the detailed descriptions of how this policy will be achieved and maintained. Policy answers *what*, while plans describe *how*. Policy is often easily obtained, with very little organizational or procedural friction, whereas plans commonly cause both.

This may seem to be a handicap of good planning, but on closer examination it is actually one of the primary benefits planning brings to a project. For if organizational or procedural impediments exist, it is much better to surface these before substantive project work is performed rather than after. In this sense, planning helps by forcing us to address project problems before those problems can grow into failure factors. These problems will exist whether we plan for them or not. Planning merely shines light on them in time for their prevention, or in those cases where they will resist control, in time for the project to be abandoned before significant resources are committed to it. There are, in fact, many projects that are feasible yet not achievable. By focusing our attention on risks and details required to implement project tasks, plans help identify these.

FF 60: Baseline Games

Baselines are our detailed expectations in terms of C, S, and T and any other primary success factors involved for a particular project. Regardless of how derived, how detailed, or how sophisticated they may be, baselines share many vulnerabilities to failure. Each of these could in itself, be classified as a separate failure factor. Because they occur so often (strike budgets, schedules, and technical base-lines at will), and are interrelated in effect, we shall discuss them here as a group called *baseline games*.

In order to be useful, all baselines should be current, represent the work planned (not the work we planned three years ago, but the work we plan to do as of now), be changable, and be structured in such a way as to facilitate comparisons between what was planned, what was accomplished, what resources were spent (time, money, labor hours, quantities, and so on), and what is expected to be needed to accomplish the remaining work. Baselines are ideally developed during the planning phase of any project and updated as project conditions change, so as to better reflect current plans and conditions and experience gained on earlier segments of project work.

Problems exist with baselines that are constantly changed, not so much to reflect constantly changing work plans, but to reflect unsatisfactory performances on past and current work. This can best be visualized as stretching the plans (baselines) to match experienced results—the old *rubber baseline* game. Rather than predict results or be used to measure results against expectations, rubber baselines *follow* results. Baselines are useless unless they help us control present work or predict future effort. Rubber baselines merely shadow the past.

When baselines are constantly revised, either in an effort to achieve accuracy or to hide expected problems, we call them *breathing baselines*. This is due to their dynamic, ever changing behavior— breathing baselines are alive. Granted, some amount of change is necessary to reflect changed conditions, expectations, and current trends. And changed baselines are acceptable; but not breathing baselines.

Whenever those working under baselines deny any authorship of them, as is often the case when the planning group is not the subsequent performing group, we have what are commonly referred to as *orphan baselines*. Every orphan has had a father and a mother, it's just difficult to find them sometimes. This is true for some plans and baselines as well. Quite often their parents wish to remain anonymous. Especially if they have become woefully inadequate or even absurd. The best way to assure absurd plans is to have them developed by someone who (1) has never experienced the effort being planned, and (2) will have nothing to do with the plans or the effort once the planning phase has passed.

Unachieveable baselines are worthless, and so are *inconsistent baselines*, mentioned earlier. Both cause loss of faith in plans and eventual abandonment of control for project activity. Plans are like leaders, they must continually gain the confidence of those under their leadership. Confidence in plans is difficult to achieve and very easy to lose. People lose that confidence when plans are perceived (they need not be proven) to be blue sky, unachievable, inconsistent, breathing, rubber, or orphan.

FF 61: Paper Tiger

Our final failure factor stemming from plans concerns the quickest way to destroy confidence in them. It just takes a few occasions where plans or their resulting procedures are blatantly ignored or circumvented, without management action, to destroy the plans entirely. Unenforceable plans are indeed paper tigers. When repetitive violations take place they may indicate either lack of management action or bad plans. Plans are no more than tools. They can be poor in themselves or used poorly. Either can crush a project before it gets off the ground.

SUMMARY

Planning is an integral element in the management of a project. More than a trite exercise performed by those who happen to be available, planning should take place early on in the project lifespan, be managed by the same cadre that will manage actual project work, and be updated periodically, according to changing conditions and objectives.

In order to reduce the cost of planning, and the time and resources it takes, we must strip the effort of extraneous purposes, games, and power grabs it often entails. We need to understand that perfect planning, for a number of bona fide reasons having nothing to do with our management capability, will never occur, nor should it ever be a goal. Our planning should result in specific project controls, and these should be selectively chosen and used as they relate to project risks. Standard controls are helpful only on a minimum basis, but must always be supplemented by specific, tailored controls resulting from an intelligent modeling of what can go wrong.

Simply because the entire project cannot be planned to the same level of detail at one time, nor can long-term risks be specified far in advance, is no reason for us to abandon the concepts of good planning. One such is that of incremental plans: the folded map. It simply makes good sense to plan the immediate future to a greater detail than the far term. As we move through time our focus shifts from near term to near term, and in this manner we plan the entire project to the same level of detail and with the same concern.

We need not be paralyzed by risk nor intimidated by project challenge, but then again, we should guard against unearned optimism that is prevalent during early stages and sometimes supplants an honest recognition of the failure that looms ahead and a determined effort to defend our project from its ravages. Plans represent our shields against failure, shields knowledgeably designed and constantly strengthened according to the needs at hand. We need not become infatuated with planning nor allow ourselves to focus on the scheme ahead to the detriment of the concurrent needs for understanding and control of that scheme as it is played out.

Planning is serious business best taken seriously. Planning is not a game; people do get hurt, along with projects. Baselines help us translate our general plans into achievable expectations in terms of cost, schedule and technical details. We must continually protect the integrity and viability of baselines. They allow us to determine where we have been, where we are, and where we are going. They give us bearing and direction, two features commonly missing from projects drifting towards failure.

INFORMATION

scapegoat and panacea

We are in the middle of an information explosion, and many projects seem to be getting hit by the shrapnel. Rather than benefit from the wealth of project-specific information made available by advances in data processing and information systems technology, these very capabilities appear to have placed yet another obstacle in the path of project success.

In this chapter we will explore the role of information in the project management mix, dispel some common and dangerous myths concerning its value and applicability, and attempt to understand why information, once considered a harmless if not neutral resource, can cause us so many problems. We will see how information is at the same time a benefit and a burden, a savior and a scapegoat, a tool and a weapon. In order to do so, we must first understand just what information is, what it is not, how it can be used and how it is often misrepresented and misused.

SAME NOISE, ONLY MORE CHANNELS

The ongoing infatuation with information is fueled by a number of concurrent events. One is the ever expanding power and availability of data processing equipment and software. There is no question that computers represent improved and increased *channels*—ways in which information can be transferred from its origination to eventual users, from senders to receivers. In this regard, they are not unlike the phenomenon of multiple channels available for home viewing by television. Where there once were three nationwide networks dominating the broadcast channels, we now have the capability, through cable, satellite dishes, and other means, to access scores if not hundreds of communication streams. The irony of this increased accessibility, however, is that no matter how many additional channels are made available both the sources of the entertainment and the time that we have to view it remain the same.

With project-specific information, the same relationships hold: we have more channels of access and more freedom to manipulate data, but the basic information sources have not changed. The same data is available as always, we merely have better ways to get to it and to play around with it: more channels, but the same noise. This is both a benefit and a hindrance to project efforts, for although heretofore inaccessible information is now available, the inherent weaknesses and failure factors associated with the production and use of information have been intensified in importance. More information available to more and more people means more susceptibility to misunderstanding, misuse and confusion.

A RESOURCE AND A TOOL

In order to deal with the topic of information in a pragmatic way, we must strip away the myths and misconceptions surrounding it—reduce it to its core, examine its value and make intelligent use of its features. In this regard we need to recognize the special characteristic of information, one which separates it from other project elements. To begin with, information is a resource. It must be obtained, refined, and managed. In this regard it is no different than the other essential resources we need to make any project successful, namely time, money, people, material, equipment, plans, and authority.

What makes information special is that, in addition to being a valuable resource, it is also a tool needed to make effective use of all the other resources of any project. We need information to prepare and use plans, budget money, create and maintain schedules, direct people, manage equipment and material, and use authority properly. No other project resource, with the exception perhaps of people, is so valuable and yet so misunderstood and misused. Unlike time, money, people, and materials, information is not tangible, it cannot be quantified, it cannot be stored, its quality is difficult to ascertain and its value is subjectively determined. Information is ephemeral. This is why it is so difficult to know, at any point in project activity, whether we have the right information, in adequate quantity, available to the proper people and whether it is being used correctly for the project's benefit.

Information then, is both a resource and a tool. Often, however, we see information, or the lack thereof, as a convenient scapegoat.

Suppression of information is often due to poor understanding of its value, inability to access pertinent data, or as a means of hiding performance results—of masking C, S, and T. To understand why projects fail we must become thoroughly acquainted with the greatest potential it brings to a project, the potential for misuse.

A LIMITED ROLE

Contrary to the advice of information cultists, this resource is not the be all and end all of project management. It has a very special role, as mentioned, but this role is a *limited* one. It is helpful to put information in proper perspective; to put it in its place. It does not take the place of management skill, planning, project controls, experience, well directed intentions, or other project essentials. It will not shore up inherent inadequacies in organizations, approaches, or individuals. Often it helps by illuminating these deficiencies, but it can also intensify them.

Sometimes more or better information has little or no value at all. A frequently cited example concerns the famous passenger ship *Titanic*. Would hourly computer printouts describing the level of water being taken on by the floundering vessel have prevented its sinking? Certainly the crew and captain would have been better informed, but would this have changed the outcome? Probably not. If anything, it would only have served to inform them as to precisely how helpless their situation was. Of course little information or information of poor quality almost always hurts project efforts, but even the best and the most doesn't assure success. To understand why we must know more about what this thing called information is, and more importantly, what it is not.

A common misconception is that data equals information. Nothing could be further from the truth. Data is merely the raw material of information. It means virtually nothing without refinement. By refinement we mean the structuring of data into meaningful elements, the analysis of its content and the comparisons we make among data and preexisting standards, such as C, S, and T baselines. Only then does data become transformed into information. Data has no value unless it is transformed into structured, meaningful, and pertinent information, and information has no value unless it leads to needed management action or precludes unnecessary action. Although it has special characteristics and a dual role (resource and tool) we should treat information in this pragmatic fashion. It is not magic, mystical, or holy. It is simply something we use to get what we want—project success. Like any other resource or any other tool, information has no intrinsic value unless it is used to improve our condition.

Another misconception regarding information is that, simply by existing, it somehow leads to management action. Again this is incorrect, for no tool, simply through its availability assures its proper use, or even its use at all. Well informed managers are better able to take proper actions, but not more inclined to do so. Information is just as impotent when viewed as a resource. For the construction of a high-rise office building, structural steel is an essential resource as well, but the mere existence of a pile of steel members at the job site doesn't assure a building. Much more is needed. The same is true for information. It hurts us by its absence, but doesn't help us merely through its presence.

To further decrease the bloated importance often given to information we must also consider its perishable nature. Information has the shortest shelf life of any project resource. As the time used to transmit information (or data) from sender to receiver increases, the value of the transmission decreases. This is why many commendable efforts in the area of project information technology are aimed at collapsing or compressing unnecessary *information float*. Yesterday's newspaper has no value. Stale information, that which tells us what happened without allowing us to improve what will happen, is worthless. Any attempts to prevent information spoilage, be they through streamlined data collection and reporting systems, advanced hardware and software, source entry or others, are helpful. So information, like bread, has value only when fresh. But being fresh isn't enough.

WHEN IS VALUE ADDED?

Every resource and tool should be self-justifying to play a role on our projects. That is, nothing should be taken for granted, untested, or otherwise assured importance unless it helps us attain our project expectations. Viewed in this light, information needs to add value to our efforts or we should not spend time, money, and management attention trying to secure, transmit and analyze it. Three distinct characteristics of information seem critical to this notion of value. That is, no information adds value to our project unless it has (1) structure, (2) meaning, and (3) pertinence. These characteristics deserve special attention.

Structure—Information is needed at various levels throughout our company and project organizations in varying levels of detail. Properly structured information allows both summarization of data from its sources at a very detailed level up through our organizational and planning structures, as well as traceability down these structures from high level reports to the detailed origins of the data. It should be stratified with each successive layer of detail supporting those above it and being derived from those below. This allows *summarization* (upward) and *traceability* (downward). In this regard, the structuring of information should allow the receiver to choose what level of detail is required, to focus his or her attention on exceptions, and to trace these to their source in a timely fashion. This concept of structured information is not unlike our earlier examples of project modeling, where the degree of detail (number and size of finite elements) is increased or decreased to correspond with risk, degree of control and amount of management interest (the folded map).

Meaning—Information that doesn't provide understanding or assist in its gain is valueless; it is mere data. Unless it helps us ascertain where we have been, where we are, and where we are headed, it may be well structured, accurate, timely, and interesting, but it doesn't advance project objectives. In order to do so, information obtained once a project has begun needs to be consistent in structure and focus with our current plans. Put another way, it needs to be *comparable* to our plans. Without this comparability, information doesn't lead to valuable understanding. It leads to bewilderment.

Pertinence—Pertinent information is applicable to our perspective, focused on our objectives and processes, consistent with the reality of our efforts, and targeted, like the rest of our efforts, on risk. Any other information is mere noise; a distraction. To add value, information must pertain to our plans, our activities, or management methods and our performance processes. Without going into examples, suffice it to say that impertinent information abounds on most projects. It may be nice to know, but useless.

A SUBSTITUTE FOR MANAGEMENT PROXIMITY

If we view information as a resource, let's presume *information systems* represent our ability to gather, refine, and manipulate this resource. It matters not whether these systems are automated (computers) or manual, extensive or minor, formal or informal, express (procedures) or implied (we always do it that way). We will use the term *information systems* to describe what are commonly broad, structured networks designed to capture data and transmit it to management; hopefully in a structured, meaningful and pertinent package. Nonetheless, a great deal of time and money is being spent designing, installing, and implementing project information systems. Like any other major project effort these systems contain inherent potential for failure. It will pay to understand them well. To do so we must apply our time-honored pragmatism: what value do they bring to the project?

Reduced to their essential purpose, information systems are substitutes for management intimacy with the project. As such they increase in importance (and often in sophistication), as management proximity to the project decreases. That is, the further away in time and distance we are from our project, the more we must rely on information systems. They exist simply to bridge this proximity gap. Were we close enough to detailed project efforts, intuitively aware of what is being done and needs to be done, and well versed in the consequences of past and present action, we wouldn't need information systems. Direct observation would suffice. These types of projects are rare. They are so small, risk-free, and technologically primitive that one person can "watch" them directly and continuously—needing no telemetry.

Even within the context of a larger project, one particular element may be watched by its immediate supervisor without the need for records, reports, or transmittals to bridge his or her proximity gap (the gap is small or nonexistent). For these cases, however, information systems are needed not to satisfy the immediate supervisor (watcher) but to bridge the proximity gap between the effort and other, higher level watchers (superiors) who are not, in fact, on top of the situation in terms of time or distance. This is why lower level performers or supervisors often resent information systems designed to report performance to others—they see them as redundant and often not as dependable as direct observation. They are not. But they do allow higher management to *understand* what is being performed at various levels within the organization, and for various segments of project work, to compare it to plans, to contrast it with concurrent work, to measure it in terms of C, S, and T and to forecast future efforts of a similar nature.

This makes sense: the farther away management the broader its focus should be. The immediate performer or supervisor should be watching the leaves, someone else must watch the forest. Structured information systems allow the forest watcher to peer down, through successive levels of detail, to the leaves that are presenting problems—to zoom in. This ability to trace problems or trends to their source, this variable focus lens called a structured information system, allows management by exception. One cannot manage a forest, except tree by tree and leaf by leaf.

When properly designed and implemented to bridge this proximity gap, information systems are extremely valuable. Otherwise they are at best nuisances and at worst disastrous. Like plans (Chapter 6) these systems are often held up as "straw people." That is, they are used as scapegoats ("we're great managers, we just don't have the right information!"), or we become so infatuated with the accompanying technology and potential that we forget their role— tools. Not idols, not toys, not project objectives, but the necessary means thereto.

This admonition aside, many projects are weakened or destroyed because information systems take on too large or too important a role. They become ends in themselves. There are several reasons for this, chief among them is the fact that information systems (unlike organizations, staffing, funds, schedules, or people) are easy to manipulate, typically safe to install (safety meaning little organizational friction) and amenable to change. Playing with information systems is not unlike playing with plans, it stalls project activity, management action and postpones more difficult management decisions. Seen this way, today's magnificent information systems are simply new versions of straw people.

A CASE FOR DIMINISHED IMPORTANCE

The goal of every project manager should be to free its project from dependence on any resource. That is, to diminish its criticality and importance whenever possible. Take the resource of time, for example. Should project management somehow accelerate work, cause more time-effective performance, or remove artificial schedule dependencies it has improved chances for project success by reducing the importance of time. We all know that the resource we call money increases in importance as we approach budgetary limits. During the performance phase of project work we can reduce this importance by economies of scale, purchasing acumen, efficiency in labor usage, or cost-saving innovation in performance methods. All serve to decrease the constraint of money. We can apply this concept to the remainder of our project resources, but most importantly to information, for there are a number of ways to reduce its criticality.

Like any other resource, we can decrease information's criticality by assuring its adequate supply. We can also secure alternate sources of this resource—mainly by improving its accessibility. And we can reduce needless, unwarranted dependencies on information—eliminating review cycles, unread reports, information circulation and the like.

We can decrease information's criticality by stripping away extraneous restrictions or encumbrances to its use. One such may be the computer itself. Another needless restriction might be organizational in nature, a group which protects and isolates use of the information system (the *information guards* or the informal *information department*). And we can also reduce information dependence and criticality by demystifying its use; by simplifying the ways in which we use it. Nothing restricts use of a system more than the apparent awe in which it is held by its sponsors, the difficulty with which a lay person can access it, and the labyrynthine procedures and approvals needed for its design and installation. When tools become so intricate, so sophisticated, and so unnecessarily unfit for use they cease to become tools at all, but are transformed to pieces of art. Art is for viewing, appreciating, and admiring, but not for using. We need tools.

USES AND ABUSES

It seems the more abstract a project resource becomes the more susceptible it becomes to misuse and abuse. For although it may be difficult to conceive of material misuse, (how can one misuse structural steel?), misuse of information is common, often sophisticated, and limited only by our imaginations. Many of the information-specific failure factors we will describe in this chapter stem from misuse, or abuse, of information and information systems in one form or another. Before analyzing each one, however, it may be helpful to clarify the commonly acceptable uses of this resource and to identify typical misuses.

Acceptable Uses of Information

When correctly used, information helps to:

1. Promote *understanding* (the project "cube")
2. Target *controls* (by quantifying risks, testing proposed controls, and initiating corrective action)
3. Dispel project *phantoms* (artificial failure factors)
4. Allow project transactions (such as progress payments)
5. Communicate status
6. Predict the future
7. Satisfy outside inquiries
8. Enhance resource usage (efficiencies)
9. Validate plans

10. Comprehend change

11. Sharpen and reinforce perspectives

12. Test expectations

13. *Recognize* failure

Common Misuses of Information

Information is often misused, in order to:

1. Deceive or confuse

2. Postpone action

3. Create empires (the "information department")

4. Justify errors

5. Slow or divert processes

6. Support the status quo

7. *Mask* failure (or dress it up)

It may prove interesting, when examining the following failure factors, to identify embedded misconceptions concerning the value and role of information (the importance of the resource) and to look for cases of intentional misuse.

FF 62: Information Infatuation

This condition is very similar to that described as FF 52: Planning Infatuation. Both focus on the tool as opposed to the tool's use and eventual objective. Information infatuation seems much more prevalent, however, and this may be due to the intricacy and dynamic growth of information systems technology. Computers and information systems are simply more interesting than plans. Whereas planning infatuation is based more on continuing the dynasty of the planning organization or on the postponement of decisions (rather than interest in the plans themselves), information infatuation seems centered around the system of manipulating data—the processing of data rather than the eventual use of information. However, some similar motivations occur. For instance, the infatuation with an information system may mask or lead to the defense of an information organization (the data processing department, the "systems project," the "project information and control group," and so on). All these impede the use of information and devalue it when used, for they simply put more distance and barriers between management and the object of management attention—the project. They further decrease management proximity, even though the purpose of information is to bridge the proximity gap. Systems, organizations, procedures, or hardware that only serve to widen that gap should be destroyed. Information tools should be as clear lenses, focusing and clarifying managements' view. They should be transparent, known for their benefits rather than their features. Whenever they turn opaque, distracting managements' attention, or diverting the view they become agents of failure.

Taken to its extreme, information infatuation leads to *information enslavement* —where, for example, everyday project activity becomes subservient to the need to feed the information system and digest its output. When this occurs the *identity* of the project, much less its outcome, may become questionable. This leads to the next failure factor.

FF 63: Pretender to the Throne

On very large and complex projects, ones for which management proximity is distant or information problems have proven costly, emphasis on the information system may increase to the point where there are two simultaneous projects undertaken: one to meet the original project expectations and the other to design and install the information system. This second "project" may overtake the first; the "pretender" may threaten the throne. That is, the information project may dwarf or shadow the original project, and the means of acquiring and manipulating information may assume more importance and attract more management attention than the purpose for which the system was intended.

This is often accompanied by an unnatural management focus on the *features* of the system as opposed to the cost it entails and the benefits it brings. It can also mask blatant power grabs by those in charge of the information system, who, by virtue of their increased importance, encroach on project management. Needless to say, a tool should never dominate its user, nor should it become an end in itself.

FF 64: Computer Chaos

Because the computer and its accompanying systems, software, and procedural elements are often the vehicles on which information is carried, there is a chance that the vehicle will become more important than the destination. Computers are extremely helpful in the field of data processing and in the assimilation and transfer of information, but virtually every major project that has failed during the past decade has employed computers. They do not assure success, nor are they essential to it. They cut both ways—helping promote failure as well as success.

We are all too familiar with so called hernia reports, those gigantic stacks of computer printout designed to depict meaningful project information for management attention, (named after their impact on the health of those who try to lift them). Often these are overwhelming in volume and complexity, and many times they merely represent a hundred ways of slicing the same old, stale bread. Again, no matter how we increase the channels, the source and use of data remains the same.

Other projects succumb to the allure of hardware; an infatuation with the features and capability, yes the power of machines to structure, sort, and recast data. Some managements are sold sophisticated information processing capability after being dazzled with the tremendous output it provides them. Little attention is given, however, to the commensurate input effort involved. That is, the data accumulation problems encountered by the lower levels within the organization—where more time is spent feeding the system than performing project work. Often the needs of the system, in terms of data input, verification, comparisons, and so forth get in the way of the work that the data is supposed to portray.

This can get out of hand, with poor work effort (caused, in part by the need to satisfy the system), causing more management concern and leading to demands for more information. In this way, information systems can compound failure. The result: computer chaos.

FF 65: The Perfect Scapegoat

If we were to blame organizations for failure, we would have the organizational sponsors or their leaders to contend with. If we were to complain that certain individuals weren't performing, we would have to confront and contend with those individuals. If shortages of funds are cited, we would need to justify and defend our past and current use of money. Each of these actions can get nasty, involve confrontations or disputes, and eventually backfire. But what of the excuse of "lack of information" or "inadequate information systems?" These scapegoats can't fight back. This is why they are commonly cited. It is also why they are often examined and changed—they are the easiest resources to manipulate, causing the least organizational friction: the safest targets.

When used in this fashion, information and its accompanying systems help confuse project inquiries as to management prudency. They help make simple inadequacies, simple problems, and simple variances seem complex and therefore difficult to correct. They delay action, for they legitimize the "do nothing" alternative. After all, it always seems wise to wait for more information to become available before taking action.

In fact if we wait long enough, complete information regarding C,S, and T will become available. This occurs at the end of every project. At that time we know exactly how we are doing in terms of every baseline. Unfortunately this is always too late. We will only know how we failed, and by how much. Except from a lessons-learned standpoint, this is useless information. Better to know if we are heading for failure in time to change our course and speed—to see failure looming ahead in time to avert it. Information systems not providing this are tools of the archivist, not of the project manager.

FF 66: Hamstrung by Accuracy

We take a pragmatic look at project tools when we expect them to justify their value. The value of information is that it helps us achieve project objectives, not necessarily optimization of project efforts or perfection of knowledge (these are operational objectives, not project goals). This pragmatism causes us to insist on *workability* or *usefullness* when dealing with project information, and many times at the expense of accuracy. We would much prefer available, pertinent, meaningful information that is fairly representative of our condition than *perfect* or *accurate* information that is late, impertinent, or meaningless. These are constant tradeoffs made by all project managements: value versus accuracy.

The search for, and resources required, to obtain accurate information often exceeds our pragmatic thresholds. Accuracy has its price, often in terms of increased cost (the cost of the information system, its care and feeding) and time (increased information lag or information float—leading to spoilage). Those insisting on accuracy need consider its price and balance that against the added value that accuracy brings. Just because we *can* achieve greater accuracy doesn't mean that we *should*. Put differently (and to amend an earlier cited quotation from Ben Franklin): Everything one has the *capability* to do is not best to be done.

FF 67: Information Mismatch

This failure factor stems from the inherent properties of the information we handle. It can occur when information has the wrong structure, meaning, or pertinence; three features necessary for information to have value. If information has no structure, or its structure doesn't allow top down penetration to the source of data, or bottom up assimilation to satisfy management by exception, it is defective. It can confuse, bewilder or even cause physical damage (the "hernia report").

Not only is structure important, but so is consistency of the information from layer to stratified layer. This is achieved through conscious, detailed design of the information system consistent with a knowledge of the using organization and the models of the project employed (finite elements, baselines, etc.).

Information not focused on risk loses pertinence. To be consistent with plans and controls, information should intensify in detail and frequency as risk increases. Our focus should be very close for those elements of the project containing high risk, and distant for those having little or none.

Information lacks meaning when we cannot use it to ascertain our past, present, or future. When compared to our plans, information allows us to determine where we have been, where we are, and where we are heading for each segment of the project and, in turn, for the project as a whole. Lack of comparability is a fatal information characteristic. It is often due to inconsistent formats between plans and actual data collected once the project work begins. It is also brought about by inconsistencies among actual data itself.

Lack of data structure, consistency, and comparability force subjective judgment to enter into information processing, a failure factor in and of itself. For the role of subjectivity is one played during information *analysis*, not information accumulation or processing. When data cannot be summarized, for example, without allocations, assumptions, or lost information, we have forfeited knowledge of details, trends and problem sources. Rather than peering down through the forest to the trees and the leaves comprising it, we end up looking at a *representation* of the forest painted by someone else.

The way information is arrayed and presented should also match the way we intend to manage the project and its components. If, for example, we are managing a construction project by managing each subcontract, we have little use of cost data arrayed by commodity or by area, when in fact, each subcontractor's work transcends commodity and area boundaries. In that case we would need cost data structured by subcontract. If we are managing the schedule of this project by planning and controlling the activities of construction crafts, it makes little sense to report on schedule progress by fixed asset code. Information should be arrayed not only to meet our management objectives but to fit our management *methods*.

Finally, when information systems place walls or veils between management and the activities under review they have failed. Information systems are needed to bridge the proximity gap, not to widen it.

FF 68: Information Shock

It may be true that ignorance is bliss, but it is also true that all bliss is temporary. Bad news is like bad food, the longer it sits the worse it tastes. The same holds for information. Many projects experience what is called "information shock," the sudden discovery of huge cost overruns or significant schedule delays. When this occurs, it seems as if these variances sprang up overnight, landing on us with absolutely no warning. We scurry around searching the recent past and the present to determine their origins. This is often fruitless, for very bad news takes time to develop, to ferment, and to grow. More often than not, the causes of information shock have been at work for months or even years, we just didn't know about them.

Information systems need to surface problems immediately, when corrective action or project abandonment is still viable. They should bridge the time element of management proximity as well as organizational and spatial distances. Most projects start to fail very early in their lifespans, and because our systems are insensitive to these beginnings we often don't realize the extent of that failure until information shock occurs. Failure is like cancer, early detection promotes cure.

FF 69: Failing Reports

Management reports are only as good as the information they contain, and that information has value only when it promotes *analysis*. No matter how they are structured, how frequently they are produced, or how many ways they can slice and graphically depict the informational pie, reports that don't promote analysis don't deserve management attention. Reports lose this capability when they don't allow progress monitoring, when they don't foster problem traceability (the cold trail), when they are untimely (the information lag), block management by exception (successive layers of detail), or don't refer to previous reports and problems.

There are several elements deemed essential to management reports, particularly on a project basis. The very best reports manage to:

1. Isolate significant variances and identify the reasons they occurred.

2. Emphasize the quantitative and specific rather than the subjective and general.

3. Describe specific C, S, and T impacts on other project elements (other contracts, areas, trades, schedules, organizations, plans).

4. Indicate impact on project baselines (what revisions are needed, when, why).

5. Describe specific corrective actions taken and planned.

6. Assign responsibility for action and give expected dates for improvement.

7. Reference corrective action plans in previous reports (what happened?).

This partial listing points out a larger concept: that management judgment is an essential element of project reporting. Simply throwing up data, no matter how cleverly cast, doesn't satisfy management's need to know. Regardless of how far we advance in the field of automated data processing, we will never supplant the need for judgment.

FF 70: Looking for the Software Fix

It is easier to get people to buy a product purporting to help them than it is to get them to change themselves for the better. Advertisers have known this for years. We are more prone to buy expensive makeup, cologne, clothing, or jewelry in order to make us attractive than to lose weight, exercise, improve our posture or change our personality. The external "fix" is easier to sell than the internal improvement. It doesn't disrupt the status quo. It gives immediate results. It is easy. People in the software business benefit from the same principle. They sell the "software fix," and they have had many buyers.

There is nothing inherently wrong with software, or with project information systems software in particular. The point is that improvements to project understanding require much more than an externally applied fix. Before buying and installing software, we need to understand what our needs are, and this reaches beyond information needs. It includes understanding of how we are organized, how we manage, and the role of information in our project perspective. Externally procured software, or entire information systems, typically fail because they do not match any of these. Procured systems or software do not, on their own, help poorly planned, performed, or controlled projects.

A good information system is rarely bought once the project is in trouble. It is based on early analyses, during the planning stages, of information needs and the role information plays in each particular project. We must always keep in mind the fact that, no matter how well conceived and implemented, information systems can only meet information needs. They cannot correct deficiencies in organizations, perspectives, people, or processes. They are important, sometimes ephemeral, but never magical. Just as no cosmetic or cologne can bring instant love, neither can an information system bring instant project management.

FF 72: The Information Diet

Information, like food, can be nutritious or fattening. "Junk information" is similar to junk food—expensive, appealing, easy to prepare, yet full of calories and of minimum nutritional value. We see junk information everywhere, especially on complex project efforts. It is high bulk, low density information (the hernia report is a great example). For many of these projects, the best advice might be to go on an informational diet; to select that information giving benefit and throw away the rest. Good information planning helps ascertain what is needed and identify what is junk.

Continued information awareness throughout each project phase brings many other valuable benefits. It helps eliminate bulk by reducing paperwork. This is achieved by eliminating unnecessary or low value data gathering, processing, and reporting. Structured information allows many layers of management reporting without the need for recasting or reentering of data. This also promotes consistency and reduces the incidence of data error.

A good information system also compresses or eliminates intolerable information float, thereby increasing management proximity. Such a system also maintains *understanding* as its paramount goal, not data availability or versatility. It seeks nutrition as opposed to taste or fat content. Many failed projects don't lack information, they merely have too much and the wrong kind. They are overfed and undernourished, and they die early.

SUMMARY

Information plays a dual role on our projects, that of valuable resource and essential tool. Recent advances in data processing and information systems technology have increased the channels through which information is available, but have done nothing regarding the sources and uses of information itself. These are management-affected variables, still requiring planning and continued attention. In order to understand the role of information and use it effectively, we need to remove the myths concerning its value and realize its role is a limited, though important one.

A good information system, regardless of its sophistication, adds value to raw data only when the resulting information is structured, has meaning and is pertinent to the work at hand. At best it is a substitute for closer management proximity. Like other resources, information can become critical to project success. Prudent project management involves attempts to restrict our dependency on any single resource, like information, and thereby diminish its criticality.

Because information systems can be installed and manipulated with minimum organizational friction, they are often abused. Most information-specific failure factors center around misunderstanding, misuse, or downright abuse of this most ephemeral element in the mixture we call project management.

PROCESSES

animating the plan

A process represents that which is needed to turn expectations into accomplishments. Every business project, regardless of the objective or the industry in which it takes place, relies upon a number of processes. Some of the least understood and most difficult to isolate reasons for project failure involve this notion of processes; how they are designed and implemented, and more often than not, how they are poorly conceived, misused, circumvented, or ignored. In this chapter we will explore general process concepts, including what is needed to create a good process, some alternate ways to convey its features, promote its use, and improve it. As before, our perspective will be guided by the pragmatism that often distinguishes project work from operations. That is, we need to direct our attention to that which works best for all concerned as opposed to that which is most efficient, traditional, or intrinsically appealing.

NECESSARY EVILS

All processes, like all tools, are important only in that they are necessary to achieve results. This will be our overriding criterion when examining the benefits of any given process and any alternative ways to transform expectations into achievements. No process should be undertaken unless it can be shown to contribute directly to the project mission. Without this contribution, it becomes not an element essential to success, but yet another factor in failure. There are enough failure factors without our creating additional ones.

Processes involve activities, tasks, functions, resource usage, the exercise of authority and judgment, and express or implied responsibility for their implementation. Elements of each are combined to form *methods of conversion*, another term for processes. The conversion sought is that from what we want to what we have, expectations to achievements. As with many other simple concepts associated with project work, processes can, and often do, become perverted in both their conduct and their direction. Before we examine the many ways this happens, it is best to understand exactly what makes a good process. Taken in the negative, these features represent not methods of conversion, but agents of failure.

RATING ANY PROCESS

We can test the value of any process, no matter what its purpose or methodology, by asking the simple question: "Does it work?" Those methods for which the answer is yes are good processes, and of course, any process which doesn't work should be abandoned. But each method can be rated on a more variable scale than one of just good or bad, workable or nonworkable. Some processes work better than others, some are more efficient, and most importantly, some are more failure prone than others. The challenge is to improve processes, not necessarily by making them more efficient or optimum, but more successful—by improving their chances of working. A good process works more often than not. Because project processes, unlike chemical or mechanical ones, rely heavily on communication, people, perspectives, information, and changing environments, we cannot judge their effectiveness by any other standard. A good process is failure-resistant, a poor one is failure-prone. In this regard most processes can be improved, but none can be made perfect. No process can be made failure-proof.

Using this criterion, there are a number of process features we can identify that reduce this propensity for failure. A good process:

1. *Is Easily Established and Understood.*   The more complex a process the more prone it is to misunderstanding and incorrect implementation. Every process requires people, and people don't do well that which they don't understand. Because each project-specific process needs to be created and implemented rapidly, given the temporary nature of project work, little time is afforded to process design and refinement. Like project controls, processes in place and working are preferred to "better" versions still on the drawing board. Expediency rules, in time as well as in result.

2. *Makes Use of Operational Aids.*   Processes to be repeated time and again can benefit from the operational concepts not often used for project work. A goal should be to segregate repeated processes from unique, one-time-only counterparts and implement operational controls on them. Some of these concepts should work. Such operational goals as standardization, uniformity, interchangeability,

efficiency, result feedback, learning and self-correction, so beneficial to the improvement of non-project work can be borrowed for repeated processes. Processes lending themselves to operational controls should take advantage of them. Simply because projects as a whole are nonoperational doesn't imply that certain methods employed to achieve project expectations cannot benefit from operational analysis.

3. *Can Be Modified Without Project Disruption.* A true test of any project process, procedure, organization, or system is its ability to respond to change. Rigid, nonbending processes are poor ones, for sooner or later they will encounter changed conditions, objectives, or expectations. Each process should be designed to accommodate foreseen changes in the project environment, and to be readily modified once unforeseen changes occur.

4. *Is Not Personality-Dependent.* The easiest way to initiate a process is to personify it—to vest the entire methodology in a person. This is done when a particular person carries the process "in his or her head," or performs extemporaneously as he or she sees fit. There is little wrong with vesting responsibility or discretion in a position (such as the project manager) but it is foolish to do so with one individual. People leave the project, the company, and sometimes even die. Or as is more frequent, their capabilities change, their interests wander, or their skills stagnate. People also tend to respond differently to different situations or stimuli. If uniformity is a process goal, the discretion of any given individual should be avoided. Later we will describe how, by necessity, procedures are employed to avoid, bypass, or pay deference to certain project or company authorities, and how these invite inefficiency if not failure.

5. *Is Goal-Oriented.* Processes are our ways of changing needs into fulfillment. Any time the link between these is broken or so convoluted as to defy understanding the process is less likely to be used or used correctly. No process should be self-justifying. Each is a necessary evil, useless if not bringing results. Like plans and information systems, processes are often used to justify organizations or sustain personal authority. These hidden purposes do not justify a process, they pervert it.

6. *Is Founded on Objectivity.* Except when absolutely necessary, reliance on subjective judgments is not recommended. Whenever possible, objectivity should be built into each process. This achieves a number of benefits. First, it makes the process personality-independent. It also reduces inconsistency and promotes standardization (two operational goals also helpful to project work), and it reduces potential for procrastination and decision-deferment. Both are characteristic of subjective methodology and both extend the time required for any process.

7. *Is Singular, Lean, and Simple.* Too many processes are cumbersome because they are actually combinations of related processes, best separated and treated individually. Or they are overly complicated and byzantine. Again, processes are tools of achievement, and whenever tools become overly ornate, exotic, redundant or otherwise unusable, they become works of art. When viewing a process, simplicity and effectiveness make it beautiful, not decoration or intricacy.

8. *Produces Identifiable Results.* We cannot tell whether a process has been completed unless we have identifiable, often measurable results. Take the process of invoice review, for example. The result should be a "reviewed invoice." But how is this determined? Only by a signature or initials attesting to that review. Otherwise the process is indeterminate—we cannot tell whether it has begun, is taking place, or is completed. Any process that fails to produce identifiable results—end products we can see, touch, or measure, is an open ended series of activities. Our goal is to close these ends— to bring every process to a conclusion. Only those whose authority or empires depend on process continuation resist this requirement. Unfortunately, there are a lot of these.

9. *Is Necessary.* Many processes produce identifiable results, but those results are inconsequential to the project effort—they are unnecessary. At times this is difficult to determine, and we end up giving the process the benefit of the doubt, hoping that although intermediate results seem superficial the end result will justify the effort. It pays to design processes such that these end results are identifiable quickly, before much time and money is spent. A good process gives not only any results, but quick results; allowing us to

judge the process contribution before excessive resources are spent on it.

10.   *Rewards Compliance.*   Perhaps the most common reason for people to ignore or circumvent a process is that the process punishes its own compliance. That is, following the prescribed process actually damages project achievement or jeopardizes the position or effectiveness of the performer. When this becomes apparent we need to examine the process to determine if system or operating problems exist; if the circumvention is merely a breaking of the rules or represents an attempt to avoid the negative aspects of compliance. Often process circumvention leads to a better understanding of why the process is poor. Those who break the rules often help us understand why they should be broken. We may need to shine light on the process before applying heat to the offenders.

TOO SIMPLE, TOO COMPLEX

Sometimes poor processes are designed when we fail to realize just how simple or how complex they need to be. This often occurs when what is treated as one process is actually more than one, each needing separate performance, understanding, and control methods. The case of material purchasing gives us a good example of how this occurs. Despite the fact that purchasing has been going on for centuries, and the essential elements of purchasing seem simple enough, and therefore easy to control, the *process of purchasing* resists standardization and control. Perhaps this is due to the fact that what we call purchasing is not merely one process, but a whole series of interrelated processes, each requiring different levels of performance, facing different risks, and susceptible to different failure modes.

Thus, to control purchasing, one must control each element of the purchasing process, or more correctly, each separate process that, when collectively performed, comprises a purchasing *function.* To illustrate the concept of purchasing being more than one process, consider the following list of component processes it might entail:

1. Material planning and scheduling (when and what to buy)

2. Quantity takeoffs (how much of each item is needed)

3. Source identification (from whom may we buy each)

4. Material specification (describing what it is we want)

5. Terms preparation (commercial terms and conditions)

6. Inquiry preparation (our request for bids or quotes)

7. Inquiry coordination (questions, changes, meetings)

8. Bid evaluation (studying prices and terms received)

9. Negotiation (with potential vendor(s))

10. Source selection (deciding from whom to buy)

11. Order issuance (cutting the purchase order)

12. Order amendments (changes, modifications)

13. Status tracking (management reports)

14. Expediting (promoting timely delivery)

15. Manufacturing surveillance (witnessing performance steps, approving intermediate results)

16. Production inspection (shop tests)

17. Delivery coordination (shipping, traffic, customs)

18. Material receipt (inspection, possession)

19. Documentation receipt/disposition (drawings, warranties, operating and maintenance manuals)

20. Payment processing (partial and final billings)

This list shows how one process (i.e., *purchasing*) can be segmented into 20 separate elements, or components. Each of these in turn requires different resources, has distinct objectives, uses special tools, and is often conducted by different people—if not different organizations. We cannot manage the *function* of purchasing without managing the elements, or processes, that purchasing entails.

Whether we segment the function into 20, 30, or just ten processes makes little difference, as long as each follows the rules established for a good process and as long as we understand the scope and boundaries of each. Once again, we cannot manage that figurative forest without managing the trees that comprise it.

Sometimes this approach leads to the identification of many more processes than originally expected (process complication), and sometimes it reduces what seems like a complex process into a handful of relatively minor ones (process simplification). In either case our understanding of the process itself is improved, and our chances of avoiding inherent process failure are increased.

LET'S WRITE SOME PROCEDURES

Once a project is initiated it doesn't take long for someone to suggest that "project procedures" are needed. This sometimes leads to a frantic, poorly focused process in itself—procedure creation. Before rushing off in this direction, most projects could benefit from a little reflection on the role of procedures; what they can do to help us and the many ways they can end up representing the rope from which we will hang. For if processes represent necessary evils, procedures are often their evil consequences.

Procedures exist solely to communicate processes. Any other purpose is secondary, and to force procedures to fulfill secondary purposes is often fatal. Such is the case when we use procedures to (1) draw or reinforce organizational boundaries, (2) bolster individual or group authority, (3) frustrate accomplishment, (4) stifle healthy innovation, (5) protect the status quo, or (6) make project objectives unattainable.

Some people fail to see the role of procedures in transmitting process information—in describing how processes should take place. This is their only purpose, and other organizational or management tools exist to meet nonprocess objectives. Among these are job descriptions, organizational charters, operational guidelines, organizational objectives, and long-range plans, to mention a few.

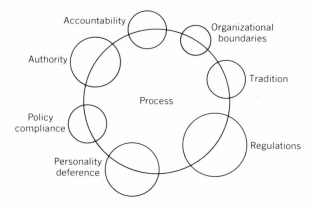

Figure 8-1 The Process as only one element of a procedure.

Two things can happen when we fail to understand the special, restricted role of project procedures. First, we attempt to address so many nonprocess elements and issues when we write these procedures that they become so topical, controversial, or offensive that they never get completed and approved. Nonprocess issues get in the way of the process description and subsequently block process understanding and control.

There are a number of these procedural elements, some of which are depicted by Figure 8-1. Note that the process itself, the reason for the procedure can be so burdened by accompanying statements and declarations of authority, accountability, organizational, and personal sensitivities, tradition, external regulations, and the need to demonstrate procedural compliance that it is almost impossible to distinguish the process itself. Rather than mere excess baggage, these issues often prevent the adoption of any useful procedure. In other cases they lead to adoption of a diluted, inoffensive procedure guaranteed not to create any organizational waves, yet totally incapable of meeting the intention of the original, unencumbered process.

The goal of anyone involved in procedure creation or analysis should be to reduce this encumbrance to a tolerable minimum. They need realize that project procedures don't exist to shore up weaknesses or inadequacies in the organization, its staffing, or management. Procedures describe processes—no more; and there are a number of ways in which this can be accomplished, some good and some woefully inadequate. A perceptive project manager knows the difference among them as well as when to apply each.

ALTERNATIVE WAYS TO CREATE A PROCESS

Like any other tools used to perform, understand, or control project work, processes should be tailored with an eye toward risk. This being the case, there is little room for "standard" processes, or indeed standard procedures except for the most standard of projects. These are extremely rare. Two extremes exist in procedure creation: (1) detailed, prescriptive *rote* procedures, and (2) general, situational or *discretionary* procedures. The challenge of project management is to strike a balance between the use of these two types; to know when rote is required and when discretion is affordable.

Rote procedures often take the form of "playscript." They are extremely detailed, describing each distinct step required, who performs it, how it is performed, and which steps proceed and follow it. They require little if no judgment, making them suited for low level personnel, simple tasks, and processes for which uniformity or nondeviation is paramount. Playscript procedures take a long time to create, review, and approve. They are also generally unresponsive to changed situations or those for which subjectivity is needed.

Commonly associated with this type of procedure are detailed "job descriptions" detailing virtually every aspect of an individual's daily performance. Playscript procedures and job descriptions suit those activities where the individual need know little except what he or she is required to do at every given point in the process. They best suit what is sometimes called "bucket-brigade work," where each individual need not know anything except from whom to receive each bucket and to whom to give it. No need to describe where the water is coming from, where it is going, why it is moving, or the ultimate group objective (put out the fire), much less alternate firefighting methods. It is easy to see why most people resent the bucket brigade approach. It only satisfies the most insecure, rote performers.

Discretionary procedures are given this name because they allow for some discretion on the part of the performer; some freedom to accomplish objectives or take intermediate steps besides, or in addition to, those described. These take the form of (1) flexible, objective-oriented procedures commonly used for middle management positions and (2) responsibility/resource procedures which typically assign responsibility and resources and leave the use of one to satisfy the other in the hands of the individual. These are the highest level procedures commonly found on the project level.

There are a number of ways to contrast these four separate ways of depicting and prescribing processes, and given enough time, we could probably contrive several others that are perhaps more representative of any given project effort. However, each of these would probably lie somewhere between rote "playscript" procedures and very flexible, subjectively applied "responsibility/resource" versions. None is any better than the other; their value, or lack thereof, lies in their use. All have proven very successful given certain circumstances and woefully inadequate given others. The task of project management is to select a procedural style, much like we select plans, controls, and information systems, that is appropriate to the risk and degree of management interest involved.

General guidelines regarding the appropriateness of each procedural style are depicted by Figure 8-2. There we show the general classes of rote and discretionary procedures compared to their applications. For simple processes, rote procedures are useful, whereas discretion is needed the more complex the process becomes. The higher up the chain of command we go, the more discretion must be afforded to process conduct; good managers resent rote directions (bad managers sometimes like rote—it gives them protection from judgmental errors and removes inquiry into their prudence). Finally, rote procedures tend to reduce most effort to an objective basis, removing the need for application of subjective judgment.

Another way to contrast rote procedures with discretionary counterparts is shown by Figure 8-3. Here we see the "analogy box" used to depict the project environment (box) and the objective (attain-

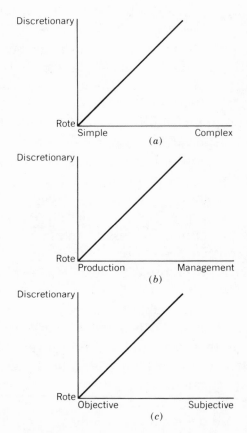

Figure 8-2 Discretionary versus rote procedures.

ment of highest position). Rote procedures (*a*) might prescribe each specific step an individual must take to assure maximum results, while discretionary procedures (*b*) would allow the individual to cut his or her own path, keeping in mind that there is more than one level of accomplishment and that it might pay to explore alternate levels before committing to any given one. These boxes depict a number of more subtle differences, ones with which project and company managements should be familiar.

Note how many steps are required for the rote condition as opposed to the discretionary one. Or thought of differently, how many more people rote procedures assume to be in the bucket brigade. Rote procedures entail little risk of misinterpretation or circumvention, thus assuring uniformity and promoting strict compliance (up

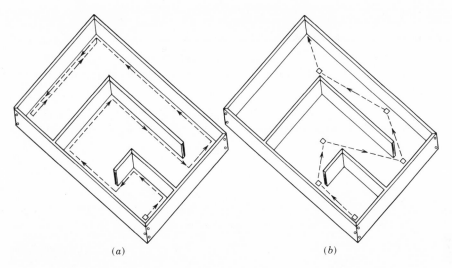

Figure 8-3 Alternate procedure levels. (*a*) Rote procedure and (*b*) discretionary procedure.

to the point, however, when the performers see alternatives that they weren't supposed to see). Discretionary procedures, on the other hand, are less voluminous, require more management judgment and insight, are easier to adopt, and involve less uniform, consistent processes. When analyzing the failure factors pertaining to processes, it is often helpful to remember these distinctions, and to determine, for any given project, whether shifting from rote to discretion, or vice versa, might be advisable when specifying the actions of others.

The concepts of rote and discretion as they apply to process control have so far been described in the the context of internal project organizations. They apply equally to the specification of work performed by outsiders (consultants, construction contractors, ad agencies, software houses, etc.). Special considerations in this regard are contained in Chapter 9.

WAYS TO IMPROVE A PROCESS

No process is perfect, and perfection is not a project goal. Accomplishment is, however, and often this is prevented or restrained by the very procedure or process designed to assure it—the necessary evil. One way to promote project success is to examine proposed processes or those in use, and determine if any pragmatic improvements can be made. This examination should focus efforts only on those processes entailing significant risk, those continuously repeated, or those for which failure has appeared—those that simply don't work. Once the process is understood there are a number of suggestions for improvement that may apply. What follows are brief discussions of the most common ones.

1.   *Shorten the Gap Between Activity and Results.*   This helps satisfy our need to see the fruits of our labor, and points out unnecessary activity—that which doesn't lead to results. No matter how rote a procedure is, people tend to get lost or give up hope of compliance when they fail to see results after a certain amount of time and effort. Even if these are artificial or intermediate, results promote compliance.

2.   *Remove Procedural Encumbrances.*   Procedural encumbrances on processes (such as those depicted by Figure 8-1) detract from process understanding, slow performance and impede progress. Depending on their nature, these encumbrances can block procedure approval or lead to diluted, meaningless procedure. Because they pertain to authority, organizational territory, tradition, or individual personalities, these encumbrances also make processes more difficult to establish and to change, more complex, and less apt to be followed by those who disagree with one or more of the encumbrances.

3.   *Create Superimposed Results.*   Anytime a single process can yield two or more separate results, the project benefits. Many processes can be combined in this manner, or made to use identical tools that, in so doing, achieve more than one objective. An example concerns the use of a form to serve as both a transaction document (facilitating the process) and as a record thereof (documenting the transaction, providing an audit trail, providing source data for information systems, etc.).

Let's take the case of a project owner who charges consultants or contractors for the cost of correcting poorly performed work. Termed "backcharging," this process involves deductions from payments made to the offender and additions to payments made to the party correcting the work (the corrector). A simple backcharge form can be used to (1) indicate the nature and extent of the offending work, (2) allow the offender to authorize correction as suggested thereon, (3) reference the correction process and the C,S, and T required, (4) record the project manager's approval of all terms and conditions, and (5) initiate both the deduction and addition to progress payments involved. This one form thereby serves several processes required for the backcharge function, in addition to providing a permanent record of each.

Superimposed results eliminate redundant processes and streamline those that are necessary. They should be sought wherever possible. However, we must be cautious not to superimpose different or nonrelated processes upon each other. Results should be superimposed, not necessarily processes.

4. *Segment Complex or Continuous Processes.* It is difficult to plan, understand, perform, or control work that is continuous, without discernible boundaries, without a beginning, middle, and end—a continuum. By necessity we must segment continuums into components and manage each. By taking this approach to the process level, we can use our finite element analogy previously applied to project planning and information systems. The finite elements we use are called process *steps,* and we should increase our managerial focus on each process by increasing the number of elements, or steps, we use to define and visualize it. The higher the risk, the higher the degree of performance difficulty, the greater the number of steps. It does not necessarily follow that more steps mean a greater tendency to use rote procedures, simply more detailed procedures. Often, however, more detail means more "bucket-brigade" mentality, and this could be justified given risk and the level of those performing each step. In order to avoid offending the intelligence of project personnel, however, we should never install rote processes just because we *can;* only because we *must.*

5. *Formalize Its Completion.* A process that never ends is merely a sustained level of activity, and there are few occasions when this is advisable. Whenever possible, we should carry the notions of shortening the gap between activity and results (paragraph 1) and segmentation (paragraph 4) to their logical conclusion: every process must end. Unending processes represent "hanging nodes"

in our project performance; we need to close these loops. The use of outsiders to perform contract work gives a common example of occasions when this is not followed. Many contracts never die, they simply fade into oblivion. It's best to shut the door, close the books, and end each contract in a formal, well-publicized manner. Just as all contracts should be formally "closed out," so should all processes. Open-ended processes evade performance evaluation, invite wasted resources, and needlessly confuse and divert management attention.

6. *Tap Human Ingenuity and Innovation.* Whenever possible procedures should specify results rather than means of obtaining them. They should communicate purpose over process by letting our people know the process objectives in addition to the process steps. Unless we are operating without people, it pays to open the process up to their inquiry, understanding, and appreciation. Only then can we expect them to commit to its operation. An added bonus is the innovation that this understanding often brings to the process. Nobody understands a process better than those performing it, (unless it is a bucket-brigade method), and these people are often able to improve it vastly. It's common knowledge that people who know the *purpose* can improve and refine the process, while those knowing the *process* only are condemned to its repetition. We can make use of this principle by reinforcing the concept of responsibility (remember the wake-up call analogy?) over that of function: that of discretion over rote.

7. *Create Useful Tools.* No process should be designed around a tool and no tool should exist without a process use. To that end, every project tool should be helpful in performing, understanding, or controlling processes, otherwise it should be jettisoned. Forms are good examples of this principle. The backcharge form mentioned earlier was designed as a useful tool, not a hindrance to those performing backcharge management. Forms and other management tools help by facilitating performance and giving it direction, or by constraining unwanted activity. Tools that prove otherwise are burdens to success: they are the tools of failure.

8. *Remove Needless Subjectivity.* As much as most of us appreciate deference to our judgment, some cases require objective, con-

sistent activity. For these the elimination of a role for subjective judgment is often a blessing. For although subjectivity is appreciated in some circles it is feared and avoided in others. Here is a case for wise use of individual deference, and even personality-dependent procedures. Should a manager be incapable of applying judgment, or paralyzed by decision-making, it may be best to give him or her less discretionary play.

We can also avoid process bottleneck by eliminating useless management reviews and approvals, all but those absolutely necessary. It's one thing to furnish concerned management "information copies" of documents, another to wait for their reviews before proceeding. Streamlined processes are never needlessly authority-dependent.

9. *Shine Light (Before Turning on the Heat).* It is an established principle that output or accomplishment is stimulated by the mere fact of its being under concerned observation (the so called Hawthorne effect). We can use this principle by letting project personnel know that management is concerned with processes and with ways to improve them. Despite the fact that mere concern often brings improvement, it also points out areas where processes need changing and leads to better results. In this regard, management's audit of the process under review should not entail another encumbrance (most processes have enough). Management should be able to witness a process stream, judging its depth and flow without damming it up.

Every effort should be made to demonstrate that process audits are geared to improvement, not to determinations of culpability. The Hawthorne effect came about as a result of experiments that increased and decreased light in the working area—not heat.

10. *Terminate It Entirely.* Every so often we find processes that are beyond redemption. These should be terminated. In many cases they persist because of tradition, or because a certain organization or individual profits by their continuation. When this occurs the process may not be the only object terminated. When such action is taken, we must assure that everyone involved understands that the termination has occurred. Unwanted processes need to end with a bang, not a whimper.

ARTISTS OF EXPEDIENCY

Project managers who succeed do so in spite of failure factors—they find ways to avoid them, outsmart them, or reduce their impact. In so doing they often take the untraveled route, circumventing established procedure or common wisdom; seeking the global solution over the local one, or seeking a workable and attainable solution over unattainable perfection.

Few topics demonstrate this pragmatic, results-oriented mode better than processes. Given an expectation and some resources, a good project manager fashions a process to convert these to results. Again, this is because a good project manager more closely resembles a prospector than a miner, one who accomplishes rather than one who refines the accomplishment of others.

With this fixation on objectives over processes, it's easy to see how project managers faced with process obstacles often seek to circumvent these rather than take the time and effort to remove them, particularly when the effort itself is a transient one (as all projects are). Although there are many, it seems the most persistent obstacles to project processes can be grouped into three categories of individuals, organizations, and tradition. Taken together, these probably account for 90% of the waste, procedural abuse, and frustration encountered with major project efforts. This is an imperfect environment, but one in which most companies operate. What this means is that, many times the enemy is us: our managers, organizations, and reluctance to perform outside traditional restraints.

Project managers, then, need to become artists of expediency. They need to get things done, to achieve despite the obstacles placed in their paths. The best project managers are often the most expedient; the scroungers, the improvisers, the ones who make it happen one way or the other.

A simple depiction (Figure 8-4), shows how a project manager might approach a series of process obstacles. Of course the unencumbered process along the bottom of the figure is preferred, but so often unavailable, leaving the project manager no choice other than to destroy or remove all obstacles or build a process over, under, and around them. Most choose the latter course. This is due to the one-time nature of their need and the self-interest (project

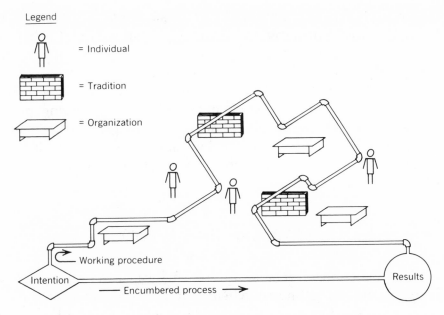

Legend

= Individual

= Tradition

= Organization

Working procedure

Intention

Encumbered process

Results

Figure 8-4   Expediency: Building a process around obstacles.

interest) they represent. This of course is also why project personnel should not be relied on to eliminate imbedded problems for the benefit of other projects or for the company as a whole. A traveller passing through a forest only once doesn't often build a highway for the convenience of those who may follow. Any steps taken to capture this valuable information before the project team dissolves should bring great and sustained rewards. In this fashion, some of the most persistent process obstacles, or failure factors, can be eliminated. These are described in the following sections.

FF 72: Procedural Infatuation

As its name implies, this factor is similar to planning and information infatuations. Like these, procedural infatuation confuses the tool with its object; in this case, the process with its intended results. Although every procedure may be improved, holding approval of a process until perfection is achieved is foolish, but also a symptom of procedural infatuation. This affliction often has a number of fatal results. One is the extended time period and effort required to get what appear to be even the simplest of procedures out the door. This in turn causes inaction or action without the benefit of procedural guidance. Procedural infatuation often leads to process paralysis.

Because it is so difficult to issue approved procedures, the project is often stuck with outmoded, inefficient, or nonworking procedures in their stead. Finally, infatuation with procedure creation often extends the rein of those responsible for it, and establishes a visible scapegoat for those wishing to postpone decisions or activity—that of no procedures.

FF 73: Disjointed Activity

Projects sometimes resemble squirrels in a cage: we see a lot of activity but no one getting anywhere. Often this activity is not linked together to produce some identifiable result—it isn't part of a process. And it is not unusual for these steps to lead in complete circles, much like the squirrel's exercise wheel. This all leads to motion without results, one of the worst examples of well intentioned people working with improper tools, or no tools at all.

Disjointed activity is often the direct result of misunderstanding of processes, lack of proper responsibility assignment, redundant perspectives, or simply organizational tradition. No activity not part of a necessary process and not leading to the accomplishment of project objectives is necessary. In fact it is harmful, for it consumes valuable resources and detracts from essential work, both contributing to project failure. No activity is neutral: it either helps us or hurts our cause. Disjointed activity fits the latter category.

FF 74: Procedural in Nature

Procedures exist to communicate processes. But as we have already seen, this communication device is often burdened with a number of encumbrances dealing with the establishment of authority, drawing of organizational boundaries, deference to certain individuals, and many others. Often it is almost impossible to save an overloaded process by extracting it from this procedural burden, especially if the latter is composed of dangerous and difficult issues.

The best procedures are simple and direct; they are little more than process descriptions. Tying extraneous baggage to them is similar to attaching unrelated riders to legislation. The result may be the eventual death of the procedure, or the issuance of diluted, transparent, or castrated directives designed to offend no one yet accomplish nothing.

FF 75: Process Piggyback

Ambitious processes designed to accomplish several objectives often fail at each. The problem with combining processes is not one of intent, but one of result. Our example of purchasing being composed of at least 20 separate processes shows how combinations of any may lead to failure of all. They are often performed by different groups or individuals, use vastly different tools and approaches, and occur in different places or times.

It's not unusual for combined processes to defy improvement, or even change. This occurs when we try to strengthen one embedded process and, in so doing, weaken another. Or when we cease performing one only to find seemingly unrelated processes suffering as a result. It's always best to segment processes and treat them individually. Superimposed *processes* often give us trouble, even though superimposed *results* stemming from one process are worth pursuing.

FF 76: Arnold-in-a-Box

This failure factor represents the extreme case of personality-dependent procedures. Its name comes from a well-known expert working for a major project management firm. When asked by potential clients how they planned to control each project, the firm's representatives went on to describe the years of experience Arnold possessed, his education, ability, and worldwide respect in the industry. Arnold was, in fact, a superlative project manager. He was an example of the 5% or 10% of our people who do well even without tools (the outstanding category—they make their own). Wags around the industry began to refer to this firm's project management philosophy as "Arnold-in-a-box."

As silly as this example may seem, the cult of personality often prevents establishment of personality-independent processes even in major corporations. The best response to the Arnold-in-a-box approach is the "Runaway Truck" corollary. It asks "What happens to the project when Arnold is run over by a truck?"

FF 77: Prisoners of Tradition

Perhaps the most persistent obstacle in the path of creation and use of valuable processes is tradition: the way we did it last time. While acceptable for operational work, tradition often stymies progress on projects. The unique nature of project work limits the application of traditional processes, for there are few traditional objectives, traditional organizations, traditional environments, or traditional risks. When tradition is our master, we often find our projects inheriting traditional failure.

What makes blind obedience to the dictates of tradition even more foolish is the fact that what happened last time often did not happen—what worked before often did not work. Traditional solutions are often perceived rather than real. Problems brought about by traditional processes are always real, however, and often avoidable by taking a fresh look at the the three essential elements of any process: expectations, resources, and results.

The use of traditional methods of conversion (processes) often ignores the specificity of risk and the concept of selective controls, those tuned to *expected* risks rather than to *experienced* ones. These are not always the same. Insisting on performance of any process activity merely because of the dictates of tradition tends to weaken support for the process and leads to half-hearted compliance. People work better at what has been intelligently designed to meet their specific, unique needs. Failed projects are often those imprisoned by tradition, not only in the process sense, but also as it restrains their selective use of organizations, people, information systems, and perceptions. Tradition perpetuates failure.

FF 78: Monkeyfied

A general rule in process design is to keep every step as simple as possible. While there is little need for unnecessary complication, there is even less for process steps that are so trite, so discrete, and so rote as to be able to be performed by a monkey. So called "monkeyfied" procedures insult the dignity of the performers and degrade their individual contribution to project success. Their performance becomes dulled, listless and characterized by narrow vision. Although we all appreciate control and consistency in our environment, no one likes working on a treadmill, or prolonged service in a project bucket brigade.

Whenever possible, monkeyfied processes should be automated, with the monkeywork performed by machines. Procedures based on rote suffer in other ways, besides from the stupification of those who must follow them. They are notoriously unresponsive to changed circumstances, for one simple curve in the process often disrupts it entirely, turning control into chaos. Monkeyfied processes are great for work involving monkeys. Unfortunately (or fortunately) we must work with people.

FF 79: Concrete Icons

When we place so much value on certain procedures that they are held up to be subjects of adoration and respect rather than mere tools subservient to a greater result, we have created icons not procedures. These are often so inflexible and unchangeable that they appear to have been created out of concrete rather than paper. A number of procedural features create this illusion.

One of these is the reliance on too high an authority to endorse or approve the process itself. A general rule is that the lower in the organization a process needs to be approved to gain acceptance the better. Too many reviews and management concurrences also contribute to this unfortunate end, as well as the need for too many compromises to finally get the procedure out the door and activated. The more people involved in blessing a procedure in the first place the more involved to change it. So concrete icons are not only difficult to create and implement, they can be most recalcitrant when it comes to change.

They are also commonly circumvented. Besides this, they often resist analysis or suggestions for improvement. They are seen as too perfect to be questioned, much less tampered with. This immunity from analysis should never be tolerated, whether applied to procedures, organizations, or individuals, for when we cease to ask "why" or "why not" we cease to advance. Projects are not houses of worship, they are bridges to accomplishment.

FF 80: House of Cards

When we try to tie nonrelated processes together, or to create needless process links and dependencies, we may be creating a house of cards—one for which the slightest breeze of change brings disaster, for one minor modification in one area can have relentless and far-reaching impacts in others. The sad fact is that most of these impacts have been artificially contrived through the needless combination of processes. Procedural houses of cards are also difficult to establish, for they require more and more reviews and approvals the more complex and encompassing they become. Our duty is to prevent this from occurring, to identify the critical elements of each process and separate them from ancillary or otherwise independent activity and restraints.

FF 81: All Fluff, No Stuff

It is difficult to establish processes or to create procedures in the absence of overriding company policy. We cannot, for example, design and use a procedure for material source selection (purchasing) if we do not know whether our company insists on competitive bidding, or whether we may select from single sources without the need for competition. Procedures communicate processes, but these must operate within the overall framework of general, higher level policy decisions. Herein lies the reason for the failure of many companies to establish procedures on a timely basis—the lack of higher management decision-making.

Often those working on the project level, mindful of this dependency yet desperate for some sort of processes to perform the work, attempt to "dance around" this inadequacy. The result is often silly, contrived, and meaningless procedure. Or they attempt the "quick and dirty" solution—simple results-oriented directives that gloss over critical issues essential to their implementation. Quick and dirty procedures are often just that—quick and dirty.

Another common response is the adaptation of eyewash procedures—those full of fluff, but containing no stuff—no substance, no meaningful directions or guidelines. As long as these don't prevent performance, understanding, or control of project work they present little problem. However, what usually occurs is just the opposite: confusion and wasted resources. The biggest problem with fluff procedures is that, because they exist, they eliminate the pressing need for actual, meaningful versions. They fill the procedural vacuum, thus relieving the pressure to create useful, pertinent and effective procedures. Add to this the fact that any procedure, regardless of its merit, is difficult to eliminate entirely. Like band aids placed over an open wound, poor procedures are very easy to install, yet extremely painful to remove.

FF 82: Hidden Purposes

It would be naive to presume that all processes or their derivatives, procedures, are created to meet altruistic goals—that of furthering project objectives. On the contrary, many exist for hidden purposes. These may be the need to respond to a negative audit finding, a low level attempt to set policy from below (rather than from the top), tradition, to satisfy internal or external regulators, to grab organizational territory, or to *preclude* the adaptation of more stringent procedures—to fill the vacuum before it is filled by something more onerous to us. When analyzing any project process, then, we need to first examine its true reason for being, not always accepting it at face value. A dose of pessimism helps separate the bona fide from the bogus.

FF 83: Narrowmindedness

Everyone has run against this attitude, in our daily lives as well as with project activity. Narrowminded management refuses to consider processes not proven, nontraditional, or at odds with their preferences. Narrowminded managers lock on to a process and become tenacious defenders, even when they fail to understand the process itself. They think "there is only one way" to do anything, and are blind to alternatives. They lack peripheral vision, courage, or just plain business acumen. But most of all they lack the pragmatism that separates success from failure in the world of projects.

FF 84: Impotent Responsibility

This is a phenomenon that occurs with surprising frequency throughout the business world. It consists of the assignment of *responsibility* without the commensurate and essential assignment of *resources* and *authority* to carry it out. To be successfully implemented, each element of the process equation needs to be assigned. That is, each process needs an initial set of expectations, the resources needed to meet the process, the process itself, and finally, the requisite *authority* to set these all in motion. Procedures that fail to establish and transfer authority and resources in the right quantity and quality are impotent procedures. They are hollow and useless.

FF 85: Ignoring Human Factors

No management process runs itself. People are needed. No matter how intricate, failure-resistant, and effective a process appears in the design stage, it will fail if it ignores human factors. These factors are simple, direct, and easy to understand. It is surprising, however, how often they are disregarded, how often people are missing from the process equation, assumed to be mechanical, consistent, and having no needs whatsoever. This is a gross error in judgment; an often fatal presumption.

People have simple needs and wants. Among these, as we have already described, is the need to see the fruits of their labor—to identify their individual contribution. Any process that fulfills that need has gone a long way toward its successful implementation. People tire easily, and they become bored even more quickly. They will accept bucket brigade duty for short durations, under emergency conditions, and for the overall good of the project, but they will not tolerate large and continuous doses. Neither will they support and cheerfully participate in processes which suppress their judgment, insult their intelligence or degrade their dignity. Under these conditions they often perform poorly, circumvent the process they are compelled to follow, or in worse cases, sabotage the process itself. Of these, circumvention is probably the most common response. People simply refuse to follow procedures that ignore them as essential elements.

An excellent example of the failure to consider human factors, and subsequent circumvention, concerns the design and layout of concrete sidewalks. Many years ago architects arranging sidewalks on college campuses persisted in laying them out in straight lines, at right angles to each other, and along inoffensive routes. Once these were constructed, students wishing to get from point A to point B (say from a classroom to a dormitory building) were required to follow sidewalks over routes that ran contrary to their initial inclinations. That is, rather than travel in a straight line from A to B, the shortest distance, they were forced to take the longer, right-angled paths. It didn't take long for students to ignore the sidewalks completely, choosing instead to follow the dictates of their intelligence and, consequentially, travel over grass and dirt.

These students weren't purposefully disobeying procedures, nor were they trying to sabotage the architect's work. They simply followed a better process, a better way of getting from one place to another. The purpose of the procedure (sidewalks) was also not to force students to walk only in right angles, but to place sidewalks under their feet—to keep them from having to walk in the mud. This being the case, a sensitive architect would have put the sidewalks where the people walk rather than insisting that people walk where the sidewalks happened to be. Procedures should follow the same approach. They should be put where they can be used by people, and whenever possible, the natural tendencies of people should be followed. The sidewalks on most college campuses now follow this advice. They wander around trees, cut diagonally across open expanses and contain few right angles. The procedure has been changed to match the process.

SUMMARY

Every project relies on the successful conduct of many processes. These necessary evils convert original expectations into accomplishments: results. Any additional encumbrances to a process limit its value and may prevent its use. Whenever possible, we should examine each project process to remove needless organizational, individual, or traditional obstacles.

Regardless of the project or industry in which each process takes place, a number of attributes contribute to improvement, eventual use, and accomplishment. Among these are simplicity, singularity, accommodation of change, objectivity, the reward of compliance, production of identifiable results, and of course, necessity. Alternate ways to communicate process elements, called procedures, range from the most simple didactic rote versions to open-ended responsibility/resource assignments. Prudent project managers understand each and know when to use one over the other. This often requires them to strike a balance between rote requirements and discretionary latitude.

Processes are not intended to be perfect, for their role is a much more pragmatic one: to accomplish objectives. As such, many operational principles do not apply to their design or conduct. Whenever possible, however, certain repetitive processes may benefit from operational analysis. Common business sense tells us that we can often improve many processes with little or no expenditure of resources. This should be pursued at all times, and often involves a number of general rules. These include the need to shorten the gap between activity and results, eliminate noncontributing activity, segmentation, formalized conclusions, capitalizing on human ingenuity, and for some processes, outright termination. Because of their need to circumvent process obstacles, to build a process around the encumbrances that are often attracted to any procedure, today's project managers need to be innovative, results-oriented, and resourceful. They need to try the expedient solution to give their project a chance at success, but can't be depended on to eliminate long standing obstacles themselves. They commonly go around or over these, choosing to become artists of the expedient rather than saviours rescuing the company from all its deep rooted problems. We should ask no more of them, for this is their charter.

Each major project endeavor or element contains both general and specific failure factors. With processes, we find procedural infatuation to be similar to other infatuations, equally dangerous, pertaining to planning and information systems. Specific failure factors include personality dependence, disjointed activity, the burden of tradition, debasement of the human element and the human contribution, procedural adoration, fluff, and impotence. But of all these, the most persistent and chronic problem found in the entire area of process design and implementation seems to be these unnecessary encumbrances tacked onto innocent processes, formalized through the procedure approval process, and made virulent through our continued acceptance of them as if they were inescapable facts of life. Those seeking project success can tolerate only so much of this burden on performance. There comes a time when we must confront the challenges of organizations, individuals, and tradition and eliminate all that impede the successful accomplishment of our objectives. When done, this will have immense benefits to the project, benefits that are intensified the earlier this confrontation takes place. Not only will the project benefit, but the sponsoring companies should be grateful as well.

CONTRACTING

surviving the marketplace

Any time outsiders are used to perform, understand or control project activity, some sort of formal or informal *contracting* takes place. The most visible example of contracting occurs when a project sponsor hires a construction company to build a physical facility. A contract is signed and work is performed according to, or in spite of, its express terms and conditions. But project work encompasses many more fields of effort and many more industries than just construction. Also many more "contractors" are used beside those who happen to call themselves by that name. If our project involves design and engineering work, we may contract with an architect or engineering firm; contractors in pinstripes. Likewise, when we engage a management consultant, advertising agency, research group, public relations organization, market samplers, lobbyists, material suppliers, temporary personnel, or even an outside project manager, some sort of express or implied terms and conditions apply to each engagement, and some distribution of project scope is made from the sponsor to the outsider: the contractor.

INSIDE, OUTSIDE

Even for those cases when work is performed internally, quasi-contracts are used to define the work, limit the accompanying authority, and set resource levels and performance expectations. Sometimes these are expressed in work orders, budgetary allocations, responsibility assignments or other internal "contracts." Although we will treat contracting from the persevtive of the project sponsor engaging another company in this chapter (classic contracting), virtually every concept, risk, and failure factor accompanying this external contracting should apply to internal versions as well. Most projects involve both, external and internal contracting.

UP AND DOWN

Contracting is practiced upward and downward. *Upward contracting* refers to the position, rights and risks associated with our company being engaged to perform for others, while *downward contracting* concerns our hiring of others to perform work for us. Upward contracting concepts apply to the group selling contracted services while downward contracting takes the buyer's perspective. In many cases project work requires us to apply sound contracting principles both within and without our companies and in both the upward and downward directions. While these perspectives may vary and our contracting objectives will differ depending upon our position and relationship to others (internal, external, upward, downward) most of the contracting principles described in this chapter remain the same.

A contract exists whenever two parties agree to contract, have a meeting of the minds as to what the scope entails, and transfer some consideration, typically money. It matters not, for purposes of our analysis, whether the resulting agreement is formalized in a written, express contract or whether a simple and implied understanding is attained between both parties. We will call this understanding "the contract," keeping in mind that it need not be formal or express in nature. We will also avoid reliance on any externally applied requirements which may pertain to specific types of contracting and constrain what otherwise is an unrestricted business practice. That is, we will not cite or depend on government regulations, jurisdictionally specific limitations, or esoteric industry practices.

Our focus will be on business agreements designed to serve the interests of both parties and necessary for the free and open conduct of project work. Our objective will be to understand and control that which works best for all concerned. Other than the guidelines under which private contracting occurs, such as contract law and commercial expediency, the descriptions and recommendations presented are governed by sound principles of project management and business acumen, both tempered by the pressures and reality of the contracting marketplace.

CONTRACTING'S FOUR PHASES

Most companies engaged in project contracting, from any side, seem to focus on two of its major phases: those activities necessary to achieve a contract and those used to manage it throughout its life. These two are commonly termed *contract formation* and *contract administration*. We will take a broader view, realizing that there are actually four major phases to the contracting function. These are:

1. *Contract Planning*. Determining how many contracts are needed, what their respective scopes of work shall be, when they should be awarded, how they shall be priced, and which terms and conditions will apply. As this list of concerns implies, contract planning is a responsibility of the buyer (project owner buying from contractors, general contractor buying from subcontractors, etc.). Contract planning is an important component of a broader effort—project planning. Whereas project planning deals with the question "What are we going to do and how will we perform, understand and control it?," contract planning seeks to answer "Whom shall we hire to do it, and how shall we understand and control what they do?"

2. *Contract Formation*. The collection of activities required to identify potential contractors, express our needs and conditions, and reach an agreement with each is called contract formation. Each contract, express or implied, is formed before its respective work is begun. In most cases this agreement, the object of formation, is reduced to a written contract and signed by both parties, but as mentioned before, this is not always necesssary.

3. *Contract Administration*. This term represents the commercial handling of contract business from the time a contract is established, or formed, until it expires, through natural or unnatural causes. Each active contract must be administered in order for necessary transactions, controls, and performance to take place. Additionally each contracting party (buyer and seller) needs to administer contracts from its own distinct perspective. Often these perspectives are conflicting or even opposing.

4. *Contract Monitoring*. This term represents the overall management of contracting processes, including those taking place during the previous three phases. It involves review of contract activity, control, and information. Distinct from the other three phases in that it does not follow sequentially, contract monitoring takes place

concurrent with each. It can best be understood as a continuous management perspective placed over each step, process and function of contracting.

THE BAD WITH THE GOOD

By its definition, contracting centers around the placement of some project work in the hands of others. This requires a certain vesting of responsibility, expectations, resources, processes, and controls in those who, we trust, are more capable of the specific performance than ourselves. When we contract we gain their expertise, capability, knowledge, management acuity, resources, and strengths. These are the benefits of contracting. However, with the good comes some bad, for we also expose our project to their lack of experience and expertise, poor business practices, hidden agendas, incompetence, and tendencies toward failure. The trick to contracting is to extract the benefits of the relationship without assuming the associated faults; to maximize the reward and minimize the risks. This is extremely difficult to accomplish, and it represents one of the greatest challenges to project success. It is also why project managers skilled in the craft of contracting are extremely rare and valuable individuals.

THE GREATEST ERROR

The greatest error in the field of contracting is not necessarily one involving lack of skill or craftsmanship. It is one of misunderstanding or underestimating: a lack of respect for the tremendous power and multifaceted danger of contracting. Too many projects have suffered or failed outright because project management failed to recognize the danger of contracting or undervalued the power of good contracting perspectives and tools.

Contracting cannot be taken lightly. It is not simple, uniform, well understood or easy to control. It is fraught with risk, uncertainty, frustration, deceit and human error throughout all four phases. For many projects it represents a wagonload of risk, risk in all shapes, sizes, and strengths. There is no other way to survive the contracting experience than to begin by recognizing this fact. Risk is a passenger in all contractual arrangements.

The most successful projects, on the other hand, are those that turn this relationship around, to their benefit. They realize that contracting brings a wagonload of risk and are determined to convert that wagon to a vehicle of control. They use the tools and process of contracting to attack inherent risks to the processes itself and to reduce other project risks not associated with contracting. They examine each aspect of contracting, looking for ways to use its nature to their advantage.

There are a number of fairly common ways in which this is done. We shall explore many of them directly, and point out their need in an indirect fashion when we describe common contracting failure factors. There are scores of these, and they vary in frequency and intensity. Many are context-specific. That is, their impacts vary with the industry, contract arrangements, and project scope involved. However, there are a tremendous number of generic contracting misconceptions, mistakes and failures that apply across the board— plaguing all projects. For some they are simple nuisances, for others they are chronic and critical. Our concern will be with the latter. To begin this process we need to sharpen our understanding of contracting and consider its role on each of our respective projects. One way to do this is to examine common misunderstandings and myths surrounding this practice.

LAWYERS DO IT ON PAPER

Because contracts are legally binding agreements, are often spoken of in terms of lawsuits, claims, and arbitration, or involve the drafting of legally enforceable clauses and terms, there is a tendency to overvalue the legal significance of contracting at the expense of the business objectives it entails. Put simply, contracts are not merely something the *lawyers* handle. They have a very limited, minor role in the creation and use of project contracts.

Project management, on the contrary, has a very vital, extensive

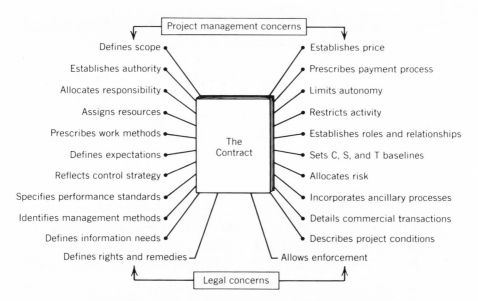

Figure 9-1   Legal versus project management concerns.

and ongoing involvement in all phases of contracting. This will be our perspective; contracting is a business practice, full of risks and controls, best managed by those sensitive to project activity and well versed in the details of project life. The contracts themselves, as well as the processes and controls they embody have significant impact on the success or failure of the project, making *contract management* an essential element of *project management*.

Figure 9-1 demonstrates the difference between those concerns relegated to the legal area and those pertaining to project management. Note that of the many concerns listed there, only two are of a "legal" nature. Considering the tremendous role contracts and contracting play in addressing and enforcing project management intentions, it is more accurate to consider them management tools and management processes than legal devices.

BEYOND THE DOCUMENTS

To understand the power and danger of contracting we must look beyond the documents themselves. When we use the word "contract" we shall use it to mean the entire series of events and positions, risks and controls, and yes operations, represented by the written or verbal agreement. Of course, the contract documents play a central role in the establishment and control of the relationships they define, but they are certainly not the objective of contracting; they are simply another necessarily evil. Poor contract documents cripple otherwise well intentioned agreements, for a number of reasons. First they are difficult to define and manage, this because they are not exactly directions, specifications, rules or guidelines. They are a mixture of all. They are often tedious to prepare, boring, and obfuscating to the reader. And they are often prepared under time pressure with little thought given to their importance. Finally, there are few universally acknowledged contract standards, or "templates" limiting their variety. They are what we chose to make them, seldom uniform, standard, or resembling what was used in the past. Within the general confines of contract law, we are free to make whatever arrangements we see fit. The documents themselves merely serve as a communications tool and a record of these arrangements. They do not guarantee those arrangements to be realistic, enforceable, fair, intelligent, or manageable. Nothing does.

THE UNSEEN HAND

Contracting is a dangerous practice conducted with no safety net to catch or protect us from our own errors or misjudgments. There is no big brother guiding our contracting efforts, no "understood" limits, no universally accepted industry practices, traditions, or overriding concepts of fairness that transcend and correct what can be very stupid moves on our part. The law doesn't protect us from our own foolishness, nor does it remedy bad business decisions. Except for a few very general guidelines restricting our ability to contract (legality, enforceability, impossibility, etc.) we are free to fail. There is no unseen hand directing our acts and guarding our interests. We must use our own. Nothing can be taken for granted.

NO PAIN, NO WOUNDS

A business truth is this: What you don't know *will* hurt you. Most of us understand this. In the contracting game, however, it is also true that what you don't know *is* hurting you will hurt you even more. Put another way, the lack of pain doesn't mean we are not being wounded in a contractual sense, and the fact that we are feeling no pain may signify that we are in more trouble than if we were experiencing some. Some examples may help illustrate this.

Change orders to contracts are the bane of many industries. They modify scope of work, commonly increase C, S, and T and are symptomatic of poor planning, performance difficulties, or indecisive management, to name a few causes. Most companies that do a lot of contracting (upward or downward) suffer from a plethora of change orders—they suffer a lot of pain. Every so often a company will minimize the impact of changed work by claiming not to have any problems whatsoever with change orders. They have none, they don't expect any and they fail to see what the rest of us are concerned about. This company may be using cost-reimbursable pricing exclusively; no lump-sum or unit priced contracts. This being the case, changed work is not necessarily identified as such. It merely represents work, and all work will be compensated—regardless of whether it was in the originally identified scope or added later. As long as it was performed, and performed correctly, the contractors will be paid for it. No change orders needed. No problem with change orders. No pain—no wounds.

Given this example, the project owner is abolutely correct to contend that change orders do not plague its projects. However, a much greater problem than change may exist, such as of excesive contractor payments and lack of C, S, and T control. Cost-reimbursable payment schemes place virtually all risk of cost overruns squarely on the buyer's shoulders. The project owner may be enjoying the luxury of no change orders at an excessive cost—that of higher prices, lack of cost visability, and no motivation for the contractor to monitor or control expenditures or improve efficiency. These are very large wounds, but without the pain system that *change control* represents, the hapless owner would continue to presume all is well.

The same concept applies in the field of contract claims. Owners that have no claim experience may attribute this to good contract management, association with amenable contractors, fair business dealings, or just plain good luck. Claims are messy, difficult to resolve, expensive, and distracting. No one likes them, save those who profit from their occurrence (lawyers, arbitrators, consultants, etc.). But a little bit of "claims pain" may be better than none at all, for the lack of claims may indicate that the owner is overly generous, giving contractors whatever is asked in terms of increased C, S, and T. It takes a dispute to create a claim, and if the owner is compliant at all times with the demands of contractors, no matter how well founded they may be, there will be no claims. Unless these parties are extremely lucky some problems will arise. A "pushover" owner never has to contend with messy claims; it merely pays too much for what it gets. This is often an expensive practice, a high price to pay for a painless passage through the contracting zone.

The analogy with our physical beings begs addressing. Many contracting systems are essentially pain systems, series of nerves that transmit pain impulses to our management. We would be in poor shape without the benefit of pain, for it would cause us to keep our hand on the proverbial hot stove until it went up in smoke. Contract pain alerts us to problems in time to correct them or reduce their impact—to pull our hand off the stove before it is severely burned. As much as we resent contractual pain (change orders, claims, backcharges, penalties, etc.) it represents an effective way of replacing the "unseen hand" with one of our own.

TIME CURES ALL

Contractual mistakes intensify over time. Contractual problems fester the longer they remain unresolved, and most contracting errors can be remedied very quickly if they are addressed early. Time doesn't mend contractual wounds, it exacerbates them.

There is a human tendency in this regard that we must counter. It is the allure of procrastination, the "out of sight—out of mind" theory: If we wait long enough the wolf will go away from the door.

Nothing is further from the truth in the world of contracting. Problems need to be confronted head on, immediately, and with determination. Contracting is very unforgiving in this regard—mistakes always come back to haunt us. We suffer during the administration of contracts when the planning and formation phases were ill-conceived or neglected. We suffer as contractors (sellers) when we promise more than we can deliver: buyers never forget promises. We also suffer as project managers when we underestimate the need for contractual controls during the early project stages.

It is always many times easier to get what you want *before* the contract is signed than after, or to get the other party to agree to change before work begins than once it has. The best business decisions made are those that occur without the pressures of C, S, and T. Once contracts are issued and work begins, these pressures always intensify. Decisions made on the run are less than optimum. Time is only on our side before we commit to contractual work, whether we be buying or selling services. Once the starting gun is fired, time becomes our enemy. It does not heal wounds, it opens them.

RISK DUMPING

Another contracting myth concerns risk. It holds that one party can offload all its project risk, for a price, on another; that risk can be dumped. It can't. Contracting is a game of *risk sharing,* with both parties ideally taking that type of risk they are best suited to manage and leaving the rest for the other. Any buyer or seller thinking this untrue hasn't been in the contracting arena long. Like responsibility, risk cannot be given away, or bought off, entirely. We always retain some, whether we like it or not.

There are a number of ways in which contracting parties share risk, pricing being chief among them. Fixed price methods (lump sum, or so called hard money) assign almost all cost risk to the seller, while cost-plus arrangements do the opposite—the risk of cost growth is the buyer's. Depending upon the information available at the time of formation, the technical and schedule risks involved, the nature of the work, and the pricing components, either method may prove entirely appropriate. And risks in the other performance areas (S and T) can be assigned differently. For example, owners who issue broad, general *performance* specifications place the risk of the finished item meeting these (risk in terms of T) on the contractor. When exclusive, limited, narrow scope, or "prescriptive" specifications are used, the risk that the finished item will work as it should (providing the specifications are followed) is the buyer's— the party drafting these specifications.

So risk in terms of C, S, or T can be assigned differently in every contractual setting, and often the assignment of one impacts the distribution of the others; C, S, and T risks are highly interrelated. But never can one be completely devoid of risk. Contracting is a process that occurs in a sea of risk. Those uncomfortable with this fact should stay away from the use of outsiders on project work, or better yet, stay away from projects entirely. We cannot avoid all risk, nor can we use contracting as a vehicle for dumping it all on the other guy.

THIS MEANS WAR

Although it sometimes seems that way, contracting is not like war. In war, the object is to kill your enemy. You win when your enemy dies. In contracting, when the other party dies you lose. Contracting is a business based on *need* as well as *greed*. Adversarial relationships and posturing belong in the courtroom, not in the field of project management. Every owner and every contractor, whether they wear pinstripes or overalls, would much rather have a completed contract than an enforceable claim in court.

Contracting then is a game of cooperation. We need each other. Without that need we wouldn't be associated, there would be no agreement, no contract. Even though each party may have differing expectations and objectives, an overriding objective, jointly shared by all, should be project success. Very seldom does one party fail miserably and the other come out on top. When the project ship sinks all passengers drown.

This is not to suggest that we should naively assume all will go well as long as both parties need each other. It is only to point out the value of cooperation and the strength of contractual controls that reinforce this notion. What works best for both parties works best for the project, and what works in the interest of only one, to the detriment of the other, generally harms the project as a whole, sooner or later, in one form or fashion.

The role of contract planning is essential in this regard. During this phase we need to establish joint and mutual expectations, communicate needs, pick amenable partners, and distribute risk in an equitable fashion. These are all factors in our subsequent ability to perform together, to understand what each respective party is doing, and to control it in the best interest of each. Contracting is like an intimate dance with another party. We need to choose the right partner, select the proper music, practice the steps, and begin with a good faith attitude. Contract planning is when we need to practice dancing and, at the same time, prepare to fight should the occasion arise. The better we are at one the less we will have to engage in the other.

THE GREATEST WEAKNESS

If undervaluing the power and danger of contracting is the greatest error in its practice, the greatest weakness is a lack of experience in this area. The project sponsor is typically entering unfamiliar territory when engaging in project work to begin with, much less the contracting of outside parties to perform portions thereof.

For the project sponsor the act of contracting has all the elements of project work. That is, it is unique, one-time-only, played in a different environment with extemporaneous rules and unresponsive to operational concepts and tools. Like projects, contracts are contrived arrangements; with created roles and responsibilities, created organizations, and created expectations. It is not our mainline business, unless of course, we are on the other side of the table: a contractor.

Contractors of all types have much more experience at this game than do project sponsors. In fact contracting is *operational* to them—they do it as their business rather than as an infrequent, adjunct exercise. It is their bread and butter. They are also good at it, for if not they wouldn't last long. Project sponsors, on the other hand, need not be good project managers or contracting pratitioners—only good at their respective operations (garment manufacturing, mining, retail sales, hospitality, shipping, pharmaceuticals, electricity generation, oil exploration, etc.). Natural selection in the business world, then, helps sharpen the skills of contractors without helping sponsors at all. Sure, the game is played with the sponsor's ball (C, S, and T resources), but it is often played on the contractors' court. This is the major weakness confronting all project sponsors when it comes time to contract, the fact that they are neophytes at this aspect of project management while their dancing partner (or eventual opponent) is in the advanced class. The world of contracting is the habitat of contractors, a world in which project sponsors are mere tourists passing through. Since when did a tourist get a real *bargain* from a native?

In order to keep up and keep in control, sponsors need thorough planning, formation, administration, and monitoring of all aspects of the contracting process. It's not enough to be well intentioned, well informed or well aware of risks. They must be practiced, equipped with contracting plans and tools, staffed with personnel who are aware of contracting pitfalls, and constantly attentive to change. They must dispel the misunderstandings and myths associated with contracting, realize its power and danger, and respect the failure factors that accompany it.

FF 86: Amateur Hour

One of the ironies of life is that for its more mundane tasks we are required to prove our skill or maturity before obtaining a license to undertake them. These include such common activities as driving, marriage, borrowing money, gaining employment, or practicing a trade. Yet even the rankest amateur is allowed to perform far more dangerous and demanding roles, such as investing huge sums of money, having children, or contracting without any preparation or practice whatsoever. Herein lies a major failure factor pertaining to contracting: even an idiot can contract.

Good contracting requires knowledge, management awareness, tools, properly trained and focused personnel, and a wealth of other traits gained through formal education, experience, or vicarious learning. Bad contracting requires none of these, just the ability to commit company funds. While it is common for companies to underestimate the risk of contracting and the power that good contracting practices give to project management, it is also common for them to assume that no particular training or preparation need preceed it. This is simply unture. Contracting is one of project management's greatest challenges, not a game for amateurs.

The concept of contract management is new, dynamic and evolving. To stay ahead of its ever changing risks, one must practice it frequently, pay attention to subtle nuances as well as stark differences in perceptions among the parties involved, and constantly search for better, more controllable methods and processes. Contracting is inseparable from project management, for it is both the risk wagon and the control vehicle applying to many project tasks. It is as much an art as a science, requiring exercise of judgment, business acumen and ethics, and risk taking in addition to a rational analytical approach to each step. Unlike pure science, there is never only *one* answer to any given challenge we may face. Perhaps this is why it is so fascinating, and at the same time, so risky a business.

FF 87: Unreasonable Contract Expectations

Amateurs often overestimate the benefits of a new activity and underestimate the costs. This is as true of contracting as any other sport, business, or pastime. Project sponsors often begin the business of contracting with unreasonable expectations, thereby assuring disappointment, if not project failure. They are unrealistic when they expect to dump all project risks onto another party via a contract, when they assume that because everyone *can* contract everyone can contract well, or when they contrive impossible scopes of work, unachievable expectations, or unacceptable contracting conditions.

They labor under false assumptions when they presume that the other party knows exactly what they want, despite what is written into the contract documents or agreed to the contrary, or when they assume that there is some magical clause, "weasel word" or legal language that will absolve them of all sins and shore up any and all of their organizational and managerial inadequacies. And they err when they trust that some general contract "safety net" exists to break their fall, to protect them from themselves, and to correct what are simply bad business decisions.

Many a project has suffered or failed when sponsors or their agents expect too much from the contracting process. This is often accompanied by a lack of appreciation of the risks and costs involved. When we feel that anyone can plan, form and administer contracts, when we presume these tasks to be "monkeyfied" or clerical only, when we fail to document and incorporate major agreements into the contract itself, postpone the resolution of contracting disputes, and downplay our responsibilities while insisting on full enforcement of our rights we are only fooling ourselves. Contracting, like a very sharp knife, is only a good tool; one which should be wielded with skill and respect. For although we can use it to cut our bread, it is also capable of cutting our throats.

FF 88: No Contract Focus

Good contract management requires many different skills from many different disciplines. Among these are engineering, law, purchasing, auditing, accounting, scheduling, construction management, commerce, and people skills to name only a few. Because it is a new discipline in itself, eclectic in skill requirements and impacts many different project and company groups, many companies approach it eclectically. That is, they assign a group of people to accomplish its daily tasks (a committee), or they treat it functionally, letting each affected functional nest perform contract tasks. This takes the approach that "contracting is everybody's responsibility" and commonly fails. To be effective, contract activities need a central focus—contracting functions need to be vested in one or a few specialists who are integrated into the project organization. They cannot assume all contracting responsibility, for this is the domain of the project manager, but they can perform most contract tasks and, more importantly, serve as the clearinghouse of knowlege regarding contracting events and risks.

Projects of moderate to large size and risk demand that contracting responsibilities be focused and sharpened. When they are spread over many diverse positions they cease to represent a disciplined approach, but merely revert to a disjointed set of ancillary activities—often secondary to other ongoing efforts. This dilutes contracting strength, dissolves responsibility, and blunts contract tools. Most project managers who recognize the power and danger of contracting also recognize this need to concentrate contracting strengths and focus its activities. We may not be contracting professionals, so to speak, but at least we can nurture professionalism in our contract specialists and take advantage of them. They represent our guides through the exotic world of contracting. They protect us from many of its inhabitants, translate for us, and lead us around traps set by our own ego, naiveté, and lack of skill.

FF 89: The Transparent Discipline

As much as we would like to use contract specialists as part of our project teams they are difficult to find. As of now there are no college degrees granted in contract management and no recognized standards by which the ability of those holding themselves up to be contract specialists can be ascertained. It is a transparent discipline, with no licenses, registrations, or professional societies except limited and local versions pertaining to certain businesses.

Companies that recognize the need for contract specialists, or for that matter recognize contracting as so powerful and dangerous that it may require specialized expertise are way ahead of those that don't. Hopefully this need will be met in the near future by a consistent supply of uniformly accredited individuals. When this happens the transparent discipline will take shape and contracting will be performed in a much more controlled, professional manner than it is at present. Amateur hour will be over.

FF 90: Winging it

Performers, extemporaneous speakers, politicians, and athletes have all done this: skipped rehearsal, failed to practice, neglected preparation or training—waiting until the real thing and just winging it. The most they risk is loss of a few laughs, some applause, a few votes, or a trophy. Major corporations facing project contracting frequently take this same approach—they wing it. They enter contract areas with virtually no preparation, rehearsal, or plans. Unfortunately they can lose more than a few laughs. They can lose their corporate assets.

Although it is easy to understand why this occurs it is impossible to defend it. Children putting on a third grade Christmas pageant practice for hours on end, rehearsing over and over again, yet major companies investing millions or billions of dollars via contracts blunder into the contracting arena with little or no preparation whatsoever. They may fail to understand the power and danger, they may assume that amateurs can succeed without really trying, or feel that any risk entailed can be offloaded to the other party provided the price is right. All these are naive assumptions.

Good contracting requires time consuming, costly and difficult planning. This precedes any formation steps, and includes decisions concerning how many contracts to use, their respective scopes of work, how they should be priced, what information must be available at the time of bidding, negotiation and award, integrating precedent activities and sensing the marketplace for competition, capacity, and availability commensurate with the plan. Contract planning must be addressed very early in the project life, for the ability to contract is usually a prerequisite to the ability to meet project expectations. It takes time, it takes skill and it demands the attention of project and company management, because contract decisions are in fact project decisions. The less time we have to make these decisions, the greater our chances of making them incorrectly, with little information, under duress of time and money. Better to rehearse and plan when the pressure is yet to come than in the heat of project initiation. Decision making on the run is often bad decision making.

FF 91: Double Vision

We have all had neighbors, friends, or business associates who refuse to turn over responsibility to others. They are like the homeowner who hires a painter to paint his or her house, then proceeds to help mix the paint, move the ladders, direct the painter's every stroke, clean the brushes, and scrutinize and critique every other aspect of the job as it proceeds. Such a homeowner suffers from double vision: two perspectives of the project held and obeyed simultaneously. In this example the perspectives are those of performing (the painter's job) and controlling (the owner's job). It's only common sense to let someone do the work you have hired them to do.

This doesn't mean you must turn over your checkbook, close your eyes and pray that it will be done according to your C, S, and T baselines. What it means is that you allow the performer to perform, limit its authority and action, express your expectations, and inspect and test the product as it is produced and when ready for your final acceptance. You consequently release payment as prearranged steps are accomplished. This is the first rule of contract buying: tell someone what you want, get out of their way, let them do it, and then pay for it. It's surprising how many owners, contractors, and project managers fail to understand the distinction between control and performance; between doing work and directing what work shall be done.

There are many corollaries to this rule. One is that the more risk you transfer to others the more authority, freedom and flexibility you must also grant in order for them to accomplish what is required. Owners who give contractors tremendous risk and responsibility (such as with lump-sum pricing, no escalation, unclear scope, and fast-tracked design) cannot expect to engage in detailed supervision and management of those firms. On the other hand, when owners take on a majority of risk (such as with cost-plus pricing, detailed scope definition, comfortable schedules) they are entitled to direct the work of others a bit more closely.

The boundary between performance and understanding is also blurred at times. Because a contractor needs detailed information in order to perform work doesn't necessarily mean that this is the type of information the owner needs to control it, or to understand what is being performed. Performance information is not always the best type of control information. Because the contractor produces this data doesn't necessarily mean it has to divulge it to others, including the owner.

Double vision is a failure factor that applies to perspectives, and it is common when one or more contracting parties fails to understand its position, rights, responsibilities and place. These often differ from contract to contract, project to project, and they sometimes change from time to time under the same project or contract. It is not enough for the contract documents to enunciate the perspective of each party; this must be transmitted to all those who fill the organizations of each, as well as to affected third parties. Roles, relationships, and perspectives must be established early in the contracting process and understood by all who are touched by it.

FF 92: The Magic of Money

Money can't buy everything, it's true, but it sure gets of a lot of work done in the contracting business. Very little ever occurs without it, or at least without its promise. Many sponsors forget or undervalue the magic of money. It represents the single most powerful control tool the buyer of contract services can ever hope to wield. For that reason, the leverage that money brings shouldn't be abandoned too early: early payment is just as foolish as overpayment.

This is not to degrade the importance of other motivating factors which might enter into a contractual relationship, factors such as pride in one's work, self respect, business reputation, desire for referrals, and honesty. All are important and should be nurtured in every contract, and none should be taken for granted, or expected to overcome the power of money as the supreme motivating factor in business.

This aspect of power should be incorporated into every contract feature possible, not merely the price of contracted services. It should be imbedded in payment schemes, progress determinations, and witholding or release of retention. We should never neglect the ability of money to make things happen and the lack thereof to stop the project machine abruptly. There are many tools we use to supplement our ability to control the other contracting party, such as persuasion, threat of legal action, promise of future work, continued business relations, or relaxation of S and T restrictions. In general, though, comparing these to money is like comparing pocket knives to a chain saw. Money is a power tool.

FF 93: Services Are Not Goods

Most companies control purchases well. That is, they manage the procurement of *goods* in a controlled fashion, have the process well defined and understood, and have few problems with it, even with project-specific purchases. The purchasing of *services*, however, is different. This is what presents contracting problems, because contracting in a project sense most often involves the buying of services, with or without accompaning goods. And services are more difficult to price and control than are goods.

Because the manufacture and delivery of goods typically takes place under controlled *operational* conditions (a factory rather than a construction site, our offices, a project site, etc.) and has generally been performed before, the purchase of these goods is more conducive to fixed-price methods of contracting. Project-specific services on the other hand, are often influenced by: (1) greater owner involvement (the King of Change); (2) environmental factors pertaining to their performance, such as weather, labor availability, access, restrictions in work space, and constant buyer interface; (3) transient, temporary work forces and organizations; (4) mobile and temporary work tools and production facilities; and (5) uniqueness of scope.

All of these differences point out the need for special awarenesses and special care when ordering services as opposed to goods. Companies who think their existing purchasing group, which buys operating materials and equipment, is somehow equipped to manage and control contracting for project services are often sadly mistaken. Contract "buying" is much more difficult, precarious, intricate and risky than mere purchasing. It requires different planning methods, tools, skills and controls.

FF 94: Bad Paper

Contract documents, their wording, misuse, and misunderstanding represent scores if not hundreds of individual failure factors, each holding the potential for project disaster. We will address only major categories of error and misjudgement applying to poor contract documents: *bad paper.*

The first has been described already: the absence of project management and control concerns in the contract, resulting from treatment of the documents as legal entities rather than management tools. Secondly, many companies rely on "what worked last time." They simply pull out a copy of what appears to be an acceptable contract and modify it somewhat for a new application. This goes on over time to the point where, in some cases, the original document grows in size and shrinks in applicability. The practice of using and reusing project-specific documents for new project applications is termed "paperdolling" because once it is cut, a pattern can yield dozens of applications: dozens of dolls. Unfortunately there was no "last time" and what worked in the past may have no bearing on what is being attempted at present. Often the differences are subtle or known only to the original drafters of the paperdoll pattern, and these may be long gone. Paperdolling also opens our contracts to "the stickyball phenomenon." This is the process of document growth as clauses and conditions are added to protect known or perceived areas of weakness, often like band aids are placed over scars. As more applications yield more specific problems, more and more new terms and conditions are applied to the paperdoll pattern, much like a stickyball attracts and holds any litter in its path. Once a term or clause has been added it takes intelligence and courage to remove it, features often missing. Contract clauses are often seen as so much chicken soup: a little more can't hurt, and might even help. Of course this is completely incorrect.

Besides being unwieldy and messy, stickyball contracts are usually redundant, self conflicting, disorganized, and unenforceable. Just as many projects could benefit from an information diet, many contract documents could use a few less clauses and lose a few pounds from those that remain.

A related failure factor might be titled "documents under dust"; the aging of contract paper through lack of use or reference. It's surprising how many major contracts being written today contain clauses and references to laws that are outdated, have been rescinded; or rendered meaningless. Yearly contract reviews are recommended.

A final failure factor concerns undeserved reliance on industry standard documents. Many organizations and associations promulgate so called standard contract paper for use by their members whenever contracting. These represent good starting points for contract and project-specific applications, but often require major modifications before making any sense in a unique project environment.

They contain embedded assumptions regarding roles and responsibilities, are not enforceable in all jurisdictions, and, worst of all, they generally favor the contractual party represented by the drafting organization (i.e., forms issued by the American Institute of Architects favor architects, those by The Associated General Contractors of America favor general contractors, etc.). It is fair to say that authority is often slanted towards the group represented by the drafting organization, and questions of liability or responsibility are slanted away from that group. When issuing standard paper, organizations tend to take care of their own. Treat these with caution.

FF 95: Ruled by Bias

Contracting is different from many other processes in that there is never any right way to do something, only workable ways. But as with other fields where lack of experience and ignorance often dominate rational processes, contracting is replete with personal bias and prejudice. Often major contracting positions are dictated by this personal bias, at the expense of understanding and fully informed business judgment. Everyone seems to have a pet method, organization, pricing structure, or administration philosophy.

Companies flirt with contract failure when they contract *by knee-jerk*—applying controls not based on analysis of risk but obedience to personal bias. Many times this bias is ill-founded, reflecting only that which was perceived to have worked before (whether it did or not is another question) or the opposite of what was perceived to have failed. A good example is contract pricing. There are hundreds of ways to price contract work, ranging from the firm-fixed methods (lump sum, hard money) to cost-plus percentage of cost, with all sorts of penalties, bonuses and performance incentives (C, S, and T) applied to each. All of these work given proper application circumstances and all fail given others. The challenge is to know their features, understand considerations for their use, and once one is chosen, apply the associated organizations, information systems, and process controls commensurate with the particular scheme used.

When done correctly this takes time, planning, and knowledge, three elements commonly in short supply. Personal bias, however, is always plentiful. If scarcity enhances value, personal bias is next to worthless. Whenever you hear someone make statements, such as "Lump sum is the only way to go" or "We always withold 10% retention, everybody does," you are listening to the noise of personal bias. It has no place in contracting, or project management for that matter.

FF 96: Rule Makers Don't Play

One concept of good contract management is often overlooked. This is the notion that people who draft, negotiate and award contracts should have some exposure to their eventual uses. Those responsible for formation should understand administration, and vice versa. It is not uncommon for companies to segregate the two responsibilities, eliminating opportunities for appreciation of one that will benefit performance of the other. Many concepts or ideas that seem viable on paper simply cannot be enacted once the contract is signed. Formation personnel need to be aware of the effect of their actions and words—the rules they have established. The best way to gain this intimacy is by playing the game by those rules.

Ideally one has the opportunity to form a contract and then follow it to the field (whether that be literal or figurative), learning through each step and putting the resulting knowledge to use by refining the next series of contracts to be formed. But this is often impossible. Whenever those who form contracts are segregated from those who administer them, some sort of rotation of personnel between the two groups will assist in the cross-pollination of ideas that is so helpful to each.

FF 97: Dancing to the Wrong Tune

This next failure factor has to do with perceptions, or more precisely, ingrained assumptions and habits. It occurs when people enter into contracts different from those they are accustomed to working with and apply the wrong controls, approaches and processes. These are often those which have been used many times in the past and, although work well for other conditions, are not suitable for the contracting at hand. We may be dancing well, yet out of time with the music being played.

Dancing to the wrong tune is the result of continuous contracting in one mode. We tend to assume that the rules transcend the differences among contracting types, parties, objectives, and risks. They don't. The best way to counter this tendency is to review each particular contract setting before work begins, and to constantly reinforce differences as it progresses. Companies that continually contract one way are most susceptible, as are those who hire contracting or project managers entrenched in other ways of doing things—of contracting differently.

An associated problem may be that, although what has always been done in the past seems to work well, a new approach, method, or technique may prove even more successful. Companies who follow consistent contracting practices might do well by trying new ones from time to time. Pilot projects, low risk contracts, or minor

C, S, and T efforts should be used to try new approaches and new ideas. Whenever done, however, we must assure that everyone understands the differences involved and changes his or her perceptions accordingly.

FF 98: Declining Gifts

There are a few benefits to contracting that should never be overlooked; gifts that shouldn't be declined. Foremost among these is the value of competition. Companies that eschew competitive bidding, revised bidder lists, new contractors, or innovative approaches often decline the benefits these bring. Competition is free, and it works.

We see it declined by companies that dictate pricing terms to potential contractors without letting competition play a part in their establishment. When a buyer tells bidders that cost-reimbursable additions to scope *must* be priced at a markup of X% it is precluding those bidders who might have offered a lower markup absent this dictum. We also see others block the benefits of contractor innovation when they dictate performance *methods* in lieu of performance *results*, thereby excluding methods that may prove better, less expensive, and faster than those specified. As in other areas, it is often more sensible to ask performers what they can do rather than tell them what they must. Again, contracting is operational to contractors, they do it all the time, and they may have better ways to achieve the results we seek than the ways we envision. Let competition and innovation play an important role in contract formation, it can be a very valuable one. Those who ignore its value may be declining the few gifts that contracting has to offer.

FF 99: Fist Fight

Contracting is a business exercise conducted by two or more parties with mutual interests and values to exchange. It is not war, nor need it be adversarial. As mentioned before, it is a relationship based on need as well as greed. While a bit of healthy pessimism is harmless, we err when this is allowed to fester into suspicion, resentment, or distrust. There is no sense to contracting with a party one distrusts or suspects. Better to choose another, or to change your project expectations.

Contracting should be done in good faith, with a mutual respect for the value that each party brings to the project. Contrary to the opinion of some, all contractors are not trying to cheat or otherwise ripoff the project sponsor. This attitude is counterproductive and tends to be self-perpetuating. Those who begin a relationship with their fists clenched often end up in a fistfight, and project goals always suffer as a result.

FF 100: The Immortal Contract

Even though most contracts begin on a formal note, often the signing of a document, many of these are never formally terminated. They just fade away. This opens both parties to a variety of risks that typically arise towards the end of each contract. Among these are (1) the early loss of payment leverage caused by release of retention or contractor abandonment of small payment items, (2) festering of contractual disputes (backcharges, claims, and liens), (3) the loss of valuable contractor performance information (which may help us select contractors for future work), and (4) the continuation of unauthorized work and associated billings, which sometimes never seem to end. To prevent these we need to slam the contract door shut—closing out all contracts with the same degree of formality that accompanied their initiation.

Contracts, like projects, should end with a bang and not a whimper. Tools used include closeout checklists, verification of compliance, performance reviews, and termination notification of both outsiders (contractors) and insiders (our company). To protect the buyer's interests, the POWER principle should be followed: *Pay Only When Everything is Right.*

FF 101: Apologetic Management

Project sponsors and contractors are guilty of this alike. They apologize for their positions, forfeit their rights, and forego remedies they justly deserve. Contractors are guilty of this when acting in good faith and wishing to preserve good customer relations, they absorb minor changes to the scope without complaint or insistence on increases to C,S, and T (change orders). This can lead to unbearable financial burdens which, composed of individual acceptances each with little cost impact, lead to cumulative increases that are intolerable. Sponsors often wonder why contractors wait until the end of the job to bring huge requests for more C, S, and T (often in the form of claims). Many times the reason for this is the net effect of changes that have been "eaten" by the contractor throughout the performance period. They either were not recognized as such at the time, or contractor management accepted each one without considering their cumulative effects until they became immense.

Buyers apologize in different ways. They fear the spectre of lawsuits. Litigation or arbitration are seen as expensive, time consuming, and distasteful. They avoid them at all costs, including the protection of their interests or the remedy to which they are entitled. Or they avoid backcharging offending contractors for work done incorrectly or not done at all.

It makes good business sense to avoid litigation or mudslinging whenever possible, to surface disputes and reconcile them as early as we can. But the fear of formal resolution should not cause either party to take on unreasonable risk or bear unacceptable costs. Sometimes enough *is* enough.

FF 102: The Other Edge

Contracting is a two-way street, a double-edged sword. Project sponsors often forget this. They seek all sorts of ways to assure the contractor's compliance with the agreement, to force the other guy to live up to his end of the bargain. But they often neglect to consider their own duties, and these extend far beyond mere payment of the bill. Of all the causes for contractual disputes and claims, noncompliance on the part of the buyer is one of the greatest.

Buyers fail to comply when they issue late or defective expectations (specifications, preferences, guidelines), when they don't give timely or adequate inspections or acceptances of performance, when they withhold valuable project information, change criteria, limit physical access, refuse to grant authority, accelerate schedules, or otherwise impede the contractor's performance.

In so doing sponsors may think they are getting away with this noncompliance, but they rarely do. Contractors have a multitude of ways to get even, many of which the sponsor will never detect. Remember they have optimized contracting (it is operational to them). They can delay performance, cut quality, refuse to accept additional assignments, interfere with the work of the sponsor or others, and in general cause confusion and grief. None of these contributes to project success. Contractors are no different than other people. They work best when given the right tools, direction, and authority, and when they are healthy, happy, and appreciated. The best way buyers can develop and maintain these conditions is to comply with the terms of the contract they have established—to respect the sword's other edge, the one that can cut them.

FF 103: Contracting with Professionals

Every contracting party should be treated with respect. This respect pertains to what they are and what they bring to the project: uniquely qualified people with specialized skills that are needed. And this respect is important regardless of whether the contractor in question is a janitor, electrician, or architect; whether he or she wears a blue or white collar.

In the game of contracting each party is a merchant. The seller of services is marketing these, while the buyer is selling money. Neither would be in the business if this weren't true, if they were not seeking to attain something larger or different than that which they already possess. There is nothing wrong with this, for all parties enter a contract with the expectation of improving their position through it—to make a profit in one fashion or another.

There are some merchants that, while they are contractors in every sense of the word, we commonly don't think of them as such. Among these are the *professionals:* doctors, lawyers, consultants, architects, designers, engineers, realtors, analysts, accountants, and the like. A general rule, seldom followed, is that these "contractors" should be managed and controlled as tightly as are the other, non-professional types. Professionals hired to help us perform, understand or control project work are no more than contractors in pinstripes. We should not let their professionalism or demeanor somehow exclude them from the jurisdiction of sound business controls. They may be controlled differently, but they need not be controlled to a lesser extent.

Rather than rebuff attempts at control, most experienced professionals in the contracting business appreciate a buyer who knows what it wants, makes its expectations clear, and controls the process consistently. Those resenting this approach have no place in project activity. They belong in the club room, the university, or some other protected ivory tower—not on the field of contracting.

FF 104: The Souk

A souk is an arab market where goods are bought and sold. It is crowded, noisy, and full of haggling, bickering, and negotiating parties. A high premium is placed on one's ability to negotiate the right price, to hold out for the lowest (or highest) offer, and to otherwise make the best deal. In the field of project management, many sponsors view the contracting arena as if it were a souk—a place where only the crafty, devious and manipulative survive. Nothing could be farther from the truth.

Contracting parties with this attitude commonly rely on a few bargaining techniques exclusively. These are *bid shopping* and *negotiation*. Bid shopping refers to the practice of using one bidder's price against its competitors, of disclosing the lowest bid to others and asking if they can beat it. It is common and sometimes justifiable, but when used to excess, or as the sole means of pricing contract work, is dangerous; often yielding consequences never anticipated. Chief among these is the poor business relationship it initiates. Contractors who feel they have been outfoxed, or have left money on the table, seldom perform well, accept additional work, or cooperate with glee. Bid shopping starts the contracting dance with one party stepping on the other's toes. Not the preferred way.

Others place undeserved reliance on the role of negotiation. They often see it as exciting, attractive, and bringing huge payoffs in terms of higher or lower contract prices. This is simply not the case. The best tool of negotiation is competition, for it allows competitors to negotiate among themselves, so to speak, bringing the price down and avoiding ill feelings between buyer and seller.

Project sponsors who are attracted to the allure of negotiation fail to realize the advantage contractors hold—they negotiate and bid prices continually, while sponsors are infrequent, and inexperienced, negotiators. Again it is operational to contractors and project-specific to sponsors. Unless the latter is well versed in the art of negotiation it best avoid it entirely. The contracting marketplace is not yet a souk.

FF 105: Good Eyes in the Dark

As mentioned earlier, contract monitoring is a continual process designed to give project and company management a view as to the planning and conduct of contracting; how well it is managed and controlled. One often used element of monitoring is contract auditing, usually performed by an internal auditing group or by outside firms (contractors in pinstripes). Auditors look for system and operating problems, contract errors, overcharges, defalcations, unauthorized payments, unsubstantiated billings, and the like. This is well and good. These need to be prevented, and prevention is conditioned on detection.

Unfortunately, however, contract auditing is often a case of good eyes used in the dark: excellent auditing principles applied by those with little or no understanding of the business being audited. In order to detect and quantify problems of contracting, auditors need to become familiar with what, in fact, it is. They need to learn and appreciate the business of contracting, its risks, its processes, common tools, and the differing motivations and perspectives involved. Many internal and external auditors recognize this potential weakness and are taking steps to educate their staffs accordingly. When done, this will not only serve to decrease the time and cost required for audits, but improve its benefits; not only for the auditors, but, more importantly, for the project under review. Every project, no matter how well managed, could use another pair of eyes, properly focused, operating in the light of knowledge.

FF 106: The Big "Get Well"

A common and chronic contracting tendency is to gloss over small failures, cover up minor errors, suppress embryonic disputes or dispense with formal, documented decisions when possible. The refusal to surface, confront and eradicate contracting problems as soon as they are identified is one of the greatest and most common failure factors projects face. It is expressed through statements, such as "we'll handle the paperwork later," "ignore it, it'll go away," or "let it slide, it'll take care of itself." Resultantly it is manifested in the claims, disputes, mudslings, early terminations, or failed performance that surely follow.

When we avoid addressing contracting difficulty we are simply waiting for the big "get well" that never comes. Time doesn't heal contractual wounds. Neglected issues and bypassed decisions always come back to haunt us, more ferocious than ever. In contracting as in other aspects of project work, failure is best prevented or avoided, but it can never be suppressed. Time is on the side of failure, it gets stronger with each passing day.

SUMMARY

Contracting is the use of outsiders to fill project needs. It is a special area of project management, requiring special perceptions, understandings, and skills. Good contracting principles apply to external agreements and internal ones, and to upward as well as downward contracting postures. While much attention is generally given the formation and commercial administration of contracts, important controls are often lacking for contract planning and monitoring.

The greatest error found in the practice is to underestimate the power and the accompanying danger it entails. For contracting is an integral part of project management, not simply a legal exercise, and contracts represent a whole host of project management concerns, risks, and processes. The greatest weakness of project sponsors entering the contract field is one of inexperience. While contracting is new and unique to them, it is commonplace and even operational to their counterparts. This in itself puts sponsors at a disadvantage, one which points out the need for thorough planning, a contracting focus within the organization, and more uniform and professional contracting skills.

Like most project endeavors contracting is not protected by an unseen hand or a final safety net that will protect us from our own mistakes, ignorance or misjudgments. The mere passage of time doesn't reduce contractual faults, it only serves to increase their negative impacts. Contracting parties who have not experienced contractual pain and suffering had best reexamine their practices and the results they bring, for the lack of contracting sensitivities and controls may lead to unnoticed yet extremely serious consequences.

Contracting is a business practice, seldom performed well under the auspices of suspicion, mistrust, or deceit. Nor can we expect, at any price, to dump all project risk on another party via a contractual agreement. Risk must be shared, in one fashion or the other by all parties to each contract. The relationship stands on need as well as greed. When one party suffers it is often at the expense of the other, and most certainly harms the project.

Failure factors associated with contracting typically stem from our inexperience, poor perceptions, personal bias, and the inability to adapt to changing rules and contracting environments. We often expect too much from the practice, forgetting that it will exacerbate rather than relieve project-specific weaknesses. Good contract management takes careful planning, properly aligned and focused perspectives, excellent documents, and an appreciation for the motivating power of money, as well as respect for the needs and services each party brings to the arrangement.

Contracting is not a science as much as it is an art. There is seldom one right way to perform any contract tasks, but many workable ways. Pragmatism should dominate any other test of contracting methods, tools or processes. What *works* best is simply what *is* best. Often what works best is simple and free, such as the gifts of competition and innovation. We should never decline these. Nor are they alone as the only gifts contracting brings to our projects. For although the practice is replete with specific risk, it also allows us to access and use outside talents, knowledge and special skills. Without the power to contract, all these would be forsaken, and because of their value we gladly accept the added challenge that contracting represents.

CHANGE

the surest test of management measures

There are few phenomena as difficult to understand and to control as that represented by what we call change. Change is a fleeting, often misunderstood element of every business project, one which can be both insidious and healthy. In general, change is nothing more than differences that happen over time. It has been said that a wise project manager is one who understands differences, and differences are not merely evident at the beginning of a project; they occur throughout its life. *Static differences* are those demanding recognition and attention when each project is initiated. These are differences in expectations, plans, risks, perspectives, organizations, processes, and tools that shape each project, give it an individual personality, and make it separate from ongoing company operations as well as any other project yet undertaken. Once these are fixed and the project begins, it becomes immediately susceptible to *dynamic differences:* changes.

Change is a project event that can be both an agent of failure as well as one of success. It causes failure when it makes our expectations and plans obsolete, renders our processes ineffective, or otherwise frustrates our ability to see where we have been, where we are, and where we are going. It helps us succeed when we change our project goals and methods to better fit reality, a reality that in itself is never static, but constantly moving, shifting, and eluding our understanding and control.

Changes then, are perceived differences that occur over time. They can occur gradually, evolving slowly so that their effect is fluid and difficult to ascertain. Or they can surface suddenly, as when tremendous changes erupt on the project scene; forcing us to notice and respond. Often what is perceived as dramatic change is simply the cumulative effect of small, heretofore unnoticed gradual change. We often see change only when we look occasionally, not when we are constantly watching. This is why we are incapable of noticing small, daily changes in our children as they grow, and yet the same changes are startling to distant relatives seeing them for the first time after a period of years. Change is perceived as difference, and difference is sometimes unnoticeable when it is continuous and fluid.

Change can also be local in nature or far-reaching. A common tendency is to localize its occurence and conceive of limited effects without considering what are often seen as unrelated, distant impacts. The highly interdependent nature of project work, the temporary and contrived aspect of project tools and processes, and the unique environment in which we work make change at the project level seldom simple, direct, or localized. It almost always reaches out and touches many other elements, whether we have the foresight to see its impacts or not. If the first step to control of change is its recognition, the second is surely to predict its direct and indirect consequences.

There are thousands of reasons for change to occur and just as many ways in which it will. Of these, however, two distinct types seem pertinent to project work. There are changes which we initiate, knowing full well what we are doing (but perhaps not knowing the effects), called *created changes*. A second category, *incurred changes* are those which are brought about through actions or omissions of any project participant, third parties, or the project activity or environment. Of these two, incurred change is by far the most elusive, difficult, and potent in its ability to bring about failure. The goal of any change control effort is to convert all incurred changes to created ones; to recognize and accommodate changes not anticipated and to understand, if not mitigate their effects. In this way, discretionary change can be created and unavoidable change accommodated. A third response is to ignore change altogether, to continue to operate despite the incidence of change. A few projects get away with this, but not many. We may be able to walk across a busy freeway blindfolded once, but this doesn't demonstrate the wisdom of the practice.

Change has often been characterized as uncertainty, our lack of knowledge as to what will occur or, our inability to predict the future. Many changes can be predicted, however, and although the control of change always involves uncertainty, there is one certainty about which we must all be aware: change will occur. It can be created, accommodated, or ignored, but it cannot be ignored away. Because we do not see change does not mean it will not occur, it only means that we will most probably fail.

Not only do we not always recognize the existence of change, but we often are uncertain as to how it will occur, what it will affect, and what our response, if any, must be. In order to increase our chances at project success we must answer these questions regarding change. In short, we must *know* change for what it is.

THREE ELEMENTS OF THE PHENOMENON WE CALL CHANGE

As with other abstract topics of project activity, our understanding of change is aided by analyzing its components, even when this analysis may cause us to create somewhat artificial categories, boundaries, and distinctions. We have done this to better understand other topics, such as perspectives and processes, and the study of change is no different. Time is a continuum, and changes, being differences manifested through time, are only understood when they can be made discrete. Of course understanding is worthless unless it leads to control, and we cannot control continuums—only discrete elements thereof. This is the approach we shall take in this chapter, breaking change into components and controlling each. We shall use some familiar techniques to do this, including finite element models, folded map planning, and a focus on results rather than methods, all governed by the pragmatism that separates project work from other endeavors. We will study change not merely to understand and appreciate it, but to control it; to use it to achieve project success and prevent it from being an agent of project failure.

An analogy which helps us understand change compares it to the phenomenon of tossing a stone into a quiet pool of water. We can dissect each element of this change by considering the stone, the resulting splash, and the far-reaching ripples, or impacts, that the splash creates. Our three elements of change, then, are the *stone*, the *splash* and the *ripples*.

By the *stone* we mean the causes of change, what happened or failed to happen, why, and through what agent (who tossed the stone, from where and for what reason?). The *splash* is the direct and immediate impact of the change, its localized effects. The *ripples* are the continuing impacts on unchanged work; by far the most elusive and difficult to quantify. This is true for the analogy and for every project we choose to undertake.

When studying the stone, we need to understand typical causes of change so that we may prevent them, or at least predict their occurrence. We also need to identify change once it occurs—seeing the stone in the air before we hear the splash or feel the ripples on the shore. For those changes we foresee, we need to understand their direct effects, their splashes. If they were created changes, we should evaluate and approve (or reject) them before we toss them into our project pool. For incurred change, we need to quantify the direct effects so that we can distinguish them from others on our projects (those due to poor performance, poor planning, bad data, etc.), attempting to tie cause to effect in a manner that facilitates our tracking of direct C, S, and T.

As for the ripples, we need to consider them before enacting created change and to separate them from other performance information regarding unchanged work—work that is affected in an indirect way. Often these ripple effects are far more damaging than their direct counterparts: the ripples can cause more chaos than the splash, lasting longer and by their nature being more difficult to trace and quantify.

All three elements of change impact not only our work and that of others, but they cause us to reexamine the viability of the tools and processes we are using to manage the project. For one of the most significant, often overlooked ripples of change is what it does to the usefulness of our expectations, plans, perspectives, organizations, information systems, contracts, and standards. To manage change we must understand its causes (stones), effects (splashes), and impacts (ripples). The latter often radiate ever outward, causing our fragile, created network of management approaches and techniques to vibrate and flex, if not tear apart.

WHY CHANGES ARE HEALTHY

None of the previously discussed material should be construed to imply that change is intrinsically evil or always disruptive of our ability to plan and control project efforts. To the contrary, change can be healthy. It can help us sharpen our view of project goals, hone our management techniques, eliminate unneeded controls (especially those based on tradition or risks that fail to materialize) and accept that which is inevitable or not worth confronting. This happens when we recognize that our original expectations are no longer attainable or even worth pursuing, when our plans become obsolete, or when the complexion of risk varies, making our entire management approach or its component control elements infeasible. The most common reason for this is not that they are incorrect or established in error, but merely because the economic or business backdrop to our project scene has changed, thus making our needs and our efforts questionable if not unworkable.

TOLERATING TOLERANCE

Because project success is the cumulative result of workable rather than perfect or even optimum activity, we should recognize that plans and approaches are meant to change; they cannot be perfect or static. To insist otherwise is a foolish position. Accuracy or immutability of plans and expectations are not project objectives; they are too expensive to attain, and their incremental benefits do not outweigh the economic costs required (C, S, and T).

All expectations and plans must be conceived with a certain degree of tolerance. We should aim for success as a range of outcomes, not a precise point of attainment. We must then, tolerate tolerances. To do otherwise would handcuff our projects to the promises of the past—promises that may no longer be valid. We must also remember that plans and methods, no matter how sophisticated and well conceived, are never to be worshipped—only used. If change causes their revision, so much the better. It is the ends we seek, not the means.

If we try to create perfect plans and unchanging expectations we will never get past the planning stage. Given enough time and resources, someone will always be able to create better versions of each. Many companies are guilty of missing tremendous business opportunities by ignoring the value of timing in project accomplishment, for often it is not just *what* is attained, but *when* that is critical.

The place for continuous study is the university or the laboratory, not the field of competitive business.

What this means is that our attempts to understand change should lead us to its accommodation and management, never to its prevention. That costs too much and returns nothing. Rather than insist on planning that foresees all change from the perspective of project initiation, we need to employ our concept of folded map planning: addressing the near term while providing for the accommodation or control of future events once they are within our range of vision and nearer our grasp.

TWO TYPES OF CHANGE

An experienced traveller knows which obstacles to destroy and which to travel around. This is also true when encountering change. The two types of change we will encounter with most projects are created and incurred versions. When we decide to accelerate our project schedule by two months in order to enter the marketplace with our new capacity, service, or product (the project goal), we have decided to change; creating a timing change. When delays caused by poor performance, rework, or lack of resources force a two-month suspension of work, we have suffered an incurred change. If the purchase price of planned equipment exceeds its estimated cost by $10,000 we have incurred cost change. However, if changing technology makes a more expensive machine feasible because of reduced operating costs, we may decide to select the newer machine, thus creating a change in our estimate. In either case, with created or incurred change, once the change has been recognized we must modify our plans and baselines accordingly. To do otherwise would invite misunderstanding or downright failure, for it is meaningless to use obsolete baselines and plans—ones out of synchronization with reality.

The goal of any project management approach should be to convert incurred changes, once recognized and quantified, into created changes, and to treat their impacts no differently. Incurred changes exist, whether we want them to or not. They must be recognized and accommodated. Because change was not chosen doesn't mean it should not be enacted. We should formalize informal changes, no matter how distasteful or surprising they are.

So many companies fail to heed this advice. They ignore change, belittle its impacts, and at times try to comingle it with originally planned work. They succeed in disguising change and masking its effects—just the opposite of what should be done. Suppressed change is no less potent or damaging. In fact it tends to grow and strengthen the longer it is suppressed. It cannot be wished away.

WHAT CAUSES CHANGE?

Acts or omissions contrary to our project models cause project change. They make our methods suspect, if not our expectations questionable. While instruments or agents of change are diverse and vary with industry, project, and environmentally specific settings, there are some general categories of change, typical causes that are worth a brief review. Here is a partial list.

Typical Causes of Change

Changing markets

Actions or inactions of business competitors

Changing consumers, buyer preferences, or demand

Moving technologies

Fluctuations in prices, costs, and availability

Economic instability

Unrealistic expectations

Poor plans

Inoperative methods, processes, tools, organizations, or standards

Defective instructions, contracts, and specifications

Late delivery or performance

Errors, mistakes, and misunderstandings

Noncompliance with contracts and procedures

Regulatory changes

Political instability

Changed or unknown site conditions

Impact of collateral work

Nonproject changes (disruption in the company)

Restrictions in work methods

Need to accelerate work

Loss of management confidence

Intermediate project failures

Some of the items listed are both causes and impacts of change, and many changes are due to more than one cause. Again, the only thing about which one can be certain is that change will occur. What is very uncertain is our ability to respond to it in an intelligent manner, and to take prudent management action under changed conditions. It is this ability that often separates successful projects from failed ones.

OUR REACTION TO CHANGE

Each business project has its own way of reacting or responding to change. Forgetting specific techniques for a moment, there seem to be a few categories of response available to us. Often we move from one response to another quickly, proceeding down this list:

1.	*Ignorance*	Not seeing change
2.	*Recognition*	Identifying changed conditions
3.	*Accommodation*	Living with the effects
4.	*Control*	Directing and channeling changes

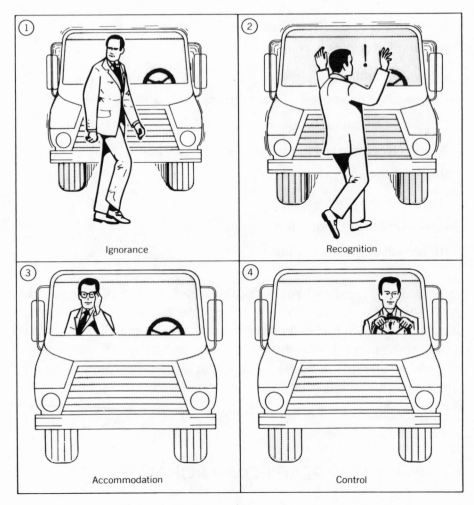

Figure 10-1   Change: Four levels of reaction.

The goal of prudent management is to move quickly from position 1 to 4 on the list. A number of techniques help us do this; help us increase our level of reaction. We can visualize each step by thinking of change as a runaway truck, speeding towards our project, much like that shown by Figure 10-1. The first level, ignorance, has a fairly predictable result. This is another case where what we don't know will hurt us. Perceiving change, giving it recognition, is helpful only if it leads to levels 3 or 4, for recognition alone only serves to intensify our anxiety if not our suffering. We need to accommodate or control, to ride or drive the change vehicle.

For some cases merely being a passenger is enough to ask for, while for others to be able to steer the vehicle, to make it go where we wish, is achievable. Any steps taken to advance our position with respect to change, from one of innocent victim to beneficiary of the phenomenon are valuable ones. We can examine our response to change for real projects by applying this simple concept, by testing our approach to see if it helps move us from the path of change to its controls. The first step is recognition and understanding, for we cannot control that which we do not understand. We need not only recognize the causes of change themselves for each project we undertake, but to develop a fuller appreciation of change itself: we need to know what change means.

WHAT CHANGE MEANS TO US

Once we have accepted the inevitability of changes and have some respect for the impacts they bring, we are able to better understand our project approaches and tools. The first understanding that follows is that success cannot be attained if we expect precise, pinpoint results. If we expect a venture to return 15.5% on our investment and it returns 15.3% we cannot pronounce it a failure, for success and failure are areas of performance, not points. There must be tolerance in any definition of either. Secondly, we recognize that, to withstand changed conditions, our management perspectives and tools must bend in the wind of change without breaking. We must design flexibility into their structures and conduct, avoiding rigid, ironclad methods, planning icons, or immutable baselines.

Here we can take another example from the world of physical science, or to be more precise, the practice of structural design. In years past it was accepted practice to design buildings to withstand the force of earthquakes by making them rigid, heavy, strong, and therefore, it was hoped, able to survive the massive accelerations and forces brought about by a quaking earth. Sometimes this worked, but more often than not it achieved two unwanted results: (1) structures so designed and constructed cost a lot more to construct (in terms of C, S, and T) and (2) the resulting buildings were often *more susceptible* to earthquake damage.

The reason for the latter effect has to do with the nature of earthquakes themselves. By moving the building foundation they in turn accelerate the structure, back and forth, time and time again. This acceleration when multiplied by the mass of the building yields tremendous forces (F = MA), forces which in turn serve to tear the structure apart. In effect the strength of these buildings, in terms of mass and rigidity, intensified the earthquake's effect. Something else was needed, for it seemed the larger and stronger buildings were made, the more they shook themselves to death.

Hope came with an understanding that it might be better to accommodate earthquake forces rather than withstand them; to use intelligence rather than sheer strength. Analysis of earthquake activity yielded the concept of *tuned* design, where buildings were designed to bend, vibrate, and flex at certain points; yielding to forces and dampening their impacts rather than contributing to their power. More slender, flexible, and lighter materials and designs were the result of an understanding of the nature and mechanisms of earthquakes. The resulting buildings were not only more earthquake resistant, but less expensive as well.

Can we borrow this idea to make our projects more change resistant? Of course. We do so when we design flexible procedures, processes with exceptions, tools that can be modified to meet their uses, and approaches that accommodate change by bending in its wake. Our key to surviving change is similar to that of designing buildings; we aim to accommodate change rather than confront it head on. An added attraction to the new earthquake design was that lighter, more flexible buildings tended to lose less parts and throw less material onto their neighbors once an earthquake came along.

History has shown that the majority of deaths experienced in earthquakes came from falling building materials. Heavier, "stronger" designs, with their load bearing walls, massive concrete and steel members, and added reinforcements tend to throw much of these down on the poor people fleeing them. In essence, that which was designed to protect us actually hurt. Rigid project measures have the same effect. They don't protect us from change, but ironically intensify its damage.

A lesson we can take from this example is that, to bring value and not failure, project measures (plans, processes, organizations, contracts, standards, information systems, and the like) need to strike a balance between the need to stand on their own, to maintain structural integrity and the need to flex to change. None of us needs limp, transparent measures nor those constantly changing with the slightest tremor, but neither do we need massive, rigid, stationary measures. The ideal approach is to choose those that can function well under expected conditions *and* under changed ones; that can bend but not break.

FLOATING ON AN ENDLESS OCEAN

Change means much more than the need for resiliency. In order to recognize change (a factor precedent to accommodation or control) we must know what exists before change occurs. Like a ship on an endless ocean, we cannot determine our direction, speed, or even location without referencing external markers—buoys, shorelines, or stars. Absent these the only way we can tell we are moving is by the consumption of fuel. This tells us nothing about where we have been, presently are, or are headed. Some projects are in this category; the only way we know we are moving is by continuous consumption of C, S, and T. This is a very poor indicator of progress, to be kind. It only tells us what we've spent—not what we bought, or the value thereof.

Tools needed for change detection, then, are baselines, markers, plans, and anything else giving a continuous location of our position. This is where information systems, properly tuned, can be of immense help. They can tell us what was *accomplished* in addition to what was *spent*. Any system which doesn't provide this information is merely a fuel gauge, telling us what has gone and what is left; not a compass, speedometer, or odometer. All are needed to understand and manage change.

FROM POINTS TO BANDS, AND THE EXTRAPOLATION TRAP

A healthy respect for change involves not merely recognizing each change incident (or possibility), but the ability to synthesize change data to see trends and predict impacts. This need is often over-looked, for companies sometimes focus on each individual change as if it were an isolated occurrence (or omission). They fail to see change trends and underlying causes of many recurring changes. Both are necessary to move from a change victim to a change man-ager, to progress from position one to position four on our reaction scale.

In so doing however, we must be skeptical of false trends and avoid a simple linear extrapolation of change into the future. It is too ephemeral and influenced by too many factors to be plotted in a straight line. Like industrial progress in our society, the future cannot be predicted through linear extrapolation (this is why we are not living on Mars or flying helicopters to work each day—the old futurists simply extrapolated existing trends). So we should expect performance *bands* rather than precise *points*, we should build flexi-bility into project measures, and understand change trends without being captured by them.

WHAT WILL, WHAT WON'T

One final awareness is needed before we can understand what change means. We must be able to distinguish, for each of our projects, between that which will change and that which won't. For although change affects a great deal of our project environment, there are some items that we should hold unchangeable. In general, specific approaches, measures, and techniques can and will change, while general concepts, principles, and proven business practices should not. A perceptive project manager knows for example, that while different changes will occur on different projects, the concept of change and the principles of change control should not change. Knowing that which is changeable from that which isn't is a key to good project management, and essential to the maintenance of sanity, for attempting to preserve a changing measure or to modify an immutable law of business can be maddening. The following list may help, in a small way, to prevent such a frustrating exercise.

What Will Change	What Won't Change
Project expectations	Role of expectations
Specific plans	Concepts and techniques of planning (i.e., the folded map)
Perspectives	Three major perspectives and the importance of perspectives
Information systems	Role of information, uses, and abuses
Specific organizations	Need for focused responsibilities
People assigned	Value of people skills and importance of peoples' needs
Project procedures	Focus on process control and results
Contracts	Power and danger of contracting
Frequency and severity of change	Inevitability of change
Project standards	Role and weaknesses of standards
Specific outside factors	Need for consideration of outside factors
Particular failure factors encountered	Failure avoidance as the key to project success

THE PROCESS OF CHANGE MANAGEMENT

Once the nature and causes of change have been mastered through understanding, we are in a position to manage specific changes our projects will encounter. Whether these changes are created or incurred, there are five general steps involved. Depending on their severity and frequency, some changes may involve intermediate steps or can be handled by merging two or more of the steps listed. In any case, the following need be taken for each incidence of change:

Created Changes	Incurred Changes
Identify	Recognize
Evaluate	Quantify
Approve/reject	Accept
Incorporate	Accommodate
Process	Process

No change can be managed unless it is identified or recognized. Discretionary changes (ones which we may or may not accept) should be thoroughly evaluated in terms of C, S, and T costs (both direct and, most importantly, *impact* or ripples). For incurred changes, commonly identified after the fact, we need to ascertain the resulting changes to C, S, and T as best we can; some may be incurred already, some may be forthcoming. Created changes then go through some sort of approval process, hopefully quickly and by well-informed managements. For incurred changes, this step is mere acceptance and notification of all parties that the change has occurred, or is imminent. Each change is then incorporated into project plans, processes and other measures, often resulting in modified C, S, and T baselines, contracts (change orders), or future plans. Finally, we must process each change depending upon its nature and impacts. Should the change be contractual in nature for example, we need to issue a modification to the contract documents. If it results in increased costs, we need to pay for it, and so forth. We process each change by changing our performance, understanding, and control of the changed item or events. These steps need not take place consecutively, for some instances lend themselves to concurrent, parallel steps. And we often are not able to follow each step in the order shown (although this is highly recommended).

Sometimes as with incurred changes, identification (step one) occurs only after processing (step five) problems are encountered. When a contractor sends an invoice for work performed yet not in the contract, for example, the payment process forces the identification of the change after the fact. Even under these conditions, however, it makes good business sense to formalize this incurred change, treating it as if it were created. This would include the quantification of C, S, and T impacts, an evaluation of submitted costs, and the eventual issuance of a change order to the contract.

It isn't always necessary to go through each of these steps for each change. Some are so minor and local as to make their formalization impractical, or more irritating than the change itself. What is important, however, is that the steps be *considered* for each change, that project management consciously decide how best to accommodate or control each separate change incident. Once we have become practiced at each, we will be better able not only to control the impacts of each change, but to foresee changes and trends in time for their prevention, circumvention, or the least painful accommodation possible. Only then will we be able to call ourselves change managers rather than change victims. This is an important title, for one cannot expect to manage projects without being able to manage change. Of this we can be certain.

FAILURE FACTORS

As can be expected there are an unlimited number of ways to become victims of change. They cannot all be described here, but we can list and describe major categories of failure. In this regard the majority of projects which fall victims to change are those that fail to accept its inevitability, do not know what it is, misunderstand its elements, and do not realize its beneficial sides. These projects often ignore change, try to confront it through sheer force (or edict), or confuse changeable measures with concepts and roles that should never change.

Finally failure strikes these projects when they do not manage change as they do any other process: by taking distinct, linked steps leading to its accommodation or control. In reviewing the collection of failure factors that follows, it should prove enlightening to consider which of these mistakes were made—to isolate the agency of failure in the phenomenon of change.

FF 107: Forbidding Change

Companies or projects that have been bitten by the change monster one too many times may try to forbid change by edict: to outlaw change. This works only when created change is forbidden and has no impact on incurred change. The practice of forbidding created change also occurs among highly mobile technologies, where to react to every possible improvement in the project goal would bring about dynamic plans, breathing baselines, and moving expectations. Even though it is possible (and sometimes advisable) to freeze each of these, it may be expensive in terms of C, S, and T to do so. Sometimes, however, expectations and plans must be solidified before they can be attained.

When we try to forbid incurred change we are simply restricting our ability to recognize, accommodate and control it. We cannot prohibit its occurrence, only its management.

Although the prohibition of discretionary change, those types of created changes we can avoid, is possible, the practice works well only for short-term projects involving low technology work, little interdependencies and simple project goals. The longer a project's duration, more complex its activities, and more organizations involved the more prone it is to both created and incurred changes.

Two unfavorable reactions need addressing whenever change is outlawed. First, people needing change may try to hide it. If budgets are about to be exceeded, the need for a new budget (change) might be circumvented by simply creating a second category of work falling outside the project budgetary restrictions (charging another account number). Or when increased contract work is needed and change orders are forbidden, we might see a new contract issued to the same contractor—eliminating the need to "change" the existing agreement. These are but two ways in which people mask changes when they are forbidden, and there are many others.

A second problem encountered is the needless padding of C, S, and T baselines when they are prepared as part of a project plan. Knowing that changes to the work will not be allowed, people may add baseline contingencies to cover its cost—thereby circumventing the need to increase budgets, issue change orders to contracts, revise schedules, and so forth. Any contractor quoting lump-sum work will add cost contingencies to its price if told that no changes will be allowed once work is started. Again the phenomena of changes will occur. Whether we choose to acknowledge them is a different matter.

FF 108: Blind to Change

We can become blind to change by ignoring it, in which case we avert our eyes when it occurs, or we can fail to see it even when we desire to do so, because we do not have the plans, baselines, or status information that would give change visibility. Often both are due to our failure to segment the project (or our models of it) into discrete, noticeable increments, elements or pieces; choosing instead to manage a continuum. Since change is often evolutionary rather than revolutionary, it is difficult to detect minor continuum movements. Change is occurring, but we cannot see it.

We are also blind to change when our models do not highlight trends or allow us to see signs of future change until we hear the splash; or worse, feel the ripples. This often leads to what has been called "information shock," the sudden and massive awareness that something has been going wrong for a long time. It also leads to the continued use of expectations, plans, organizations, and other management measures that may have been deemed obsolete long before, if only we knew what was happening earlier.

It is not unusual to see companies managing the wrong project with the right tools—that is, they are using measures appropriate for the project they originally planned, but the current project bears no resemblance to it. The project has changed underneath them, without their knowledge. They have been blind to the cumulative effects of change; managing a project that exists only in their memory.

FF 109: Spurning Change

This failure factor is similar to change blindness. It happens when we ignore changes we have seen, hoping they will go away if we give them no attention. Even though most managements would admit the need to cope with recognized change, they often do not recognize it because of system or process weaknesses that hide it. Management reporting is an example. Many reports list only those project changes that have been approved; ones already processed through the five steps of change management. Pending, potential, disputed, or nonquantified changes are often unreported and thereby ignored. For management to have change visibility, they need not only see those changes already accepted or approved (these are history), but changes about to occur. These should always be listed and described.

FF 110: Hiding Behind Change

Although the phenomenon of change has a healthy side, it can also be subverted, bringing benefits to those using it for their own purposes and often at the expense of the project. This is seen when people use impending or occurring change to (1) defer needed action, (2) discredit plans and management measures, (3) ignore project policy or procedures, or (4) mask or conceal defalcations and fraud.

The most common example of management procrastination in view of impending change has to do with the myth of reorganization. If a reorganization is about to occur (or has recently occurred) it is often seized upon as reason enough not to proceed with needed activity or decisions. We know this is happening when we hear statements like "No need to fix that now, it'll only change once we reorganize," or "I know that needs to be done, but we just reorganized! Give everyone a few months to settle into the new organization and then bring it up for review."

Because plans and baselines are not exactly attained is no reason to abandon them. Unfortunately some people use a failure to achieve exactly what was expected (which in itself is not failure, per se) as reason to discredit the plans and the measures taken to achieve them. Projects that insist on precise achievements, not bands with tolerance levels, are most susceptible to this defective rationale.

Flexible, change-oriented procedures often contain exceptions to be used under certain conditions. When these exceptions are abused people are taking advantage of our need to accommodate change in a process sense.

The confusion, misunderstanding, or even chaos resulting from massive or continuous change also provides a cover for theft, conversion, fraud, and other forms of dishonesty, if not crime. Swirling change is like a smokescreen, disruptive and harboring opportunism; making it difficult to determine exactly what is going on until it is too late. Sometimes those hiding behind change are avoiding time behind bars.

FF 111: Brittleness

Brittleness is a characteristic of management models and measures that are not responsive to change. A general rule is that which will not bend must break, and many a plan, process, contract, or other measure, while excellent under static conditions, will simply snap at the first sign of change. We cannot tolerate inflexible methods or unchanging perspectives. They have no business in the world of projects.

Brittleness is also seen in intricate, highly detailed processes and performance schemes. These often resemble a house of cards, in appearance and stability. Needless process or procedural interdependencies lead to brittleness and rigidity that has no contribution to project strength. When the smallest of exceptions cause the house of cards to tumble down, the house should never have been built.

A brittle attitude is also damaging. It is represented by a refusal to bend perspectives, modify approaches or amend concepts, even when change has rendered them obsolete. Sometimes we hang onto our old notions so tightly that we simply do not know when to let go. Change should cause us to question our grasp, if not loosen it.

Sometimes a brittle attitude is called stubborness. This is not a very scholarly term, but an accurate one.

FF 112: Local Vision

When we fail to see or consider change impacts, the far reaching ripples of each incidence, we are restricting our vision and our grasp to local effectiveness. We are also localizing our control efforts when we fail to see change patterns or trends, for ripples of change extend spatially (to other parts of the project) as well as across time. Poor change visibility also refers to our inability to isolate change causes from their effects. We sometimes confuse symptoms with causes, making the traceability of problems to their sources difficult. As with disease, change is best managed through cure rather than mere treatment of symptoms.

FF 113: Encouragement, Amplification, and Arson

Believe it or not, we are not all trying to prevent or control change. Some of us actually promote it, stir it up, and amplify, rather than dampen its effects. Why? For a number of reasons, all contrary to project objectives. The first, deferral of action or decisions, has already been mentioned. Sometimes this is done to shift attention away from areas of poor performance or toward areas of good performance. More insidious reasons deal with the manipulation of outsiders (contractors, the public, the company) and attempts to discredit those responsible for the change.

When a lot of costly mistakes have been made, massive project change allows them to be buried in a common grave, along with meritable plans and activities. Changes hide evidence. Those wishing to bury their mistakes look forward to the possibility of a slate wiped clean by change. Finally we must never forget that there may be project enemies lurking on the fringes, in the company or outside, trying to discredit the entire effort. By encouraging and amplifying changes they could be building a case to terminate the project entirely. Change is not always a naturally occuring phenomenon, void of any human intent; it can be contrived, guided, and manipulated to serve the needs of its benefactors. These tend to give the spark of change fuel, fan it with oxygen, and hope the resulting conflagration will consume the entire project. In this regard change is like a fire. It can occur spontaneously, through accident (mismanagement), or as the result of arson.

SUMMARY

Once every project begins it becomes susceptible to dynamic differences: changes. They inevitably occur, and we cannot wish, hope, or order their absence. Most changes fall into the categories of created or incurred change, the latter being the most difficult to identify or accommodate. The analogy of a stone tossed into a quiet pool serves to isolate three change elements: the cause (stone), local effects (splash), and far reaching impacts (ripples) that inevitably radiate across time and distance.

Some changes are healthy rather than disruptive. These are the ones that result in more appropriate, representative project models or measures—ones better fitted to current project risks and conditions. Because changes are bound to occur, we create expectations and plans that can be met through a range of achievements rather than precise points of value. We tolerate some tolerance in our definition of success. Our reaction to each change incident can range from simple ignorance to practiced control, with the goal of change management to increase this level of reaction as quickly as possible, whenever we can.

The fact that changes occur also means that flexibility should be built into our project measures, allowing them to flex without snapping in the wake of change. We need continuous status information to detect our project positions and to notice change while it occurs. Prudent project managers are always scanning their baselines to determine where they have been, where they are, and where they are headed, trying to understand what has been gained in addition to what has been consumed in terms of C, S, and T. They also recognize that while specific approaches and techniques may change from time to time, certain business principles and sound management concepts always remain valid. Some things should change and some should not. A wise manager is able to distinguish between these.

Successful projects cannot forbid change entirely, nor can they avert their eyes to it or spurn it once seen. They must manage change as they do other project risks, by establishing and operating a change process consisting of a series of linked steps leading from its identification to eventual processing. Lastly, a bit of healthy skepticism is needed to guard against those who might hide behind change or encourage and amplify it to achieve personal benefit. Change can be contrived and manipulated.

It can also be ignored or managed, unexpected or foreseen, accommodated or controlled. It can never be prevented, nor suppressed once it occurs. We must address change; it will not allow us to do otherwise. Should we choose to ignore it we do so at our peril, and in so doing convert change itself from an interesting and challenging phenomenon to a powerful and relentless agent of failure.

CHAPTER
eleven

STANDARDS

shadows of shadows

Although the nature of project work limits the role of standards, they are used nonetheless, and a great deal of insight into project failure can be gained through their consideration. The term *standard* is used here to represent any management measure brought from outside the project to help shape its conduct. The study of standards, as they are used in project settings, is especially intriguing because they represent a reversal of common methodology used for other project activity.

Standards are patterns that we use to *create* and *define* reality. Whereas planning, perceptions, information systems, and the like (other project management measures) typically use some sort of models to understand and control project work, models that approximate reality, standards are used to make reality approximate the model. In this manner standards can be thought of as reverse models, seeking not to represent reality but to be represented by it. The resulting reality (measures used successfully) is often used as a model for the next project. If we think of a model as a conceptual *shadow* of a project, standards are often shadows of those shadows. In studying standards here, we must constantly refer to this orientation, for there is a good chance that reality and its representations can become confused, and we may be unable to distinguish between them. Of course that condition itself (confusion between reality and its various representations) is often very typical of actual project life.

LITTERS OR LINEAGE

Standards then are used to shape reality, and often they have been shaped by previous reality themselves. That is, a model of one project (hopefully a successful one) is used to be the standard for the next project. The resulting measure (plan, process, system, tool, etc.) is then used as a standard for the project that follows. In this way a project standard is carried down through many "generations" of projects, with each project "product" being used as the standard for the ensuing project.

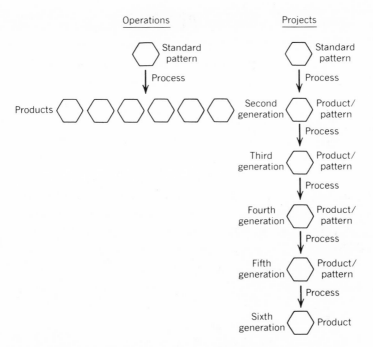

Figure 11-1 Litters versus lineage: Using standards to reproduce results.

This lineage of standards is quite different from the reproduction
of standards used in the operational environment. As shown by
Figure 11-1, operations create one pattern (standard) and use it to
produce multiple results (products) simultaneously or through repetitive means. A simple example might be a casting die for engine
blocks. Once a master die is created it is used time and time again
to produce thousands of products, what we might call a product
"litter"; several offspring at one time.

In the project world we seldom have the benefit of reproduction
by litter. Instead we find one standard used to produce one offspring, and that offspring being used in turn as the standard for the
following project. Projects use standards as a series of generations,
one following the other over time. Operations tend to reproduce by
a batch process, with one standard producing many simultaneous
results. Herein lies the major difference between these two types of
endeavors regarding standards, and embedded in this difference are
many subtle causes of failure.

WHAT ARE THEY?

Standards can also be thought of as *managerial templates,* tools used to ensure consistency or uniformity from project to project. They can be high level, summary policies carried from one project to another, or at the other extreme, simple, specific, and very detailed process steps. Any measure transcending two or more projects within any given company can be termed a standard. In order to fully understand the variety of standards found on any project and the broad scope of the term "standard" itself, we should consider some examples. The following list is by no means intended to be all inclusive, representative of any particular project, or arranged in any priority whatsoever. It merely serves to identify some types of various standard measures we might see among many projects.

Types of Standards

Policy	Specifications	Processes
Procedures	Designs	Responsibilities
Organizations	Change categories	Budget levels
Staffing levels	Procurement types	Audit types
Funding criteria	Quality programs	Research steps
Plans	Written copy	Personnel management
Graphics	Scheduling levels	Pricing methods
Contracts	Materials	Accounting codes
Equipment types	Proposals, bids	Information systems
Reports	Configurations	Work breakdowns

WHO NEEDS 'EM?

If projects are all different, the value of standards that exist to create similarity among projects might be questioned. But this is not the sole purpose for their use. Standards have many purposes, and whether any given standard fulfills each contributes to its individual success. Before we dispense with standards or minimize their application, we had best understand their many reasons for being. Most standards are employed to achieve one or more of the following objectives.

1. *Gain Project Understanding/Approval/Acceptance.* Every project must be funded or otherwise approved by the sponsoring company, and, in turn, by other participants as they are invited to join the project effort. By standardizing certain aspects of a project we are able to better describe it to the funders or approvers—to translate specific project goals and activities into terms they understand. The more we can express the project in terms understandable to them, including standards, the greater our chance of acceptance or approval. The more the project appears to be nonstandard, abnormal, or "weird," the more difficult acceptance will be. Project managers trying to gain funding or other approvals know this, and color their project descriptions and expectations in terms understandable to their audience, and ones with which they are comfortable. Every project involves going out on a limb. Approvers are more likely to follow the project out on that limb if they believe it to be a short trip, over familiar territory.

2. *Facilitate the Creation of Tools and Processes.* As opposed to most business operations, project work requires the creation of tools and the establishment of processes before either can be used. From time to time certain elements of each can be transferred from one project application to another. These allow the creation or establishment of project-specific measures to proceed at a faster pace and less cost.

3. *Avoid Scratchwork.* Any time we have to start from scratch, go back and reinvent the wheel or otherwise retrace steps taken for previous projects we are increasing C, S, and T and reopening new

doors to failure. Standards let us begin project-specific work without starting from scratch. Consider the need to build project tools and processes. Suppose these can be compared with the need to construct a certain brick wall, of specific height, width and length; one never before constructed. Because this "project" is so unique, we could presume nothing done before may apply—an assumption causing us tremendous additional work if followed.

We would have to create the building products from scratch—inventing the brick-making process, securing a source of clay, building a kiln, crafting brick molds, developing the proper material and water mixture and experimenting with the best firing techniques. Then we would have to invent mortar, find its components, combine them, and use the result to bind our bricks together. A lot of work for a simple brick wall! How might the use of standards have helped, yet still allowed us to create our very own, distinct and unique project?

The answer lies in the concept of components, or standard components to be more precise. Standard mortar mix and standard bricks would have greatly eased our wall-building project. These uniform components would have eliminated the scratchwork just described, allowing us to concentrate on the *differences* that our project entailed: the length, height, and width, or perhaps the pattern, finish, and configuration of the bricks, openings, and layout of the wall itself. The fact that standard components (bricks and mortar) were used in no way lessens the uniqueness of our result, it merely allows us to be similar at a level that doesn't restrict us in any way and helps us in many—at the detailed component level.

For actual projects there are many figurative "components" similar in their use to the bricks and mortar of this example. These include schedule networks, budget classifications, estimating line items, planning steps, audit steps, and project change categories to name a few. We use them to "build" specific schedules, budgets, estimates, plans, audit programs and change controls respectively, without starting from scratch for each project.

4. *Bridge the "Intuitive Leap."* When mathematicians set out to prove a certain theorem, they begin with few known equalities, and build, in a step-by-step fashion known as *rigor,* through a series of incremental proofs leading to the final conclusion they seek. Rigor-

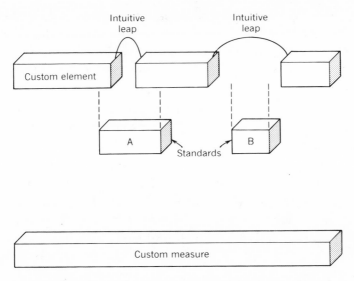

Figure 11-2 Using standards to bridge intuitive leaps.

ous proofs are correct, irrefutable, self-justifying, and sound. They are also tedious, time consuming, and dull. When we build project processes or procedures rigor has little place. Its use would create perfect processes at too high an expense in terms of C, S, and T. We need to shortcut rigorous determinations and create useful, available tools or processes that work now, not in the future. Standards help us do this. They "bridge the intuitive leaps" that are left by nonrigorous processes.

This somewhat abstract notion can be better developed through the illustration found in Figure 11-2. Suppose the top series of bars represents a project estimating process. Because we are dealing with a unique business endeavor we cannot use a standard process, but would like to use standard components thereof if possible. In this regard our intention is to combine custom components with standard ones to create a project-specific pattern (estimating process to be used whenever estimates are needed for our project). The alternative of creating an entirely custom-made process (scratchwork) is too costly and time consuming. We have rejected it.

When writing the description of the process, we come to two areas that are fairly common, low in risk, repetitive, and best handled through standard "subprocesses," shown here as "A" and

"B." Suppose "A" is a list of material categories, and "B" is a series of standard productivity factors for certain types of labor-intensive work. The estimating process would refer to these standards. Rather than list them, describe their creation, and take the estimator through a rigorous determination of the material categories (why they were chosen, why others weren't, how common each is, when to combine certain ones, how to distribute common materials among them, etc.), the procedure would merely refer to the standard list and dictate its use. The same for labor productivity factors. No need to sample other projects, perform a statistical analysis, and rigorously determine which factors should be used; our process would simply adapt an existing standard, called "B" here.

These two standards can be thought of as the bricks and mortar of our procedural wall: our project-specific management measure called estimating. Note, however, that the lengths of bars labeled "A" and "B" appear to be shorter or longer than needed to fit the intuitive gaps in our process. This is done merely to point out that the use of standards in this fashion (as building blocks for management measures) is never perfect nor always efficient, or even successful. Since "A" seems to be larger than the gap it is used to close, it may be deemed more than needed; useful but a bit wasteful. On the other extreme, "B" seems inadequate to fill the gap for which it is used. Perhaps it contains not enough steps to take the process across the intuitive leap needed.

In any case, standards don't always "fit." Of the two misfits shown in the figure, "A" is wasteful but successful, while "B" is a failure. As with mathematical proofs, often those intuitive leaps that one takes for granted, identifies with *rote*, are the ones that give us so much trouble. The intuitive leap is often a stumble.

5. *Achieve Consistency if Not Uniformity.* Consistency and uniformity are ultimate operational goals. Although projects are nonuniform and inconsistent by their definition, there is room for (even need for) uniform or consistent project elements. Of these (uniformity and consistency) consistency is probably the most applicable. Uniformity implies sameness, similarity, and identicality. We see very little of this from project to project, but some. Consistency implies similar aspects among different elements. Here projects can be consistent in component used and yet nonuniform in final configu-

ration. This occurs when standard elements are used across projects; when certain similarities bridge the overall differences obtained.

Consistency has tremendous value for those undertaking more than one project. It allows certain rules, laws, and assumptions to transcend projects; having application to all. It allows a certain degree of comparison between projects, perhaps not comparisons of overall achievement but of performance of certain similar, component activities. Consistency also allows mutual understandings among project participants as to what is to be done, how, and by whom. Consistency is, in effect, a common project language. Whenever standards can be used to promote consistency, without interfering with achievement of specific, different project objectives, we are better able to communicate, measure, predict, and control project work.

6. *Highlight Important Differences.* If one project is totally different than others (never possible) it would be impossible to separate and concentrate on significant differences. We would have no yardstick, no normality baseline against which to measure and understand differences within the project. It would also be difficult to point out significant differences to others, including outsiders. The ability to do so often helps prevent incorrect assumptions regarding success or failure, the imposition of standard controls that don't fit, or the use of standard tools which don't work. We need to understand, and quite often to articulate, differences that are important and distinguish them from the "background noise" of minor differences. Standards suppress this noise. They eliminate unnecessary differences, or differences that cost more than they are worth.

7. *Assist Nonproject Efforts.* Project participants and project managers are not so self-indulgent and project-obsessed as they might sometimes be portrayed. From time to time they do raise their eyes from their primary tasks (projects) to other needs. Standards that are used on projects satisfy some of these. By contributing to consistency in project results, they help those who eventually inherit the project objective from the project team—the operations organization. These people come from other operations and would like to apply a few of their techniques and understandings without having to familiarize themselves with an entirely new operation,

from scratch. Anything done to improve consistency in results improves their eventual understanding and use. There is no need for a successfully achieved project goal that cannot be used. If we think of the goal as a physical facility (say our bicycle factory), operations of the factory would be assisted if we built standard processes, used standard equipment, designed standard plant layout and line configuration, and supplied interchangeable parts. Much more difficult would be the job of operating a totally different, unique facility. Standardization helps ensuing operations—another reason to look beyond project success.

Standardization also helps concurrent and future projects to the extent that successful measures can be transposed to them, or when their performance can be intelligently compared to another project. And it lends itself to production of project spinoffs that might have nonproject applications, such as within other areas of the sponsoring company. If everything were foreign, little could be adapted to external uses. Standards make intermediate project products, tools, measures, processes, and the like identifiable and understandable by outsiders, thereby increasing the possibility that they will be taken and used elsewhere.

Never to be forgotten is the eventual consumer of the project goal. We have addressed internal consumption by other organizations within our company (the operations group using our new factory), but have so far omitted consideration of the customer—that oft-overlooked entity down at the far end of the project chain. If standards used through the project phase assist in customer identification, understanding and, most of all, acceptance of the resulting product or service their use has been justified—even if it causes temporary project discomfort. We may be able to build a better mousetrap, but if it is so foreign, different, or "weird" to the potential customers that they pass it by, it is a failure.

In summary then standards are very useful to project efforts in many regards. Often the value gained through their use outweighs their cost, and causes us to suppress our natural, project-oriented aversion to externally supplied patterns. They help achieve our immediate, local goals by helping gain acceptability of the project, create tools and processes quickly and cheaply, avoiding scratchwork by bridging the intuitive leap in processes and highlighting important differences, separating these from nonessential ones. They also help achieve more global, company-wide efforts by making operations that follow project work easier, assisting in the planning and measurement of other project results, and making the eventual customer more willing to buy our products or services. Standards allow us the benefit of being different without the stigma of being "weird."

STANDARD WEAKNESSES

For all their benefits, standards do bring a measure of weakness to each project. To fully understand this it is not enough to acknowledge that standards can be incorrectly chosen, poorly formulated, or improperly used. These are obvious failure factors. Instead we must probe further into this notion of standards, finding subtle, commonly overlooked problems, for it is these that frustrate projects more. And like projects themselves, standards carry inherent weakness as well as the created variety.

1. *Infrequent Use.* Creation and maintenance of standards governing project life is a fairly cost-effective process for those companies involved in continual project work or those facing a future of more and more project experiences. Infrequent project participants cannot absorb the cost of creating standards with one or a few project applications. Standards are the luxury of companies heavily into project work. Neophytes need to borrow or buy standards from others. Otherwise they must forego their benefits.

2. *Development C, S, and T.* The fact that many companies operate on a short-planning horizon, looking at immediate costs and benefits rather than long-term versions also prohibits investment in long-term gains brought about by continued standard use. It often takes many incremental uses to justify the first cost of a standard, and unless the company has a way of spreading the absorption of these costs among several "users" most project managers cannot assume them alone. This budgetary myopia thwarts the develop-

ment of many company standards everywhere, not merely project ones. Long-term vision is needed, but often missing.

3. *Obsolescence.* Obsolescence renders standards useless over time. We must be on constant guard against this. One way to limit the effect of obsolescence is to use higher level, less susceptible standards, such as standard policies, approaches, and concepts as opposed to detailed standard processes, steps, activities, and documents. The former survive the test of time longer than the latter, riding out temporary fluctuations that often destroy specific standards.

Certain projects and industries are more prone to the obsolescence of standards than others. These include high tech companies, ones tied closely to consumer preferences (i.e., fashion, entertainment, dining, and hospitality), and those which require extended project performance periods (nuclear power plants, cross country pipelines, and civil infrastructure projects). The more our projects or their eventual products are prone to changes in technology, time, or consumer preferences the more susceptible they will be to the obsolescence of standards.

4. *Mutation of Standards.* Standards not only become obsolete, but they change through continual use—they mutate from generation to generation. This happens when they are tailored to specific uses and those tailored changes are not removed before the result is used as a new standard. It also occurs when people perceive results differently, and their perceptions are used to create the ensuing pattern. And it occurs when errors or undesirable features are amplified or exaggerated through their passage down the generational lineage of standards. This is how many foolish processes or meaningless tools have been given legitimacy, a legitimacy based on the fact that "they seemed to work alright last time" or "we've been doing this for years, why change now?" (Interestingly enough, this is also how many a foolish or useless monarch was given sovereignity—a legitimacy based on the legacy of generations without regard to merit. But that's a subject for other books.)

Figure 11-3 depicts what commonly happens as a standard is used generationally, as is the case for most project applications (as opposed to the "batch process" used with operations). Notice how the input standard, the six-sided figure, is slowly changed as project

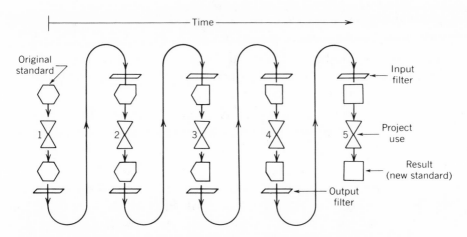

Figure 11-3 The mutation of a project standard though its use.

after project (1 through 5 in this example) uses the output of one effort as the pattern of the next one—the progression of pattern to model to pattern to model, making shadows of shadows. In this fashion the six-sided object is gradually altered over five generations to resemble a square; the cumulative effect of many gradual mutations.

Sometimes changes develop as part of the project use itself, but more often they are the result of some sort of filtration step that exists between project applications. This figure shows two types of filters acting to modify the standard, called input and output filters for simplicity. These might represent the analysis of project results to determine the value of the standard (output filter) or the selective modification of an existing standard to fit perceived needs for a new project (input filter). There are other filters worth mentioning.

One of these is the filter of time itself. Standards become stale, losing applicability and respect the longer they rest between uses. Perception is also a very potent and unpredictable filter, for how one perceives a standard, whether it is judged to be good or bad (in need of modification or not) is more often than not the result of individual prejudice than calculated objectivity. Misunderstood standards are often changed incorrectly, or unnecessarily.

Finally, changing perspectives impact our ability to use standards and often lead to their further mutation. Should we be using a certain device to manage work *performance* for one project, for example, and on the next project are given responsibility for *control*, the device should be changed to reflect the needs of that perspective. Taking the thus modified standard back to a project requiring a performance perspective (without changing it back again) would invite unnecessary error or lack of usefulness.

Thus we see error, misuse or lack of effectiveness added to what might have been an otherwise excellent standard as it is used over and over again. Mutations compound themselves in this manner, eventually leading to the abandonment of the standard or the failure of a project under its application. The action of various filters creates this change from one pattern generation to another. These are the filters of time, perception, misunderstanding, error, perspective, and project use itself. If the notion of pattern filtration or mutation sounds a bit foreign or academic to the business ear, business terms that have the same meaning may sound better. These are *modification, tailoring, using what's applicable, appropriate parts thereof,* and *according to specific needs*. Filtration and mutation, referred to by any term, almost always lead to a weakening and loss of distinction and effectiveness among standards. Seldom are they improved accidentally.

6. *Often Disposed.* Like returnable bottles in a no-deposit no-return economy, project standards are often discarded after one use. We live in a disposable society, and projects are often the worst offenders—what with their immediate, pragmatic orientation exclusively focused on project-specific goals. Project managers tend to use standards and toss them away with little regard for those who follow.

The problem with this approach is that there is often no guardian of standards, no keeper of the standards library, so to speak. In order for standards to transcend immediate uses and be valuable to other projects besides the one at hand there needs to be a protected, "vanilla" version that maintains its integrity despite project-specific modifications based on it. Unfortunately many companies do not create such a version, nor do they maintain a repository, literally or figuratively, of standards. Those that do often neglect them, allow them to gather dust and become obsolete, or make their use prohibitively difficult and involved.

Like library books, standards are best used when they are free, open, easily accessed, and used without a lot of onerous restrictions. Otherwise, like their library counterparts, they will sit on the dusty shelves untouched. Standards have value only when they are used, not in and of themselves. An unused standard is like an unread book—a waste of paper.

FAILURE FACTORS

Some of the failure factors related to standards are inherent and some are created. That is, some have to do with the very fact that standards are standards, while the rest occur when standards are used and abused by people. Many of these are common and others are highly unusual, depending upon the reader's perspective. All have occurred, however, and all have the potential to corrupt project work as well as to legitimize failure.

FF 114: No Profit Involved

The absence or scarcity of viable project standards which can be used across any given industry is often the result of there being no profit involved in their creation. The most likely candidates for production of standards are those companies providing project services on a continuous basis, ones that transcend projects and gain a wealth of knowledge in so doing—knowledge that can be shared for the benefit of all. Unfortunately this proposition works contrary to the interests of those companies, for their profit is made through creation of project-specific (read as "customer-funded") standards or measures.

Figure 11-4 attempts to illustrate this point graphically. Although by no means does it purport to be accurate or even representative in quantitative terms (the relative size of billings in the four categories shown) it does depict fairly typical project services that we may buy from any number of providers (architects, engineering firms, project managers, advertisement agencies, real estate developers, realtors, software houses, information systems consultants, etc.). Rightly or wrongly, these firms typically bill on a cost-reim-

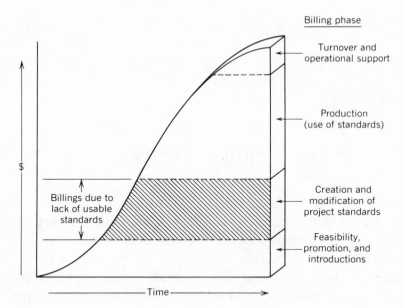

Billing phase

Turnover and operational support

Production (use of standards)

Creation and modification of project standards

Feasibility, promotion, and introductions

Billings due to lack of usable standards

$

Time

Figure 11-4 Standards development as a component of project fees.

bursable basis. That is, they charge by the hour for services and either pass through or markup expenses.

This being the case, the less work they have on any one engagement the less money they will make from it. Their profit orientation, therefore, is to maximize the amount of billable effort required for any given project—up to the point where the project either fails the funding hurdle or exceeds the sponsor's billing tolerance. The creation of project measures for performance, understanding, or control is a significant element of their work, and as such they do not wish to abandon it or reduce it through application of off-the-shelf standards. Consider the legal profession for example, where hourly billings are very typical. Would a lawyer benefit if there were standard wills, standard trusts, standard contracts, standard personal injury claims, or standard divorces? Of course not. They thrive on specificity as do other firms operating in the project environment.

This does not suggest that sponsors (customers of these firms) are not their own worst enemy in this regard (The King of Change), for they often are. It only points out the motive of inefficiency behind a lack of standards. More standards means less work and less profit for those providing project services under a cost-plus arrangement. This is true whether these contractors are professionals or craft workers, accountants or carpenters; it makes no difference.

If our contractor is pouring structural concrete for example, it can do a much less costly job if standard formwork is to be used with standard reinforcing configurations than if custom design, foreign material, or abnormal configurations not lending themselves to economies of scale are employed. For a cost-plus contract, a contractor with plenty of excess capacity and a good fee markup would not complain about these exotic methods. But give the same contractor a lean, lump-sum agreement (where savings accrue to the seller) and it would much prefer to install common, consistent, "standard" formwork, and reinforcing steel.

By streamlining operations and cutting costs, standards help a contractor gain profit under hard money arrangements and, to the contrary, lose profit potential under soft money versions. This should never be overlooked. Wise consumers of project services should be aware of the tendency of sellers to discard standards under cost-plus contracts and insist on their use under fixed price conditions. It is a fact of life. Money motivates—it is a power tool; and its presence or absence often explains many conditions that seem otherwise odd in the business world. Lack of project standards is merely one of these.

FF 115: Creative Vacuum

A certain creativity is needed to produce project standards, creativity often lacking in the business community. For to be creative involves risk taking, exposing oneself to ridicule and derision regarding the product, its applicability, and inherent weaknesses. Those who never create a thing are often the first to criticize those who try to develop standards. Their development is a high profile activity, often with little direct payback for the individuals involved. This is why most standards are not developed for eventual project use, with the needs of many applications in mind, but are the result of specific project measures made generic after they have proven successful. Standards require creativity and pragmatism, and people characterized by both are often assigned project work. They are too valuable (in the narrow vision of the short term) performing project-specific work to participate in the development of generic project standards. As with project planning, this leaves the task of standards creation to those who "are available" (read "not needed elsewhere"), are not qualified to perform actual work, or are otherwise "second stringers." And as with plans, the worst products come from those who have no experience in the field for which the products are intended.

FF 116: Lost in the Translation

Standards migrating across company barriers often don't apply. This is because they are often so company-specific, incorporating extraneous company policy, methods or quirks that they need extreme modification to work in another environment. The same is true, although to a lesser extent, when standards span projects. So often each project (and company) develops its specific "culture," way of operating, perspective, and personality. Standards thriving under one company or project culture often fail to make the transition elsewhere: well intentioned people end up speaking to each other in different languages.

The lack of individual continuity caused by transfers, attrition, and peaks and valleys in staffing levels (see Chapter 3) also contributes to the loss of standards. Once a person begins to understand a certain standard he or she may leave the project, interrupting the standard's "learning curve." Standards that aren't understood aren't used. They can be lost in the translation from project to project, company to company, and person to person, such as when one replaces the other.

FF 117: Standardphobia

Many people involved with project work (or any work for that matter) don't like the notion of standards. Sometimes they view standards as restrictive, limiting their freedom. This cannot be denied, for that is their intention. Hopefully they restrict our freedom to fail and not our ability to succeed. Others dislike standards because their existence promotes the concept of accountability; something many would rather live without. Standards promote accountability by setting levels against which we can be measured, or our work can be judged. Whether the standard be quantitative or qualitative in nature, a general rule is that the more our performance approximates the standard the better it is viewed. Without standards it is difficult to judge, and some people would rather not be judged. Often these are the ones who would fail the test of standards, for those who continually exceed standard levels of achievement welcome them.

Standards are the joy of achievers and the bane of failures. They define normality and therefore abnormality, raising questions regarding any deviations. Those who deviate on the positive side welcome this exposure. The rest hide from it. Fear of standards is legitimate when they are repressive, overly restrictive, inapplicable, and obstructive of performance. When it represents fear of accountability, however, it possesses those who fear failure or are prone thereto. Whenever the suggestion of more standards is met with screams and other signs of resistance, we should evaluate whether this is due to the fact that standards restrict achievement or spotlight the lack thereof.

FF 118: No Templates Fit

Resistance to standards also exists among those projects where the culture exudes difference, giving project participants the impression that they are untouchable, unmanageable, or beyond the reach of the company. These are the proverbial "projects from outer space" where even the law of gravity, much less sound business practices, such as standardization, isn't supposed to apply. It does, and should. Despite project differences, there are always some components, elements, steps or tasks that can benefit from application of standards.

FF 119: Not Properties

This failure factor is similar to FF 114 in that it involves the role of profit and the motivation of money. In general, whenever something can be made into a "property" (a tangible, salable item) it can be given value. Otherwise it has none. This distinguishes marketable items, such as books, videotapes, software disks, and the like from live performances, good ideas, concepts, and management approaches. If it cannot be transformed into a "property" it cannot be sold. To extend the logic, if it cannot be sold, why bother? This happens to standards. Many of them deal with intangible or nonpatentable, noncopyrighted (read "nonsalable") attitudes, methods, approaches, concepts, sensitivities, views, and applications.

The same motive that restricts the development and sale of nonproperty standards also limits their adaptation by others, even when they are free. Tangible, externally-provided, and often "packaged" items are easier for most managements to grasp and use than more ephemeral products. This explains the fixation on so called "hard properties" as opposed to "soft." It also explains the booming software market, because most software is nothing more than ideas made into property via the disk and documentation sold. Any project standard has a much greater chance of adaptation if it can be "propertized," given a package, and labeled. People buy (or managements accept) things with handles, literal or figurative ones. This also explains why a number of concepts or ideas are given names or pneumonic titles—these are mental handles increasing their chances at being grasped and used.

FF 120: The NIH Syndrome

This failure factor is best described as a sort of "concept xenophobia": fear of ideas *Not Invented Here*. It becomes more common the larger, more established, more successful and arrogant a company or project becomes. It's another way of saying "no templates fit here," not so much because the project is seen as so different, but because it is viewed as so good—so good that anything originating elsewhere is judged inferior.

Hidden reasons for this attitude include the fact that a proposed standard may threaten to replace a measure in use or championed by a project individual or organization. They may not so much dislike the standard but prefer what they have created instead. Also there are always those needing to make their mark, one way or the other, on a project, and externally prepared standards may supplant these personal touches. Finally, it takes time, effort and intelligence to understand a proposed standard. Those rejecting a standard by kneejerk might be so doing to prevent the need for either. In other words, they might refuse a standard under the guise of the NIH syndrome, when they actually do not want to spend the time or effort understanding it, or are incapable of so doing regardless of how much of either they have.

FF 121: Nit Pick

Standards are visible targets for those who would like to attack them. They are often defenseless, having no identified "champion," and often do not work perfectly or efficiently. This fact, or the existence of minor faults in the standard sometimes fuels or legitimizes ridicule and disparagement.

The irony of this common practice is that regardless of how faulty a given standard may be, it is often superior to what is presently in use. The fact that it isn't perfect doesn't mean that it is not better, but that lack of perfection sometimes prevents its adoption. Whenever examining proposed standards we should look for their *incremental* value rather than their absolute value—comparing them to what we have rather than what we *could* have. As long as a standard improves the status quo (which is sometimes nothing at all) it should be accepted. Those who choose to nit pick the defects have no role among pragmatic projects.

FF 122: Industry Esoterica

One might look to industry associations for the promulgation of standards, and sometimes this pays off. Often, however, the cupboard is bare here too. The failure of industry associations (societies, institutes and the like) to fill the standards vacuum has been attributed to any number of factors. One is the tendency of these organizations to be, in effect, marketing forums rather than those designed for the improvement of the members as a whole. Attendees at conventions and meetings are often there to meet customers and make contacts rather than to contribute to the general well being of the industry of profession represented. Often the leaders of these associations are prominent members of the status quo, resenting attempts to standardize or remodel their successful concepts, methods or practices. Associations are typically fund-poor, not able to afford efforts aimed at standardization, or their members thrive on profits derived from customer-funded standards (see FF 114).

Industry associations are commonly made up of business competitors not wishing to share efficiency or the competitive edge that standards or shared processes represent. Many are lobbyist in nature: pointing externally towards others rather than internally, towards self-improvement. Finally, many industries are esoteric and refuse to accept generic, nonindustry specific methods or results. Standards transcending industries are not viewed as sensitive to specific industry needs. This is a broader variation of the attitude that "standards don't apply to the project from outer space."

FF 123: Blunt and Brittle

Blunt standards are those that resemble a club: unfocused, unsharpened, and not very precise. In other words, useful only in emergency situations but certainly not preferred. Other standards are brittle, resisting change or unadaptable to changing environments. Whenever a standard doesn't respond to particular needs by tailoring (sharpening the blunt tool) or by flexing to withstand change it is limited in its use and acceptability. Blunt and brittle standards operate in direct opposition to the concept of controls based on risk, of selectively chosen measures meeting the needs at hand. Sometimes they are the result of an attempt to create an all-purpose tool or all-encompassing process. In order to be useable in many situations these are often rendered useless for each. Universal tools don't work. Neither do universal standards.

FF 124: Next Time

Although listed last, this is perhaps the most common failure factor associated with the concept of standards. It has to do with the fact that we are often too busy with recurring problems to prevent their reoccurrence. In other words we are so busy putting out fires that we have no time to install a fire protection system. We see hundreds of examples of this throughout project life.

We are too busy creating specific plans to create standard planning methodology (which would streamline future planning efforts). We are too busy auditing contractor invoices to create a standard invoicing procedure and format (which would streamline future invoices and reduce auditing time). We are too busy amending and correcting specific contract documents with obvious errors to "waste" our time creating error-free, standard contract documents for future use. The list of examples could go on and on. It would only serve to demonstrate the prevalence of this condition. The response of those in it is usually something like "we'll have to do that next time," or "if we ever go through this again we'll be sure to create some standards." Unfortunately, however, just like there is no "last time" in the lexicon of projects there is also no "next time." It never seems to come. No project has ever failed "next time." They always seem to fail this time around. If we could only postpone failure the way we postpone its avoidance project work would be much easier.

SUMMARY

Even though standards have a lesser role in the environment of business projects than they do for operational efforts, that role is distinct, special, and unique in its fostering of failure. Standards themselves are sometimes difficult to conceptualize, for they are used in a project sense as both models of reality and patterns by which we try to shape reality. The shadows of the past are used as guidelines for the future. We use this term loosely, for standards are meant here to mean any management measures, no matter how conceptual or specific, that originate outside the project but are used for its conduct.

We use standards for a number of reasons, some direct and some a bit less obvious. They assist in gaining project acceptance and funding, avoid scratchwork when creating project tools and processes, help us avoid tedious rigor when prescribing controls, and give us some degree of consistency, if not uniformity, which transcends projects and even companies at times. But muting nonessential differences, standards focus management attention on important differences demanding that attention. From time to time standards promote the adaptation of project successes to nonproject settings, such as when spin-off products or techniques can be understood and adapted elsewhere in the company.

No benefits are derived without risk, and standards are no exception. Their value is weakened and their proclivity towards failure enhanced when they are infrequently used, are expensive to obtain, become obsolete, or suffer sometimes hidden and deadly mutations through continued use. We contribute to this mutation when we filter the products of past projects (patterns) through time, perception, error, or misunderstanding and end up transforming the standard into a new, lesser pattern. Even those that escape this mutation are often disposed of after one or a few uses, chiefly because project users are exclusively interested in project success and the fact that many companies do not have guardians of standards, the ones who maintain up-to-date, vanilla versions.

Of all the failure factors surrounding the use or misuse of standards, none is more prevalent than the "next time" syndrome, where projects are so busy solving specific problems that they cannot install standards that would prevent whole series of like problems. This being the most common reason for lack of standards, the most powerful concerns the lack of profit motivation for those marketing project services.

Creating standards is a risky, high profile task which subjects one to criticism. It is best undertaken by creative individuals, experienced in the fields towards which their standards are directed and able to withstand the attacks of those who have it in their interests to prevent adaptation of standards. There are many of these. Whenever a standard is proposed or rejected, we must understand both the obvious and the hidden reasons either is done. Standards are very helpful yet very dangerous elements, for although they can help us circumvent error and avoid failure, they can also legitimize error, giving it currency by embedding it within standard measures. Like bad genes standards can also spread failure, like a genetic weakness, through generations of projects, often making it impossible for us to detect and prevent its reoccurrence.

Successful projects use standards whenever possible. They consider the incremental value of standards as compared to what they have used in the past or are using and apply a very pragmatic criterion: if it's better they use it. Of all the advice this chapter contains, none is better nor more universally applicable. This is how we should all approach the subject of standards—not seeking perfection, not necessarily seeking standardization, but seeking improvement. This is why standards exist: to improve our chances for success.

OUTSIDERS

beyond the circle

Anyone or any organization not directly involved with daily project work should be considered an outsider. Whether they be business competitors, government regulatory agencies, funding sources or the general public, project outsiders can have a tremendous impact on our chances of success or failure. For although their distant or tangential participation is seldom directly related to C, S, and T performance, many outsiders can hamper a project to the point where it becomes either unfeasible or impractical. When assessing project risks we should never neglect nor underestimate the power of outsiders.

The larger a project, the longer it takes and greater its visibility the greater risk posed by any number of outsiders. Seldom neutral, most outsiders take a stand either favoring or opposing one or more aspects of the effort. And once their support has been gained it should never be taken for granted, for although their support may be questionable in terms of direct value, their opposition will always hurt. Seldom can we consider them to be indifferent to our project, for that is a temporary attitude. It soon changes to support or opposition.

A general rule is that the farther a group is from daily project interests the more ephemeral its allegiance can be. Project management needs to understand the importance of outsiders and to respect their views, if for no other reason than to protect the project from them. In effect, a good project manager should direct two sometimes distinct efforts—one inside the project perimeter and the other beyond it; to manage outsiders as well as insiders. Some are good at one and not the other. Consistently successful managers excel at both.

DIFFERENT LEVELS

Just as failure is not the opposite of success, neither is an outsider the opposite of an insider. There is more than one outside position, and different levels of what we might call "outsidedness." In general, the more removed or indirectly participating a group or individual becomes from the project core, the more it can be considered

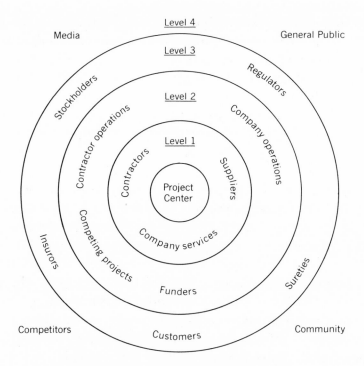

Figure 12-1 Outsiders at different levels.

an outsider. So there are different "levels" of outsiders, ranging from those frequently involved to those with little or no interest or stake in the project efforts or eventual outcome. To help visualize this concept of outsiders at different levels, Figure 12-1 depicts examples of groups lying outside the project center, away from daily project efforts, yet at differing distances and in different locations. Although this is a contrived, somewhat arbitrary illustration, it does remind us that certain groups are more involved than others, and that it would be a mistake to group everyone as either an outsider or an insider. There are different levels of both.

Considering the project center to be the organization directly working on project efforts on a daily basis, we might arrange contractors, material suppliers, and company services (personnel, accounting, etc.) in the inner circle of outsiders—those having frequent and sustained involvement but only when needed. These are called "level 1" outsiders. Next there are companies and other business entities that have less involvement and, in general, less impact on project activity. These "level 2" groups might include both company and noncompany groups, such as competing projects (sponsored by our company, but with other goals), the operations people within our company, contractor operations (those not associated with the project), and those who have funded the project. "Level 3" groups could include company stockholders (eventual project "owners"), government or industry regulators, insurance underwriters for the project effort, bonding companies issuing bonds for it, or eventual customers of the added capacity, new product or whatever result the project has been created to accomplish. Finally, we could arrange the rest of society in a "level 4" ring surrounding the others, and include here the media, general public, business competitors, and the local community affected by project work.

Depending on the industry involved and nature of the project itself, these relative positions and indeed the identity of outsiders would vary. What shouldn't change, however, is the concept of outsiders existing at different levels of concern and impact—that "outsidedness" is a relative, often dynamic characteristic.

It is dynamic because groups tend to migrate toward and away from the conceptual project center, becoming over time more or less involved in detailed project effort. An example might be project funders, those groups (internal or external) providing the funds for the effort. During the feasibility stage of project life they are very involved in defining and restricting exactly what the project may entail, what its expectations should be (the funding hurdle) and whether it can become a bona fide project or merely someone's impractical suggestion. Once these hurdles have been cleared, however, the funders drift towards the outermost levels of involvement—only to reenter the inner zone when more and more funds are sought. A similar movement concerns government regulatory bodies, those groups responsible for approving or licensing various project efforts. They move into and out of project prominence and concern as various licensing steps, inspections, or approvals approach and pass.

If our project involves increased plant capacity (such as when a new factory is constructed) the local community may play a role of interested bystanders during the design and construction stage, perhaps at levels 3 or 4 on our figure, and then move into the project center once the finished facility is to be operated; filling that organization with managements, supervisors and a workforce taken from that community. Two major principles need be noted then: (1) there are different outsider "levels," and (2) groups and individuals move across levels over time.

EXPOSURE AND REACH

Outsiders can help or hurt our projects. This is fairly easy to understand. We need be more concerned with ways to avoid needless *exposure* to outsiders; to protect our projects from them. Some projects are simply more vulnerable than others. These are the ones that maintain a high profile, take years to complete, involve tremendous costs, are extremely visible from the outside, and involve a number of dependencies with groups beyond the project core. Shorter, lower cost, "private" projects executed within the confines of one or a few companies and holding little public impact until completed are by their nature less exposed.

Another term we might apply to outsiders is *reach*. Reach concerns the impact of the project on others, and increases as the number of outsiders increases as well as in direct proportion to the impact the project will have upon them. No projects take place within a vacuum; there is always a role for outsiders at various levels, even if it is a postproject one. A general rule, however, is that a project's exposure to outsiders (and therefore its vulnerability to their damage) is directly proportional to its reach.

If outsiders are viewed as potential enemies, the greater a project's reach the more of these we will face and the more we will interface with each. Reach is a term representing both the number of outsiders impacted and the degree of impact as well. Needless to say, failure generated by outside sources increases in frequency and strength as reach increases. Some examples might help illustrate this concept. Suppose we were building an addition to an existing facility in a fairly large metropolitan area. If the project is worth only a few thousand dollars and will result in no new positions at the factory (no new jobs), we may conclude the reach is short. However, if to transfer a large piece of equipment through the community for eventual placement in the addition necessitates the removal of a bridge located on the main thoroughfare, and the rebuilding of the bridge will take several weeks, the activity involved has tremendous reach to commuters in the area. Given enough warning and visibility, they can interfere with or even prevent this critical project element.

Suppose another construction project requires the importation of foreign marble into a country, marble to be used for the facade of a very large office building. Although the cost of the marble may be high, it is deemed insignificant in relation to the total construction price. But if the amount of marble so imported consists of twice the amount produced nationally, the national marble producers may feel the reach of the project very directly, and take steps preventing this importation and encroachment into their market.

Reach is a concept related to the ripple effects of change. It often radiates from the project center, having strange and unpredictable impacts on outsiders. Attempts by project management to foresee, limit, or control the negative elements of reach usually pay direct dividends in failure avoidance.

NEED AND CONTRIBUTION

None of this should color our impression of outsiders as only those capable of harming project efforts or thwarting our goals. Many outsiders actually help, contribute to, and protect our project. Some of these have been mentioned, such as funders, contractors, suppliers, and eventual customers. Most projects wouldn't exist without all of these. What can be said, however, is that the more we need outsiders, and the more of them that we need, the greater our dependency and therefore the greater our exposure to them. If we need them and they help us, we succeed, but if we need them and they don't perform, we fail. But need is not the only element in the relationship. Contribution is one as well.

A basic and erroneous assumption often made by project management is this: "If they don't contribute we don't need them." Those taking this view tend to neglect noncontributing outsiders, an often fatal error. They manage outsiders, but only those who are, at one time or another, project contributors. What this assumption fails to recognize is that noncontributing outsiders can be, and often are, project detractors—agents of failure that must also be managed. In this regard, our concept of need should be readjusted to include all outsiders, both contributors and noncontributors, for we *need* the latter if for no other reason than to suppress their criticism, prevent their interference, or defend against their attacks. We need them to leave us alone.

A new assumption, then, might go something like this: "Every person and every group can contribute to failure." Simply because all can't contribute to success doesn't mean any can be ignored. We must maintain our vigilance of all outsiders. Failure often originates from the most uninvolved, least participating quarters. Because it can't be prevented doesn't mean it should be unexpected.

BENEFITS OF OUTSIDERS

We must look at each outsider as a potential detractor as well as a contributor, even if that contribution is nothing more than silence, acquiescence or noninterference (this has tremendous value in many areas). But outsiders at all levels contribute more than just their passivity. We should review some of their contributions and remind ourselves of them often, throughout actual project work. This will help counter the smugness, defensive, and polarized attitudes that tend to develop among people working against the odds on a critical project effort. No project is an island, nor is it a foothold in an enemy's camp. We need the contributions of those beyond the fence.

Some of their most obvious contributions are project resources themselves: money, people, goods, and services. But outsiders also give us valuable information. In this regard we should never overlook other groups who can share information concerning project risks and controls with us (typically not competitors), such as other projects within our company or served by our contractors, and compare prices, methods, processes, standards, and the like. Too many projects extend the notion of uniqueness to that of isolation. Just because we are different doesn't mean we cannot benefit from the experience, knowledge, or mistakes of others. Outsiders help us access these through the networks they represent, the connections and contacts they can give us. We should take advantage of them whenever we can.

The whole subject of "ideas" and perspectives is one that holds a role for outsiders. Many projects, isolated as they often are, tend to become inbred, stagnant, and self-focused. Fresh new ideas from the outside break this pattern, freeing us to consider another way, another approach, or another process. In most cases this infusion of newness is free, easily obtainable and valuable. Much like the fresh wind blowing all about us, all we need to do to get some is open a window here and there.

Within each project we have already defined three distinct perspectives, those of performance, understanding, and control. As important as the distinctions are among these three internal perspectives, there is a larger distinction to be made. This is between *internal* perspectives and *external* ones. Just as the global solution is often unseen by one with narrow vision, so is it often overlooked by one who is constantly focusing on the project center and not its peripherals. And often those on the outside attempt everything possible to show it to us, screaming the answer to our questions, only to have us ignore them. We need to look at and listen to outsiders to gain the advantage of this perspective. It is sometimes the most valuable and least costly information obtainable.

Finally, we need consider the fact that no project starts fully staffed, funded, and equipped—everything comes from the outside. Every person on the project team, including the project manager, began as a project outsider and, once the work is over, will become so once again. We are all outsiders at one time or another. That being the case, it's surprising how many of us forget the outsider's perspective.

TURN THE CAMERA AROUND

Earlier we defined a good project manager as one who acts like a moving camera, moving through the project by taking different perspectives (performance, understanding, and control) and by adjusting its focus from near to far term. One final enhancement to this metaphor is needed. Once in a while, while he or she is moving and adjusting this project view, the project manager should step in front of the camera, have his or her picture taken, and view the results as an outsider does. Or turn the camera around, looking outward rather than inward all the time. It's amazing how the view can change and the perspective enlighten. This enlightenment can be gained through other techniques as well, most of them involving an increase in intimacy between the project manager and the outside—the rest of the world.

A number of methods help in this regard. One such is the simple practice of pulling management away from the project core for a few days or weeks, allowing them to mingle with outsiders, listen to them, and understand, if not accept, their concerns, questions, and fears. Project people need to associate with outsiders, breaking down this artificial and damaging barrier we see separating them. A sensible project manager keeps one ear to the project and the other to the ground, listening for sounds from the outside.

The most valuable technique, however, has already been described: Networks! Project personnel are involved in all sorts of social, religious, cultural, economic, and recreational networks. They "mingle" with outsiders at all levels, all the time. If we tap into these networks, our project will learn much about its reputation, potential problems, and failure factors, not to mention the harvesting of many valuable ideas and suggestions. People in the project center have no patent on experience, knowledge, or wisdom. Like failure, these too can spring from the most overlooked, least expected places.

SELLING THE PROJECT

Here is one time-honored rule that should guide all business transactions: If price exceeds value we should sell, and if value exceeds price we should buy. What does this have to do with outsiders? We can view them as each representing potential buyers or sellers of the project "idea," the project itself. When they perceive the value of the project to be less than the price it extracts from them, they want to sell it—to get rid of it. Should they perceive the value and contribution it brings to them to exceed whatever personal or group cost involved (the price) they will usually accept and even welcome it.

The message for us is simple and direct: we must sell the project to outsiders, we must do this continually because their senses of value and price change, and we can only do this when we create the perception of value as higher than cost. We want to blunt the criticism of outsiders, if not enlist their support, by increasing value while decreasing price.

Of course, this must be done on a situational basis; we cannot sell the entire project to the entire world at once. Each outsider has a different sense of value and different ways of assessing or perceiving project costs. We must know what these are, emphasize the value (or create it, if it doesn't exist) and deemphasize the cost (or decrease it, if it is in fact too high). No other wishing, extolling, or exhorting will accomplish this sale—we cannot trick outsiders. We can only play to their sense of value and their perception of price. This is what every good salesperson has been doing throughout the world for as long as time itself. And no sale is final, nor should any be taken for granted. We must continually sell the project notion, and in so doing, turn outsiders (sellers) into "insiders" (buyers).

ALL ABOARD

In selling outsiders, in making them supporters of project efforts rather than detractors, we can think of them as passengers on our project ship. They need not replace the captain (project manager) set the course or assist the crew, but as passengers they will have a vested interest in a safe passage. We enlist their support when we bring them on board the ship, combine our interests with theirs, and create mutual goals and needs. This is the most any project can do: sell outsiders tickets to the same destination, aboard the same ship. And the selling must be continuous, for even the best outfitted and crewed ship has experienced murderous mutiny before land-fall.

When we use terms like "selling" the project idea, or "perceptions" of price and value, we should never presume to be manipulating outsiders, fooling them, or tricking them into supporting or buying something that is no good for them. On the contrary, outsiders are not fools, and they resent and repel any attempts to be manipulated. No one need be manipulated to allow a valuable project to succeed. Should manipulation, deceit or patronization be essential, the project is probably ill-founded, ill-advised, and ill-fated. Outsiders are intelligent. Remember we used to be them, and will be again. Whether we return among outsiders with a triumph or a failure often depends on how we treat them while we are "inside" the project.

FF 125: Them!

This failure factor polarizes outsiders and insiders, making outsiders guilty of all transgressions leading to failure. It is an attitude taken by managers who not only want to protect their projects but to blame those outside the project center—to use them as perfect scapegoats. Often this is done by directing the enmity of one outside group towards another, such as when the local community's desire for economic infusion (seen as a project value) is pitted against environmentally concerned groups' interest in wildlife protection (a project "cost"). Any project manager who immediately points to "them" as the reason for failure is also pointing at him or herself for not managing "them," for not foreseeing their needs and either (1) counseling against the project undertaking or (2) changing project activity, methods or measures to reduce cost while increasing perceived value.

The alignment of outsiders against each other may take place internally as well. This could happen when the sponsor's financial management is pitted against the operational executives: the funders against the users of new projects, or when projects competing for the same funding dollar battle for exclusive approval.

Many projects attack outsiders before ascertaining their concerns or objectives. They practice a version of "project xenophobia," always assuming outsiders to be intervenors. Unfortunately this assumption is self-fulfilling, for a neutral party treated as an intervenor typically becomes one. Project management is not a game of war, neither should those outside our camp be depicted as the enemy. Outsiders are distinct, with differing interests and objectives, and existing at different levels of our project reach. They are not simply one class: those not us, "them." The management and accommodation of outsiders is also not a simple, direct task. It is a multidimensional management challenge, requiring continuous effort, perceptive approaches, and an understanding of its dynamism and complexity. It's just never as simple as "us against them."

FF 126: Neocolonialists

No project is an island, and neither should one be considered a colony. Colonies in the past have provided cheap raw material, labor, and little or no resistance to their "reach" on the local inhabitants. Colonization in a business project sense is about as antiquated a practice. We cannot succeed in any project endeavor if we treat outsiders as ignorant, unsophisticated natives to be exploited.

Uninformed outsiders are often our worst enemies, for to keep them in the dark usually fuels suspicions far worse than reality. This is often a case of "what *they* don't know will hurt *you*." Nor can we treat them as some sort of fortunate recipients of our beneficience for having chosen their location, community, market, or sources.

And finally, we cannot succeed in building mutual interests if we insist that all project material, ideas, personnel and management be imported—brought to the project from sources beyond immediate outsiders. Whenever all talent and systems are imported and injected upon outsiders they justifiably resent the intrusion, the neglect, or even the social offense this represents. All reduce their support. It makes no difference the nature of our project nor its location, whether its a construction site in a developing nation or an advertising campaign formulated on Madison Avenue, it will fail if we treat it as a colony and outsiders as ignorant subjects.

FF 127: Cut and Run

The practice of hitting a lucrative market or exploiting a valuable business opportunity and then leaving outsiders in our wakes is a foolish one. It can only be done once with any given set of outsiders. Similar to colonization, cutting and running (a term applied to lumber companies guilty of harvesting forests and leaving nothing to replenish them) neglects the continued value and contribution of outsiders.

It is seen in a geographical sense when companies build new capacity in an unfamiliar area, and in a conceptual sense when they enter a market with a new product. Politicians with higher ambitions have also been guilty of using local or state offices as stepping stones to higher positions. Whatever the setting, cutting and running on a project level is dangerous and characteristic of short-term exploitation. Outsiders don't mind being persuaded, sold, or even enlisted in the support of any project, but they never accept exploitation. No one wants to be someone else's stepping stone.

FF 128: Ruled by Regulators

Almost every project effort is ruled, in some fashion or other, by outsiders with regulatory authority. They may be internal to the sponsoring company (feasibility boards, quality assurance departments, internal audit, corporate review committees, etc.) or externally based, such as those of governments, industry bodies, associations, or councils. These must be appeased, satisfied, and obeyed most of the time, for to confront or correct their injustices is often a task greater than the project itself. And project managements, owing to their pragmatic, results-oriented focus, cannot be relied upon to remove historic or chronic obstacles—merely to transcend them. So regulators must be dealt with, typically on their terms. This is often unfortunate and the cause of many business project failures. Knowing this, however, two general failure factors can be avoided.

The first takes the attitude of "us against them," forcing confron-

tation and conflict from the very beginning. This is rarely successful, for it commonly serves to increase the resolve and harshness of
the regulators. Many have adjustable, situational, or selective controls of their own, and reserve the most onerous for those projects
deemed "offensive." It is best not to encourage their wrath, no matter how obstructive and "unfair" they may be. Brick walls are easier
to step over or around than through.

On the other hand, however, an acquiescent, intimidated project
is not guaranteed success in dealing with regulators either. Apolo-
getic management often regulates itself, bringing harsher restrictions than any actual regulators would impose, simply out of fear or
because they would rather anticipate problems than face them if
they should arise. Neither approach is recommended unless absolutely necessary. That is, confrontation or obsequience are equally
undesirable when dealing with regulators. Wise management learns
quickly how to accommodate regulators without fighting them or
falling at their feet.

This often requires taking an active role in the regulatory process
rather than a passive one; rather than simply waiting to be regu-
lated. It means learning the regulations, understanding the exceptions, and following them to your advantage—not allowing your
ignorance or assumptions to the contrary to serve them. It also requires attention to detail and documentation on the level acceptable
to regulators, for in order to "beat" regulators we have to play their
game.

All of this, of course, varies with industry setting and regulators
involved. Suffice it to say that regulators need be managed like any
other outsider, only their reach differs. Perhaps they are the classic
outsider after all, ones that can contribute nothing but failure. This
is why we need to treat them with care.

FF 129: Self-Flagellation

Projects are difficult enough without whipping ourselves, especially
in front of outsiders. This is a case where what is healthy in private
is not wisely performed in public. We need to surface and correct
our problems internally, limiting outside exposure when possible.

No need to enlist the aid of outsiders when it comes to suffering. We have enough without them.

Projects constantly disregard this advice. They whip themselves, or give the whip to others, when they carry around horribly obsolete baselines—ones surpassed months or even years earlier (budgets busted, schedules missed, etc.). These should be exponged from the public record, so to speak, and replaced by realistic and attainable goals. We see other examples of self-flagellation when projects give themselves no performance alternatives save utmost success or dramatic failure, where they allow a grade of A+ or F, no Bs, Cs, or even Ds. Every project should maintain a variety of fall-back positions, alternatives that can be chosen part way through the effort should dramatic changes occur rendering original expectations and plans obsolete. When a project begins with ambitious expectations, proclaims assured success, and creates legions of enemies among outsiders as it progresses, it is merely setting itself up for a long fall.

This phenomenon also occurs in a more subtle fashion. It happens when management constantly focuses the attention of outsiders on price as opposed to value, on what they must give rather than what they will receive. It occurs when we point to processes (costs) rather than their results (value). This doesn't mean that we should ignore project C, S, and T costs and fool ourselves or outsiders with exaggerated claims of perceived value. What it means is that we should emphasize value whenever price is discussed and results when processes are mentioned. In other words we should *know* price but *show* value. We should also *manage* processes and *display* results. A good salesperson never discusses price until value has been established.

FF 130: Defensive Perimeter

This final failure factor is seen with isolated projects, ones that cut off all ties to nonproject, or outsider networks. They set up a hostile "defensive perimeter," a fortified barrier between "them" and "us." But breaking all rules of military engagement, they fail to send out scouts, spies, or even to establish "listening posts" to detect the motion of those outside the perimeter. In other words, they generally ignore the role of outsiders altogether. Except in the most insulated of environments, this is fatal.

For in order to be accepted, helped, or at least left alone, projects must bridge the boundaries between the inside and the outside, whatever they may be. We need to bring outsiders in, to decrease their levels of "outsidedness" and thereby to place an interest in project success in their hands. There are a number of fairly simple, inexpensive ways to promote this approach. Some of them include progress meetings with nonparticipating company management (internal outsiders), tours of the project site or project work areas for nonproject personnel and their families, the earnest solicitation of ideas and suggestions from beyond the "defensive perimeter," and transfers of personnel across project boundaries—often across the matrix axes.

Whether these or others, any steps taken to prevent project goals and outsider objectives from being mutually exclusive are recommended. We must always remember, however, that manipulation or offensive patronization doesn't work. Mutuality of interests, or at least peaceful coexistence between outsiders and insiders must be perceived and genuine in order to be accepted.

SUMMARY

Outsiders are persons or groups of all types who do not participate in daily, direct project efforts. Although many cannot contribute, and have little positive impact on the project, virtually any outsider can impede or even prevent our success. Like many executives in corporate environments, outsiders can always say "No," even when they haven't the authority to say "Yes." Not every outsider can contribute to success, but most can assist failure. The higher our project's profile the more exposed we become to the influence of outsiders. As our project's reach extends to many more levels of outsiders so does our vulnerability to their actions or neglect.

Few outsiders are neutral regarding our project. While they may begin this way, their indifference is a fleeting attitude. It soon gives way to tacit support or rejection. The impact this may have on project efforts will vary from insignificant to critical, depending on the level of dependency between insiders and outsiders and the reach of our project. In any case, it is always best to treat each outsider with the respect due a supporter and the care due a detractor.

We must not only become constantly aware of outsiders, but realize they are different, having different levels of "outsidedness" which vary over time. There are never simply two sides to any project (an outside and an inside), but many varying levels of each. The boundaries between them are dynamic and the groups tend to migrate across each.

Our goal regarding all outsiders is to reap their benefits and avoid their dangers. They bring us critical resources, information and innovative ideas when we have the wisdom to listen. We need to tap into the networks touching outside groups, finding out their needs, perceptions, and goals. And we need to periodically take their perspectives, turning our manager's figurative camera around, off the project center and point it towards the outside. The view can be astonishing.

FAILURE AVOIDANCE

putting knowledge to work

Failure avoidance is the ultimate prize of failure's understanding. It is that skill, the ability to avoid failure, that separates those projects headed for successful conclusions from the rest: those that will fail.

Our study of failure as it pertains to business projects has exposed the symptoms of failure (how to detect it), the inherent tendencies toward failure that projects represent (why projects fail) and the specific failure factors accompanying common project elements (how projects fail). It is time for us to capitalize on this knowledge, to put it to work. We will use the same pragmatic approach found on all successful projects: few things have value except those that help us succeed. The knowledge of failure is useless unless that knowledge helps us avoid failure and its consequences. We shall put that knowledge to work by addressing general approaches to success, attitudes, alternatives, and suggestions that are called "Success Factors" (SFs). Consider them the products of failure's understanding.

SF1: Learn Failure, Don't Practice It

Failure is a condition that need not be experienced to be appreciated. Our approach has been to illuminate failure, to identify its symptoms, tendencies, and the inherent or created project weaknesses and exposures most of us will encounter in the world of business. This is a continuing course of study, not one that ends here, for failure and all its aspects are project-dependent, varying with setting and time. It pays to learn the common mechanisms of failure, how one small error in attitude, approach, or perspective can propogate throughout a project environment, how the ripples radiate to far flung areas of effort, and to recognize typical failure patterns.

The direct and ripple effects of failure constantly teach us about its sources and habits, but waiting until they are available usually means that failure's damage has been done. We study them only to prevent their reoccurrence elsewhere, with other parts of our projects, or beyond the project circle. Above all, we study failure so that we can learn of it vicariously, a much easier and less expensive lesson than one gained through practice. Successful project managers spend a great deal of time analyzing failure, its methods and its traits, only to avoid it. Any analysis of failure that doesn't lead to its avoidance is an empty, academic exercise. It must contribute to success, otherwise it is not worth undertaking.

SF 2: Know What a Project Is

We cannot manage an effort unless we know what it is, in addition to its goals and processes. We need to understand the special, intrinsic characteristics of projects, as opposed to other business activities, in order to recognize risks, choose selective controls, and discern between that which can be avoided, accommodated or controlled.

Many projects fail from the very beginning because their very nature, as projects, is not understood or enunciated throughout the sponsoring company. Projects are different, unique, and nonoperational. They make use of created and often contrived tools, processes, and organizations. They are temporary, fleeting, and dynamic; always changing.

While these are attractive characteristics, making project work challenging and intriguing, they also open the endeavor to failure. Existing concepts, approaches, techniques, standards, measures, and procedures simply cannot be automatically applied without study and selectivity. Projects do not usually respond to off-the-shelf solutions or operational controls. Each must be understood and assessed separately, with the result being risk-based measures tailored to the needs of each.

Projects also must be judged by different standards, for they represent pragmatic endeavors seeking attainment of goals rather than refinement or optimization of results. This is for the operational exercises that follow. Neither can standard personnel skills, functions, or disciplines be readily assigned project work, for it often requires eclectic versions thereof, people who can focus on results and the steps necessary to achieve them, regardless of functional barriers or limitations.

Finally, once we know what *a* project is, we need to know what *each* project is; the special characteristics that make every project

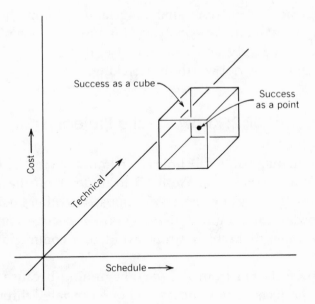

Figure 13-1   Defining success as a zone rather than
a point.

different from every other one. This includes identification of special risks, sensible expectations commensurate with the setting and
the resources required, and the particular weaknesses attributed to
the project by the work involved or brought to it by the project organization and personnel. To succeed we must know generic and
specific project elements, and focus our measures accordingly.

SF 3: Aim for Areas, Not Points

A reasonable, achievable set of expectations is needed for most projects to succeed. There is no need attempting perfection, for that goal
is never achieved without repeated attempts and constant redefini-
tion. Again, perfection is an operational goal, not belonging in the
lexicon of projects. We must be more realistic, aiming for acceptable
levels of performance (C, S, and T) rather than absolute values
thereof.

Figure 13-1 illustrates this idea. There we see a cube representing
brackets within which we expect to perform, as opposed to a dis-

crete, unforgiving point of attainment in each of the three dimensions. It is foolish to expect exact project results when each project is based on partial information, guesswork, unattempted processes, untried plans, created organizations, newly defined responsibilities and all the other uncertainties that make project work what it is— an art and not a science.

Our ultimate expectations should not only be defined in a reasonable manner, including the tolerance of certain variances, but we should strive for intermediate expectations as well. That is, we should never, except for the shortest of efforts, wait until we have succeeded or failed to determine which it is. We should establish goals that can be reached long before the final ones, goals that give us some feedback as to performance in time to make corrections if needed before all is lost. And we should always create contingency plans, fall-back positions that give us some options should failure to attain original expectations seem imminent. No wise project manager accepts only two courses of action: proceed as originally planned or cancel the project. Alternatives should always be programmed into the project scheme. These become more important the longer, more costly, and more exposed a project becomes.

Finally, for those times when failure has made its presence known, when the project ship is sinking, we need to let go, to abandon the mission with some degree of dignity. This includes mitigation of damages, reduction of costs, and any steps available to lessen the burden of project cancellation. A wise project manager, and sponsoring company, know when to admit failure and continue to pursue success where it may be gained: elsewhere.

SF 4: Consider Alternatives

Because it is an art and not a science, because it succeeds when general areas of expectation are met (and not precise points), project work never hinges on the choice of *right* options, only on *workable* ones. There are none of the former and many of the latter. Our challenge is to try something which has every expectation of serving its purpose—of getting the job done, regardless of whether a "better" choice could have been made. We seek to achieve and not to optimize. For these reasons, we should always consider alternatives, other ways to accomplish our objectives. Fixation on "the right way, the only way" is one way to fail.

By alternatives we mean different expectations, methods, organizations, processes, or personnel. We mean that it might be better to cancel the project once it has proven feasible, due to the fact that it is impractical, by recognizing that simply because something will be beneficial when accomplished doesn't mean that it can be accomplished.

We mean that each project manager should examine the project closely to determine if it should be *one* project, and not two, three, or more. Perhaps some operational elements of the proposed work can be isolated and removed; given to another group and performed concurrently. Or maybe two or more concurrent project efforts sponsored by the same company should be combined. There is never anything sacred about the definition or scope of any project, it is as inexact and contrived as any methods used to manage it. Examine this scope to see if it makes sense. If not, change it. Again, workability is much more important than exactitude. Nothing is sacrosanct in this business.

Some companies take this advice to the extreme. When failure strikes they kneejerk—take the exact opposite approach, process, organization, or contractual type the next time. They swing the pendulum of management measures from one extreme to the other. Seldom do they seek middle ground, alternatives somewhere in between the extremes. Success is generally found there, between the outermost limits. Successful companies know that sensible, informed adjustment of approaches or methods is preferable to kneejerk reactions.

SF 5: Move the Camera

To be successful we must know the importance of perspective—the differences a change of view can bring. We must practice peripheral vision, and continually change our management models and our focus of attention, moving closer or away as the need arises. We should always remember that a global solution could exist beyond our daily vision or our limited planning horizon, one far superior to the local version.

Not only must we realize the existence of many different perspectives, we must change or modify our approaches and management activity to assure it is aligned with our own. If we are charged with performance, we need performance-based plans and controls. If we are responsible for understanding, we need different tools and we need to use them for different reasons. If control of others is our aim, our measures must vary as well. The awareness of different perspectives is important only if it helps us align our management and activity with our own and respect the differences of others.

Lastly we need to consider the perspective of those beyond our inner project circle: the outsiders, existing at different levels, and each having special needs and contributions. The camera should point outward from time to time, to capture the special perspective of those who, though not directly participating, can block or hamper our efforts. They hold up mirrors for us to examine ourselves, as well. The view is worth the effort.

SF 6: Uncover the Process

Below all the procedural coverings and nonessential wrappers we find the essence of project work: the process. This is that which is needed to achieve results—and nothing more. The more successful projects strip away process encumbrances and put processes into effect quickly, with immediate results. They focus on these results, and tune the processes only when the need is result-driven. The rest of the attachments clinging to most processes are encumbrances often preventing their use. Strip them away.

When defining processes and assigning responsibility for their conduct, progressive managements typically lean toward the use of discretion as much as possible, avoiding dependence on pedantic, rote or playscript directives. They defer to the judgment of those they have hired to exercise judgment: management. Once again pragmatism is a key practice, and project managers often find that to succeed they must do so despite procedures. They become artists of expediency, finding a way to the result, even when this means going over, under or around organizational, personal, or traditional obstacles. For this they should be commended, not rebuked. Their charge is to obtain results, not to comply with procedures.

Procedures not result-driven are worthless when it comes to business projects. Most project-oriented managers are not very compliance conscious. They seek the answer, not the steps that may or may not lead to it. To be successful we must follow this example, focusing always on result, considering the process only when it is necessary for the attainment of project expectations.

SF 7: Leverage and Multiply Your Success

Ideas that work, skills that are needed, and attitudes that promote accomplishment should be treasured. But more importantly, they should be leveraged—expanded and multiplied to other areas, bringing more and more success. We utilize this principle when we place tools in the hands of good people, tools which vastly expand the work they perform. We use it when we contrive organizational structures that assist and add to the work accomplished rather than frustrate it. And we see wise project leverage when a company harnesses the power of contracting, of using outside help, to its advantage. All these steps, and more take the attitude that shared success is larger and more enjoyable than private versions. Any steps, methods or management methods that exploit this concept of leverage are to be commended. They help assure success.

This advice applies not solely within project boundaries, for it makes sense to exploit intermediate successes throughout the company as well. To that end, any time that standards or workable solutions can be put in terms that translate to operational areas or can be modified so that their benefits transcend the project boundary this should be encouraged. Successes shouldn't be kept in the closet, they should be exposed, leveraged and multiplied.

SF 8: Accept Some Failure

Failure is unwanted, but it is not as bad as death. We can go on in business, even after some colossal failures. This is said to remind us that failure is not terminal and not absolute; it is only relative and usually short term. Never should we study or analyze failure to the point where the fear of it controls us, or freezes us into inaction. This would be the greatest failure of all. To be successful in any area one must tolerate, even expect failure, for the lack thereof doesn't generally mean total success, just total paralysis.

Consider some degree of failure as the price for exploitation of business opportunity; the price for projects. Resist timidity and the safety that accompanies the do-nothing approach. Do not be afraid to expect, to want, to attempt: to have expectations. This hopelessness and fatalism is far worse than any conceivable failure. For as unfortunate and repugnant as *unmet expectations* may be, these pale when compared to the condition of *no expectations*.

SF 9: Build the Adjustable Analog

Throughout this volume we have stressed the need for maps, models, representations, and depictions in order to shadow the project work and predict or understand it. We've used the analogs of finite element modeling, the folded map, the manager as camera, the movable lens, and the analogy box. All of these are simply tools used to grip the project, to study it and to better pattern our subsequent management measures. Two points need to be remembered in this regard: (1) all models are simply that, models. We should never forget that reality exists out there, and it is reality that we are trying to manage—not models, and (2) fixed models, like fixed and brittle measures, are bad models. They must accommodate change, new perspectives, the need for closer attention, and the practicality of use.

The same is true for most project measures that are based on models. We have mentioned the need for variable, risk-based controls and for the adaptation of standards to specific, project-unique applications. We need to know the limitations of all project analogs, choose adjustable ones, and continually change them to suit our needs. In addition, we should be able to distinguish between consciously chosen alterations and those that are the result of mutation; changes that happen inadvertently, with no realization of their effects.

All our project measures must be conceived with flexibility and accommodation to change in mind. Blunt and brittle tools and controls are not appropriate for projects that will change in every regard, constantly. Our tools and our views must bend with the winds of change. And we must constantly seek ways to move our management position and our management analogs to higher levels of change response, from sheer ignorance of change to its eventual mastering and control.

SF 10: Bridge Project Gaps

Failure typically starts in project gaps, cracks, and crevices. There are all sorts of these in our management models, organizations, processes, and perspectives. If project management has one overriding challenge, aside from attaining project expectations, it is to provide the force to close these gaps and the strength to keep them closed.

Examples of attempts to bridge project gaps begin with organizational weaknesses. Without repeating these, suffice it to say that networks, those voluntary associations of people with mutual interests, help bridge holes and cracks in our contrived organizational structures. The fabric of networks helps cover organizational tears. Astute management knows this, knows that networks exist and are free for the using and taps them.

There are gaps between expectations, perceived needs, and perspectives held by project insiders and those beyond the inner circle: outsiders at various levels. Their contributions can be accessed and their potential threats mitigated or avoided if we bridge the gaps between them and us, *annexing* their positions into the project, much like inviting them to be passengers aboard our ship. This concept of annexation, of making our interests mutual by superimposing the positions of inside and outside (making the boundary disappear) is shown by Figure 13-2.

We bridge process gaps when we use standards to eliminate rote or rigor when creating those processes, plans, or other measures. Standards help us bridge the intuitive leap otherwise filled by tedious reinvention of the wheel. And we bridge or at least narrow the gap between activity and accomplishment when we design intermediate goals in addition to final versions, bringing the fruit of

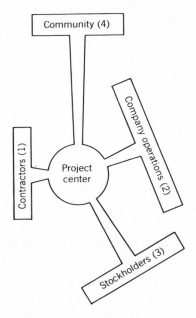

Figure 13-2   Annexing outsiders.

people's labor closer to the people themselves. Again, people who can see themselves succeeding are inclined to succeed even more. The gap between what they are doing and what they are accomplishing should never be allowed to engulf them.

Nor should we tolerate large gaps or breaks in the learning curve among our project personnel. Any steps taken to transcend the "replacement gap" (short of slavery) are highly recommended, for every project skill is vested in project people; they are the only repositories we have.

SF 11: Foster Project Intimacy

One very important conceptual gap requires special attention. This is the one that separates project management from the project itself. Few projects can be managed as all encompassing units, they must be broken down into smaller elements and each of these managed separately. Here is where adjustable analogs help. Aside from their use, however, successful projects bring the project closer, in time and space, to those working with it. This closeness is known as project intimacy, the condition of increased proximity, and it is extremely valuable. Project intimacy shortens the literal and conceptual distance between that which is being viewed and the viewer, between that which is being managed and the manager. As proximity lessens, the view becomes less clear and the effectiveness of management measures decreases.

No one ever manages a project; we must manage representations or pieces thereof. Proximity brings those into sharper focus, removes distortions and allows the impact of measures taken to be ascertained immediately and directly, without the need for various filters and transcriptions. This is why some managers can handle small, intimate groups or projects and cannot do the same for larger ones. They have not conquered the problem of proximity.

We have mentioned some techniques and approaches that help in this regard. Among them are physical relocation, information systems, consistent project "languages," and the refinement of each project continuum into manageable finite elements. All help increase proximity and therefore suppress the failure that often replaces it.

SF 12: Keep Your Bearings

Every business project undertaken is similar to a journey, for we begin with a set of expectations, travel around obstacles, use various measures of conveyance, and hopefully arrive at a destination. In our case the destination of choice is called success, not failure. No journey, actual or figurative, can be accomplished without some benchmarks, baselines, guideposts, or bearings. A lost project is a failed one. We need these markings to detect where the project is and where it is headed—to tie our efforts to progress and performance as opposed to the consumption of fuel (C, S, and T).

Bearings and baselines help us plan our project and identify our location; our status. We use them to understand where we've been and to predict, with some uncertainty, where we are headed; to forecast the future. None of these tools or techniques helps unless they are reasonable, achievable and rationally devised. Unachievable baselines (schedules, budgets, etc.) are worthless, as are arbitrary guidelines or inappropriate standards of performance. These should be rejected.

Some managements would rather avoid these measures entirely, relying on trust or hope to "guide" the project, perhaps as if by an unseen hand. We know that this often covers an aversion to accountability and that the only unseen hand to touch these projects is the cruel hand of failure.

Successful projects take constant readings as to their status and location. They keep their bearings, they refold their maps, they change their speed, adjust their instruments, and they proceed in earnest. They are accountable and welcome any test of accountability. Successful projects also travel by daylight, in the open, in full view of those who may want to measure or judge them. They realize that the ability to see baselines and landmarks helps them arrive at their destination, regardless of the fact that they may, in so doing, help others to measure their progress. Failing projects travel under cover of darkness, eluding exposure, and thereby missing the markers that would also point them in the right direction. They have no bearings to lose.

SF 13: Learn From YOUR Mistakes

Although practicing failure is not recommended, there are worse pursuits. One of these is to ignore the lessons that failure, once practiced, teaches. Many companies simply do not learn from their own mistakes, do not walk away from failure with any understanding of how and why it struck them. Failure doesn't fall from the sky; it doesn't select its victims at random. It is devoid of intent, choice or will.

In this regard failure is like rust; it only occurs where we have failed to take steps to prevent it. But rust, like project failure, doesn't pick where to strike, nor does it strike at random. It's simply a phenomenon we must avoid. We do this by learning from it in a general sense, as in reading this volume, and by tailoring that knowledge with specific information concerning our own weaknesses, cultures, and proclivity to fail.

Every company makes mistakes; fails to some extent. The ones that avoid repetition of these problems make conscious efforts to compile and analyze their failures. They collect and study them, looking for general traits, common agents, or predictable signs. This information is then used to make future project efforts more failure-resistant. There are a number of ways this is done.

Among them is the cross-pollination of ideas from one organizational structure to another, from operations to projects, and from different levels of outsider to insiders. Simple discussions with other projects (within or beyond company borders) engaged in similar activity are highly recommended. Many companies could also benefit from some formal clearinghouse of project information, a repository of knowledge where standards, or workable approaches, techniques or measures are given visibility and available for study and selection by others. Finally, solicitation of the external viewpoint, from the uninterested observer, or the distant outsider can help point out many mistakes we never see ourselves. Sometimes the very proximity that assists in managing projects blinds us to their faults.

In summary, we should conduct postproject analyses, sessions where the entire project is examined and discussed in order to isolate errors (not place blame) and reap the expensive lessons of failure. The focus need not be negative, only on error or problems. We should highlight and commend measures that worked—that leveraged success. The purpose of such exercise is to extend our knowledge of failure from one of a generic, fairly predictable occurrence to specific ways in which we will fail if we don't change.

Each company should be thus building a list of specific failure factors, those which pertain to their own settings and methods. The ones listed here have been only a start—those most common but certainly not all to be encountered. It is by no means an exhaustive compendium, and must be supplemented with your own special failure elements. Once created such a list can be summarily discarded, for in and of itself it has no value. The value obtained is in its creation, in the accumulation of knowledge that is secondary to a much higher objective: success.

FAILURE
SUCCESS
INDEX

FAILURE SYMPTOMS

FAILURE TENDENCIES

SUCCESS FACTORS

I N D E X